Rooted as they were on a radical voluntary principle of membership, they felt a special need of concern for their brothers and sisters. In taking seriously the biblical injunction to care for their own responsibility to members in need, these groups were also involved with the broader human dilemma. Their leaders were vocal in condemnation of injustice, economic oppression, and societal shortcomings. They have been credited with major impetus in attacking such evils as slavery, militarism, mistreatment of the mentally ill, and the like. The record of these groups is also outstanding in providing relief to war sufferers and refugees, in responding to natural disasters, and in giving aid to abused minorities.

The Free Churches are enjoying great attention today precisely because many of their emphases are seen as highly relevant for today's world. The widespread movement among young people which rejects middle-class customs and values of private ownership and individualism parallels the history of the Free Churches. Some of the Christian-oriented communes look for their inspiration specifically to the early development of groups here depicted.

DONALD F. DURNBAUGH is professor of church history at Bethany Theological Seminary in Illinois. He is the recipient of the Colonial History Award and is well known for his many articles and books on the Brethren and on Radical Protestantism.

**Every Need
Supplied**

Documents in Free Church History

A Series Edited by Franklin H. Littell and George H. Williams

"That collections be timely made for the poor . . . from which every need may be supplied . . . that no private ends may be answered, but all brought to the light, that the gospel be not slandered." (Article 5, The Balby Advices, 1656)

Every Need Supplied

Mutual Aid and
Christian Community in
the Free Churches,
1525–1675

Edited by
Donald F. Durnbaugh

Temple University Press
Philadelphia

To the memory of W. Harold
Row, 1912–1971, who personi-
fied the spirit of mutual aid

Temple University Press,
  Philadelphia, 19122
© 1974 by Temple University. All
  rights reserved
Published 1974
Printed in the United States
  of America
International Standard Book
  Number: 0-87722-031-X
Library of Congress Catalog Card
  Number: 73-94279

Contents

v

Contents

Illustrations

Series Foreword

Studies in the Radical Reformation continue to grow in number with each passing year. This fact reflects not only the response of scholars to the quantity of primary sources discovered and published in recent decades but also the shifting center of gravity in world Christianity. On the mission fields and among the younger churches, from which delegates at ecumenical conferences and councils play a much larger role than they did even a generation ago, there is a pronounced sense of recapturing and reliving the life and spirit of the New Testament and Early Church. European "Christendom," whether medieval or sixteenth century, seems far more strange, far more distant in time and space than the congregations to which Paul wrote his Epistles. Thus the scientific effort, whose beginnings might be dated in America with Harold S. Bender's founding of *The Mennonite Quarterly Review* in 1926 and in Germany with the publication of the first volume of the *Täuferakten* (Anabaptist Archives) in 1930, has been sustained by a growing awareness in the churches that in Protestantism, at least, there are two distinct church types and life-styles dating from the earliest years of the movement. One continued in modified form the territorial and parochial patterns of the medieval period, while the other used the New Testament and Early Church as a model. One was essentially concerned for reformation of doctrine and reform of ecclesiastical institutions, the other was devoted to the restitution of pristine Christian polity and faith.

In June 1964 a seminar on the Church in the World brought together a number of Free Church scholars—primarily from the "historic peace churches" (Mennonites, Brethren, Friends) at Earlham School of Religion. In June of 1967 a large number met for a week at Southern Baptist Theological Seminary.* In late June of 1970 the Second Believers' Church Conference met at Chicago Theological Seminary.† Beginning in 1971 a section of Free Church Studies established itself as a regular feature of scholarly sessions at the annual convention of the American Academy of Religion.

Parallel to this development of cooperation and consultation among American specialists, the work of the German commission sponsoring publication of the *Täuferakten* has gone forward steadily. A Dutch counterpart, *Documenta Anabaptistica Neerlandica*, has been initiated. At the meetings of historical societies held during the holidays in 1964, the suggestion that a comparable American organization be formed was discussed. In April of 1965 the North American Committee for the Documentation of Free Church Origins was launched, and the dates 1525–1675 chosen to bracket the era of concern (including the *TAK* attention to the sixteenth century, but adding also the Polish Brethren, the beginnings of radical Puritanism, and Pietism).

Of first importance among the Committee's publishing projects has been a series of sourcebooks of Free Church materials on themes of contemporary concern, such as the status of women, the genesis of the modern conscience, revolution, war and violence, religious liberty, the mystical basis of religious dissent, mutual aid, and democratic government (both church and civil). These are matters on which the Free Church pioneers took quite different positions from the established churches, both Catholic and Protestant, and on which their testimonies sound strikingly contemporary.

Today Catholics, mainline classical Protestants, and many others are finding in the Radical Reformation principles and motifs of vital importance whose adherents their own spiritual ancestors were liable to punish by fire and sword.

Franklin H. Littell
Temple University

George H. Williams
Harvard University

*The 1967 conference papers, edited by James Leo Garrett, Jr., have been published as *The Concept of the Believers' Church* (Scottdale, Pa.: Herald Press, 1969).

†The 1970 papers, edited by Clyde L. Manshreck, were published in The Chicago Theological Seminary *Register* 60 (1970): 1–59.

Preface

From the wealth of documentation now available on the Free Churches, I have chosen a variety of materials—letters, treatises, church records, examinations of prisoners, chronicles—to reflect the lively historical panorama.

As would be expected, there was a wider choice available for certain groups than for others. The book could have been filled with selections from the Anabaptists or the Society of Friends. Considerations of balance made necessary the exclusion of some excellent documents. I have also avoided the inclusion of writings readily accessible elsewhere.

Free Churchmen were steeped in the scriptures, and what they wrote is full of biblical reference and allusion. For easier reading, only those scriptural passages specifically mentioned or quoted have been identified. Verse references have been added to chapter citations, as an aid to readers. The great number of biblical references may appear burdensome, but serve to emphasize the importance these groups placed in justifying their beliefs by the authority of the bible. Their choice of passages and their interpretation make an interesting study in themselves. The Revised Standard Version has been used for biblical quotations, although on occasion this has meant a slight variation from the phrasing used in the originals.

Throughout the book bracketed numbers indicate the page number of the original source from which the material referred to was taken.

Fairly full notes on the documents have been provided for those interested. It did not seem helpful to burden readers with a formal bibliography of the hundreds of books and articles consulted in the course of research. Instead, I have provided a note on bibliographical materials and a reading list of literature in English.

I am grateful to Franklin H. Littell and George H. Williams for the invitation to write this book and for the freedom to shape it. The Board of Directors of Bethany Theological Seminary and the Faculty Fellowship Commission of the American Association of Theological Schools made possible a sabbatical leave in Germany for its research and writing in 1971–72. Professor Ernst Benz, director of the Ecumenical Seminar and the Seminar on Church History, Philipps University, Marburg, placed at my disposal the library resources of the theological school, which include the valuable Sippell collection on English nonconformists.

I am further indebted to the following persons for assistance: Edward H. Milligan and Margot Bronner, Library of the Society of Friends, London; G. W. Rusling, Baptist Historical Society Library, London; Dr. G. J. M. Pearce, Senior Tutor, Regent's Park College, Oxford; Dr. S. L. Verheus, Zaal Mennonitica, University Library, Amsterdam; Mrs. Y. de Swart-Pot, Library, Verenigde Doopsgezinde Gemeente, Amsterdam; Prof. Irvin B. Horst, University of Amsterdam; Dr. Cornelius Krahn, Mennonite Library and Archives, North Newton, Kansas; Frau Elisabeth Zilz, Theological Seminars, Philipps University, Marburg.

The staffs of the following libraries allowed use of their collections, either through personal visits or through photoduplication (or both): University Library, Marburg; National Library, Marburg/Berlin; British Library Reading Room, London; University Library, Ghent; Harvard University Library, Cambridge, Massachusetts.

Hedda Durnbaugh corrected my translations and typed the drafts of the book.

The following holders of copyright material have graciously permitted republication here: Herald Press, Scottdale, Pennsylvania; and The Plough Publishing House, Rifton, New York.

Donald F. Durnbaugh

**Every Need
Supplied**

Introduction

According to W. A. Visser 't Hooft, former executive of the World Council of Churches, the three functions of the church are witness (*marturia*), service (*diakonia*), and communion or fellowship (*koinonia*).[1] The church fulfills her mission in the world only when all three are vitally present. The Second Vatican Council popularized an interpretation of the church as the pilgrim people of God. In these as in other recent ecumenical statements, a definition of the church has emerged which differs from those earlier dominant. Pre-Reformation Christendom characterized the marks of the church as "one, holy, catholic, and apostolic." Of highest importance was unity (coerced, if need be) of doctrine and organization, a unity defined strictly by traditional teaching. The Lutheran Reformers held the church to be present wherever the "word of God is properly preached and the sacraments properly administered," with emphasis upon regulation of this propriety by established authorities. The Reformed (Calvinistic) communions added to these two minimum standards a third—"proper discipline"—intended to ensure an uncorrupted church. It is clear that a shift has taken place between the traditional and Reformation understandings of the church, on the one hand, and the modern ecumenical understandings, on the other hand. Recent interpretations place much more weight upon the life and witness of the total body, where earlier definitions looked more to static criteria of legitimacy, office, and order.[2]

These modern ecumenical descriptions of the church converge, in the unexpected manner which history sometimes displays, with those put forth in the sixteenth and seventeenth centuries by radicals and dissenters suppressed by the "mainline" Reformers and the older

3

church. One point on which Protestants and Catholics could agree during the Reformation and Counter Reformation was that dissent must be crushed by all possible means for the sake of christian society. The widespread acceptance today of once-radical thought on the nature of the church might be thought a vindication of the brave motto of the Anabaptist leader Dr. Balthasar Hubmaier, burned in Vienna in 1528 as a heretic and rebel: "Truth is immortal" (*Die Warheit ist untödtlich*).[3]

These dissenting movements—titled variously by scholars the Radical Reformation (George H. Williams), the Free Churches (Franklin H. Littell and others), and the Believers' Churches (Max Weber and others)—were primarily indebted to the Protestant Reformers for their basic theological insights and initiatives.[4] Yet the Radical Reformers parted company with their mentors, Luther and Zwingli, on certain important points. Among these were their beliefs that wholesome change in the church could come only through a rejection of ties with the princes and magistrates (separation of church and state), that the church consists solely of voluntary members faithful to their freely given confession (believer's baptism and church discipline), and that the model for their covenanted congregations was the early christian church as revealed in the New Testament (restitution rather than reformation).

These principles, which brought their champions such savage repression when they first put them forward, have become commonplace as the foundation for the self-understanding of most modern churches and their relations with the state. This fact helps to explain why there has been such a remarkable rehabilitation of the reputation of the Free Churches.[5] A surge of scholarship has uncovered the processes by which their credos were worked out in the heat and turbulence of their times. Not only were the radicals threatened by fierce and effective suppression, they also had to contend with potential excess from within their own ranks. The very severity of the persecution they underwent made possible the emergence of reckless or misguided individuals as initial leadership was killed. The alarming cries and sporadic aberrations of these fringe elements —which violence helped to produce—were pointed to, in turn, by the established authorities as justification for even harsher measures, in a circle vicious in more than name only.

Despite all these stresses, a rather complete and coherent church view was developed. To be sure, this may be observed better in the lives and deaths of the dissenters than in their published writings, which were rarely formal theological discourses. Some evidence is found in their books and tracts, although confiscation and destruction have made them very rare. Other data can be distilled from the government records of questioning, often under torture, of captured radicals. Seventeenth-century movements standing in the Free Church line, such as the Baptists and the Society of Friends (Quakers), were more fortunate in regard to publication, although here too much of the early printing was illegal.

From the portrait that can be assembled from these mosaic stones certain features may be clearly distinguished. Among these are the two closely connected characteristics which form the subject of this book—mutual aid and christian community. It is evident from the record that these two themes were then and are now considered to be among the central marks of the church and not secondary attributes. Spokesmen for the Radical Reformation underlined their importance. The Frisian leader Menno Simons added to Luther's marks (proper preaching and sacraments) these as well: holy living, brotherly love, unreserved testimony, and suffering.[6] His colleague Dirk Philips compiled a similar list which included christian works, discipline, and benevolent gifts.[7] In William Penn's account of the "particular" doctrines of the early Quakers the first point was "communion and loving one another." Penn reported the common sayings about the Friends: "They will meet, they will help and stick one to another" and "Look how the Quakers love and take care of one another."[8] It is the purpose of this book to introduce a representative sampling of statements from various sources to document this emphasis.

Leaders of the Protestant Reformation were of course not blind to their responsibility of meeting physical as well as spiritual needs of their parishioners. The same pastoral concern which marked Martin Luther's criticism of indulgence practices (thus precipitating the Reformation) was brought to bear upon appropriate ways of caring for the needy. The first Protestant ordinance for the care of the poor was issued in Wittenberg in the early days of 1522. This measure was taken upon the urging of Andreas Bodenstein of Carlstadt in Luther's absence, but certainly with the understanding that the action was in harmony with the intention of the reformer. It was later that the colleagues became enemies, when Luther attacked Carlstadt for pushing ahead farther and faster than the former thought wise. The Wittenberg ordinance of 1522 can hardly be claimed as a document of the Free Churches, but because of its

importance for the theme of mutual aid, it is included as an appendix. John Calvin too was mindful of the church's obligation to the
sick and indigent. The *Ecclesiastical Ordinances* which he drafted
for the Geneva church in 1541 contain detailed responsibilities in
this vein for church officials, in particular for those called to be
deacons.

The radicals could thus point to pronouncements and actions of
the major Reformers urging mutual aid and community. Luther,
for example, called for "earnest Christians" who would perform
christian works, practice and accept discipline, and actively aid the
poor. But, more importantly, they used Luther's slogan of scripture
alone as authoritative (*sola scriptura*) for the basis of their call for
sharing and loving action. They repeatedly contended that what
they were attempting to do was nothing more nor less than to follow faithfully the teachings and example of Jesus Christ and his
disciples. Like the early Christians they wanted to be recognized
by the love they showed for one another. Peter Riedemann wrote
in his first *Account*: "Love has this nature that it cannot conceal
itself; because it is a light it has to shine and to show itself in action.
Its office impels it to all men, to serve them and to further their
welfare."[9]

Their opponents often had to admit, grudgingly, that the radicals'
claims of a high level of mutual support were well founded. Henry
Bullinger, Zwingli's successor as head of the church in Zürich, wrote
(critically) of the Swiss Brethren that they teach "every Christian
is under duty before God to use from motives of love all his possessions to supply the necessities of life to any of his brethren."[10] A
contemporary wrote of Anabaptism in Augsburg: "This thing grew
most rapidly among the common man so that, if the town council
had not taken action, in a short time the greater part of the common
folk would have joined the sect and been seduced by it, for they
based their cause on great helpfulness, that each should serve the
other from brotherly love."[11] Critics granted them this quality, but
alleged that it was a trick to mislead the unwary.

Sometimes government officials acknowledged the practical aid
these movements gave them. By caring for the poor they relieved
the authorities of part of their responsibility. George Fox related
in his journal that several judges and captains came to a Quaker
meeting in the North of England with the intent of disruption; but
when they saw "how we took care one county to help another, and

to help our friends beyond the seas, and provide for our poor, that none of them should be chargeable to their parishes, etc., the justices and officers confessed we did their work, and passed away peaceably and lovingly, commending Friends' practice." This helped to stop the mouths of the "priests and professors" who criticized the Quakers' gathering in large numbers for meetings "for they were afraid, that when we had eaten one another out, we would all come to be maintained by the parishes."[12]

Those in the Radical Reformation contended that service to the brother and sister was at the heart of Christianity. It was impossible to speak of faith and belief without the practice of christian love. They claimed that the Protestant stress on justification by faith resulted in a merely outward orthodoxy or actual immorality. Bernard Rothmann, the Münsterite theologian, complained about the common Protestants "who boast so much of their faith. They cling to this with such lack of understanding that they very rarely pay attention to obeying the commandments of God and [doing] good works."[13] Balthasar Hubmaier made the same criticism in his treatises: when Luther rejected the "works-righteousness" of the old Catholic ethic, he removed the last limits to ill conduct on the part of the common man. Laymen were unable to follow the subtlety of Luther's call to "sin bravely" and misunderstood his real intent of encouraging a new kind of morality. Peter Walpot of the Hutterian Brethren charged that in the case of the typical Protestant "each looks to his advantage, to his own favor and greed, that he gathers to himself and fills his sack."[14]

When the historical record of the early years of these movements is considered, it is not surprising that mutual aid and community played a large part in their development. The heavy penalties levied upon them—seizure of goods, expulsion from guilds and professions, long imprisonments, expatriation, capital punishment—caused hardship and misery to be the common lot of the believer. Although it is not accurate to say, as is often done, that these movements at first consisted only of the disinherited, the poor, and the outcast, the results of their treatment soon made this all too true.[15]

From the beginning the leaders and their families were particularly threatened; care for dependents was a standing concern. The Anabaptist Strassburg discipline of 1568 called on the ministers and bishops to "visit, provide for, and comfort the wives and children of those ministers who travel in danger or are in prison, so that the ministers may be comforted and gladdened by the assurance of brotherly love and care, whether he be in prison or absent for other reason." Michael Sattler, writing from prison shortly before his execution, urged the congregation at Horb (1527): "Be generous to all those among you who have need, especially to those who labor with the word among you, and are driven away and are not able themselves to eat their bread in peace and quiet."[16] Similar care provided for the families of Hutterite missioners has been recently assessed as one of the factors contributing to the dynamism and success of their wide-ranging mission tours.[17]

The Society of Friends developed perhaps the most elaborate organizational means of coping with such problems in their Meeting for Sufferings and their Men's and Women's Meetings. That this was necessary is made evident by the calculation that even in the later seventeenth century when the fires of persecution had cooled, some 450 Quakers were killed or died of mistreatment and at least 15,000 suffered grievously. The number of deaths of dissenters in the previous century was much higher.[18]

For these reasons, the argument which has occasionally been put forward—that the surprising growth of these movements is partly due to the economic benefit which proselytes could expect from the open-handedness of the brotherhood—is surely false. As informers and denouncers were customarily rewarded with a share of the confiscated goods of religious radicals, financial incentive was on the side of the oppressors. It would have been a foolish person who accepted the certain penalties and dangers accompanying membership in these groups for the sake of immediate support.

Moreover, they uniformly held to the stern Pauline precept that he who does not work should not eat (2 Thess. 3:10). Just as they made it a point of principle never to allow a member to be reduced to begging, so they made it a point of discipline to expel anyone who was able to labor but was unwilling to do so. An Anabaptist at Regensburg, Augustine Würzlburger, testified that anyone able to work but attempting to profit from the aid of the congregation, would be excluded and considered to be a heathen.[19] The Quakers were ingenious in providing jobs for members, even those in prison. They distributed raw material and found markets for completed products, also arranging apprenticeships for youths. At the same time, they were firm in dealing with anyone shying from an honest job.[20] These references to expulsion make it necessary to discuss how the Free Churches understood aid and christian community.

Aspects of Mutual Aid and
Christian Community

The several aspects of mutual aid and christian community may be summarized under these somewhat overlapping categories: brotherly love, material support, admonition and discipline, and concern for outsiders. From what has been stated thus far, the first two could be expected to be important to the life of the Believers' Churches. Some readers, however, may be surprised to find admonition and discipline listed under the heading of aid and community, since these terms today often have a negative and punitive meaning. For the members of the Free Churches, true love for the brother most definitely included fraternal correction, reproof, and, if need be, sharper penalties. John Denck put their conviction in bold words in 1527:

> If a man loves someone, but not according to God's truth and love, he hates him. If, however, a man hates someone for the sake of love, he loves him more than the former. Yet a man may not hate someone for the sake of love further than that he earnestly disciplines him. And if he does not wish to listen, one avoids him with a sorrowful heart. This also is being loved in the truth.

The most severe penalty was exclusion from the fellowship.[21]

Given their programmatic separation from the state, the rejection of involvement by secular powers in church matters was to be expected. The Polish Brethren asserted that the

> congregation or church of Christ (insofar as she is the church of Christ) acknowledges on this earth no other court, government, authority, or regulation than this church discipline. . . . Therefore the Papists, Lutherans, and Calvinists are badly mistaken on this point, when they go to great lengths to call upon the secular arm . . . to aid them against those whom they consider the . . . heretics.

What passed for love among the false churches, all radical groups maintained, was simply a selfish unwillingness to care enough for the brother to go to him to point out his faults. They conceded that such an act was an uncomfortable proposition for the natural man. Yet a parent who truly loved a child, they reasoned, did not neglect to discipline him. Just so, a loving church provided for the timely correction of erring members. The Regensburg Anabaptist John Umlauft wrote in 1539:

> How can it be a christian congregation, if christian order and commandments are not maintained, with separation, ban, discipline,

brotherly love, and other [practices], also that one after another may speak openly to give his gifts and revelation freely, for improvement, to the people.[22]

The Free Churches' charter for the practice of church discipline was found in the eighteenth chapter of the gospel according to Matthew, cited with almost monotonous regularity in all writings on the subject. In the famous letter of Conrad Grebel and his friends to Thomas Müntzer (September 5, 1524) is this passage: "Go forward with the Word and establish a Christian church with the help of Christ and his rule, as we find it instituted in Matt. 18:15–18 and applied in the Epistles." These churches followed this literally in dealing with problems of misconduct or lapsing. A distinction was often made between private and public sins, each demanding a different process of reconciliation, but the goal in either case was the restoration of the brother or sister to full unity. In this connection, they took very seriously the warning of Jesus that the celebration of the Lord's supper (offering the gift at the altar) should not take place if there was disunity (Matt. 5:23–24). The ultimate in discipline, expulsion, was intended to cause restoration by bringing home to the member his alienation from the body. In the unhappy case of a member's recalcitrance despite patient efforts at redemption by his fellows, exclusion would be necessary to protect others in the congregation from being misled. They saw the lack of discipline in the established churches as a major weakness. This criticism appears repeatedly in the records, and was responsible for corrective efforts by Reformed churchmen in Strassburg, Geneva, and the landgraviate of Hesse.[23]

Within the Radical Reformation the proper use of discipline, especially regarding the banning of members, caused great problems. There was the recurrent danger and actuality of legalism and harshness, and resulting schism, which mar the history of these bodies.[24] The long-suffering concern for reconciliation and unity is nonetheless impressive. A typical expression is that of John Smyth, early Baptist leader, who wrote in a confession of faith (1612): "None are to be rejected for ignorance or errors, or infirmities so long as they retain repentance and faith in Christ . . . , but they are to be instructed with meekness."[25] William Penn described the proceedings of Quakers "against one who has lapsed or transgressed." During a visit by other church members, the facts were first "laid home to him"; then the visitors would "labour with him in much love and zeal for the good of his soul, the honour of God, and reputation of their profession, to own his fault and condemn it, in as ample a manner as the evil or scandal was given by him." If the person proved impenitent, "after repeated entreaties and due waiting for a token of repentance," the meeting issued a paper to "disown such a fact and the party offending, recording the same as a testimony of their care for the honour of the truth they profess."[26]

Expressions of brotherly love loom large in the annals of the Believers' Churches. Harold S. Bender, dean of American Anabaptist studies, stressed their importance in his well-known paper, "The Anabaptist Vision." He held the essence of Anabaptism to lie in (1) the concept of the church as a "brotherhood of committed disciples," (2) the central role of discipleship (Nachfolge), and (3) the ethic of love. An important aspect of love for the brother was the willingness to risk reputation, property, and life itself. The risk was great for simple membership and gathering for meetings, but was increased sharply by the zeal for witnessing displayed by ordinary members, which led them to extensive and hazardous travels. The willingness to lose one's life for others was so pronounced that a German scholar characterized the Anabaptists by a "theology of martyrdom." One way this was practiced was by offers to take the place of imprisoned brethren. A dramatic example of this occurred in 1659, when 164 Quakers presented themselves to the English Parliament as substitutes for the large number of their friends held in jails and dungeons.[27]

There were other forms which brotherly love took in the lives of Free Churchmen. One was the manner of meeting for worship. There was ordinarily no set liturgy; all were to "exercise their gift" for the edification of the brethren. Care was taken that all things were done in order, after biblical precept. Meetings were to be held often, and they were usually lengthy. The Baptist group in Amsterdam led by Smyth met on Sundays from eight to twelve, and again from two to five or six o'clock in the afternoon. The meeting always concluded with a prayer reminding the congregation to care for the poor, and a collection to make this care possible.[28]

Many students of Quakerism have remarked that the silent meeting incorporated both an intense personal relationship with God on the part of the worshipper and a keen sense of group consciousness. Neither was complete without the other. The latest expression of this communality asserts:

If Quakers sometimes achieve what other Christians merely aim at, it
is because we start in a different place. For us the meeting itself
is central; the Spirit we know or meet there is simultaneously inward
and personal and also shared and thus objective. We *know* it
as an experience of reality, "within but not of" our private selves,
partly because it is a shared meeting with the Spirit. . . . A person
who feels a burning and compelling message within him must
nevertheless wait to make sure that this is meant for the group as a
whole, not merely for himself personally. Conversely, it is too
easy to speak as if a message from Christ's spirit were not
for oneself, but only for others.[29]

The same spirit was sought in meetings for business, which were
often indistinguishable from meetings for worship. The ideal was
stated by the Quaker Edward Burrough in 1662:

But in the wisdom, love and fellowship of God, in gravity, patience,
meekness, in unity and concord, submitting one to another in
lowliness of heart, and in the holy Spirit of truth and righteousness,
all things [are] to be carried on; by hearing and determining every
matter coming before you, in love, coolness, gentleness, and dear
unity . . . assisting one another in whatsoever ability God hath given.[30]

To make this kind of meeting possible, the Free Churches believed
that congregations should be small enough so that each believer
knew all of the others. Periodic subdivision could preserve this as
growth occurred in membership. The Confession of 1611 of the
English General Baptists led by Thomas Helwys said in its sixteenth
article that "a Church ought not to consist of such a multitude as
cannot have particular knowledge one of another."[31]

The most common phrase used by these churches to express their
material support was "community of goods," reflecting the passage
in the Acts of the Apostles (4:32): "They had everything in common."[32] Almost uniformly this was understood in the sense of holding private goods ready for sharing with those in need. A classic
expression was that of Balthasar Hubmaier in 1526:

Concerning community of goods, I have always said that everyone
should be concerned about [the needs of] others, so that the
hungry might be fed, the thirsty given to drink, and the naked clothed,
etc. For we are not lords of our possessions, but stewards and
distributors. There is certainly no one who says that another's goods
may be seized and made common; rather, he would gladly give
the coat in addition to the shirt.

This and similar responses were in answer to the charge voiced by
Zwingli, Melanchthon, Menius and others that the Radical Reform-

ers were communists plotting to seize the property of the wealthy.
Contemporary evidence from the hearings of Anabaptists questioned
on this point shows that Hubmaier's position was that held by almost
all.[33]

The Anabaptist leader Ambrose Spittelmaier testified in prison:
"A real Christian should not own more on earth than he can cover
with one foot." But he went on to say that this does not mean that
he should own no property at all. "Rather he should use nothing for
himself alone, saying, 'This house is mine, this field is mine, this
money is mine.' " He pointed out that all Christians begin their
prayer with "Our Father," not "My Father."[34] Another Anabaptist,
the Augsburg patrician Langenmantel, made the same point about
the Lord's prayer and called those hypocrites who forgot that they
prayed "Give us this day *our* daily bread." This attitude was linked
to their baptismal pledge. A tailor of Rothenburg stated in 1529:

The Anabaptists baptize one another in the name of the Father, the
Son, and the Holy Spirit, and those who are thus rebaptized,
covenant together to show christian love to one another, first to have
love for God and then love for the neighbor; he who sees his
neighbor suffer scarcity or need, would and should aid him and show
love for the neighbor.[35]

A characteristic rejoinder to the charge of communism was that
of the Swiss Brethren in Hesse, who told the government in 1578:
"We believe, acknowledge, and witness that the believing, new-born
Christians and children of God are required to maintain and to care
for the nourishment of their poor members, fellow believers, old,
ill, widows, and orphans, and also to show common love to other
needy persons."[36] John Smyth concluded in his Amsterdam confession of faith "that in the necessities of the church, and poor brethren,
all things are to be common (Acts 4:32), yea, and that one church
[congregation] is to administer to another in time of need."[37] Smyth
himself practiced what he taught. He earned a meager living as a
refugee in the Netherlands with his knowledge of medicine, but took
no fees from the poor for his services. "He was so mindful and so
careful for the poor, that he would rather live sparingly in his house
(or as we say) neglect himself, his wife, and children, than that any
should be in extremity."[38] Ulrich Stadler summed up the feelings of
more than his own group (the Hutterian Brethren): " 'One,' 'common' builds the Lord's house and is pure; but 'own,' 'mine,' 'thine,'
and 'his' divides the house and is impure" (*Ain und gmain bauet*

*des Herren hauss und ist rain; aber aigen, mein, dein, sein zertrennt
das hauss und ist unrain).*[39]

The one group that did extend this communism of sharing, called
a "communism of love" (*Liebeskommunismus*) by Ernst Troeltsch,[40]
to a full community of property and production were these Hutterian Brethren. Although they organized communally first of all
because of pressing economic need while refugees in Moravia, they
went on to make total community of goods a condition of membership. They contended with the Swiss Brethren and other evangelical
Anabaptists, with whom they were otherwise united in faith and
practice, that total obedience to Christ can only take place in community. A favorite image for them was the use of bread and wine
in the Lord's supper. Just as grain must be ground and grapes be
crushed to make bread and wine, so the individual Christian, to be
faithful, must lose his identity and possessions in the larger whole.[41]

Community is or means nothing else than to have everything in
common or everything alike out of love to one's neighbor, and for
none to have anything of his own. Which thing can take place in
no higher, more perfect way than that each should give himself that
the other may have the same benefit (as himself), as they that
desire henceforth to endure together evil and good, yes, joy and
sorrow. Each desires to be the other's neighbor, faithful debtor,
member, and devoted friend. That is the Christian church and
community of saints.[42]

The emphasis upon sharing with the brother was sometimes turned
against the Free Churches by critics who concluded that they were
narrowly devoted to their own members and thus ignored the rest
of the world. George Fox once answered such criticism from a
clergyman in this way: "I told him, 'we loved all mankind, as they
were God's creation, and as they were children of Adam and Eve
by generation; and we loved the brotherhood in the Holy Ghost.'
This stopped him. After some other discourse, we parted friendly."[43]
Menno Simons responded to a similar attack by writing that "we
are prepared before God and man with all our hearts to share our
possessions, gold, and all that we have, however little it may be,
and to sweat and labor to meet the need of the poor, as the Spirit
and Word of the Lord, and true brotherly love teach and imply."[44]
The Collegiant Plockhoy attacked the false Christianity of those
who not only failed to lighten the burden of the poor around them
but actually profited from their misery. His communitarian scheme

was intended to ease the suffering of some of the many paupers in England.[45]

An interesting testimony to the willingness of these groups to aid the afflicted is found in Voltaire's *Candide*. Although he otherwise viewed with distaste the early Anabaptists as fanatics, Voltaire used the figure of the "honest Anabaptist" Jacques as a foil for what he considered to be the hypocrisy and narrowness of orthodoxy. It was Jacques who played the good Samaritan to Candide and Dr. Pangloss when they were in bitter need after being turned away by churchmen. Later in the narrative, Jacques gives his own life to save an ungrateful sailor at sea. Voltaire's praise of the honesty and plain-spoken merits of the Quakers is well known.[46]

A largely unwritten story is the aid given by Dutch Mennonites and English Quakers to beleaguered religious minorities on the continent in the seventeenth century and later. In the case of the Mennonites, the early toleration they enjoyed in the Netherlands enabled them to achieve a prosperity which they more than once put at the disposal of those still persecuted in Switzerland and elsewhere. It is probably not an exaggeration to say that no groups in christian history have contributed so much to others in proportion to their numbers as have these and other Free Churches.[47]

Another way in which these groups showed their concern for those outside their number was their prophetic criticism of social evils. They were outspoken in their condemnation of the carelessness and ineffectiveness of those responsible for the public welfare. Such ills as debtor's imprisonment, usury, unemployment, and poor housing were objects of their attacks. Anabaptists repeatedly scored high rates of interest and the neglect by townspeople of their poor. None was more active in this regard than George Fox, who wrote tract after tract calling for action to the magistrates, merchants and statesmen in seventeenth-century England. Significantly, even Karl Marx wrote approvingly of some of the Quaker initiatives for social reform. An important area of their activity was to create a climate of concern for needs not yet considered public responsibilities, such as employment offices.[48]

Yet another way in which these groups have shown responsibility for those not in their ranks was their interest in missions. Franklin H. Littell and others have documented the seriousness with which the Anabaptists took the missionary imperative.[49] This was also true of the other movements under study.

The practice of mutual aid and christian community was intended to produce sturdy Christians, capable of making their witness wherever they were in the world. The quality of spirit hoped for is reflected in a letter which George Fox directed to ministering Friends in 1656:

This is the word of the Lord God to you all, and a charge to you all in the presence of the living God; be patterns, be examples in all countries, places, islands, nations, wherever you come; that your carriage and life may preach among all sorts of people, and to them. Then you will come to walk cheerfully over the world, answering that of God in everyone; whereby in them you may be a blessing, and make the witness of God in them to bless you. Then to the Lord God you will be a sweet savour and a blessing.[50]

The Scope of Selections

The chronological range for selections in this book is one hundred and fifty years from 1525 to 1675. The geographical area is the Continent and the British Isles. The first date comes from the conclusion that the Free or Believers' Church movement starts with the Anabaptists. Although there has been a persistent effort to place the origin of left-wing Protestantism prior to the Reformation, most historians agree that the Swiss Brethren or Anabaptists in Zollikon near Zürich began the movement in 1525. The noted Reformed scholar Fritz Blanke summed up this view when he wrote: "In Zollikon a new type of church had begun to differentiate itself, the Free Church type. Zollikon is the cradle of this idea, which from here entered upon its triumphant march through four centuries and through the whole world."[51]

For most Europeans the name "Anabaptist" is synonymous with Münster, the walled city in Westphalia. This was the scene of a violent but abortive attempt in 1533–35 to establish a "Davidic kingdom" or "New Jerusalem." Modern scholarship has shown the essential difference between the Münsterites and the pacific Anabaptists, but it is also clear that there were connections, primarily through the mild but apocalyptic teaching of Melchior Hofmann, between Dutch and German Anabaptism and the revolutionaries. It is therefore appropriate to include part of the writing of the Münsterite theologian Bernard Rothmann, who was influential in bringing his city into the Protestant camp.

A Catholic priest in the Low Countries who had become dissatisfied with traditional belief and ceremony, Menno Simons was aghast at the catastrophe into which the revolutionaries in Westphalia and the Netherlands had blundered. He decided to throw his life into an effort to guide their deep religious desires along saner paths, knowing quite well that in so doing he was giving up a position of prestige and ease, and that his life henceforth would be that of a hunted criminal. He expressed his intense pastoral concern in voluminous writings as well as in his undercover visits and ministry. A grateful following took his name for their movement (Mennonites); it also served to distinguish them from the feared and hated Anabaptists of Münster.

Although closely connected in both origin and belief with the Swiss Brethren and South German Anabaptists (as previously indicated), the Hutterian Brethren developed a communitarian way of life. They came together first in Moravia, where they sought refuge on the lands of the independent nobility from bitter persecution in the homelands—Austria, Switzerland, South Germany. After great initial difficulties and sharp internal rivalries, they were put in order by the Austrian Jacob Hutter. Their chronicler recorded that the community took their name from Hutter because he directed them for some years and left them "gathered and edified in the Lord," before his cruel death as a heretic in his native Tyrol.[52] The Counter Reformation forced the community into an epic and tragic migration through Eastern Europe to the Ukraine, whence they migrated to North America in the latter part of the nineteenth century. They dwell today in the northwestern United States and in several Canadian provinces as the oldest continuing christian communes.

A group of different ethnic background which developed into an Anabaptist movement in its own right was the Polish Brethren. Here the initiative came from Reformation-minded elements in sixteenth-century Poland that combined with liberal theological currents from Italy to form the forerunners of the modern Unitarians. For a time after 1569 they practiced a fully communitarian economy in the new town of Raków, which became the religious and intellectual center of the movement. Under Faustus Socinus (from whom the group received the name Socinians) the movement took on a more moderate social posture and deepened its anti-trinitarian view of the deity. The beliefs these Poles held in common with the Anabaptists led to several attempts to combine with the Hutterian Brethren, but social as well as doctrinal differences prevented full unity. Certain of the Polish Brethren were also in personal contact through visits and correspondence with Anabaptists in South Germany and the Netherlands, especially Christopher Ostorodt, whose writings are represented in this volume.

The Polish Brethren also had relationships with an amorphous but important religious society in the Netherlands known as the Collegiants or Rijnsburgers, after their place of origin. From their beginnings in 1619–20 the Collegiants were influenced by the Poles, including their adoption of the practice of immersion baptism, stressed by the Brethren. When the Socinians were stamped out in their homeland by Counter Reformation forces, with the final expulsion in 1660, some refugees found asylum in the Netherlands, although Calvinist theologians there continually alerted the Dutch government to the dangers of the newcomers' liberal theology. There was strong Socinian-Unitarian linkage with the Collegiants and with the closely associated Dutch Mennonites.

One of the more interesting Collegiant figures was Peter Cornelius Plockhoy of Zierik-zee. He became an international personage in 1658 when he tried to interest Oliver Cromwell, Lord Protector of England, in his plans to bring religious and economic peace to the troubled Puritan commonwealth. When Cromwell died later that year, Plockhoy approached the son and successor, Richard, but the restoration of Charles II in 1660 squelched his hopes of utopian reform. On returning to the Netherlands, Plockhoy was able in 1662 to persuade the city council of Amsterdam to grant him land in North America (in present-day Delaware) to start a colony on christian principles. Whether his plan would have proven successful in the long run is impossible to know, because the young settlement was destroyed by the British a year after in 1663, when the English displaced the Dutch in control of the Middle Colonies.

The Dutch Collegiants and Mennonites, in turn, had many contacts across the channel with England. Among these were their ties with the English Baptists. The early Separatist leader, John Smyth, brought his independent Gainsborough congregation to Amsterdam in the early 1600's to escape the repressive hand of Anglican authority. He formed there a congregation along Baptist lines when he rejected his early baptism, baptized himself, and then the rest of his flock. Later regretting this action, he sought membership with a branch of the Dutch Mennonites, but died in 1612 before negotiations were completed. Most of his followers did in fact unite with the Mennonites, but a group led by Thomas Helwys returned to England to form the English General Baptists. These English congregations remained in touch with the Mennonites in Holland but doctrinal differences prevented the desired union.

A second link, however, was established with the rise of the Particular Baptists in 1640–41, distinguished from the General Baptists by a narrower view of atonement. The Particular Baptists came to the belief that immersion was the only correct form of believer's baptism. They sought a way to secure this mode. Learning of the immersionist Polish Brethren they sent representatives to Silesia, only to find that the Brethren there were in need of renewal themselves. They therefore looked to the Collegiants, who had baptized by immersion since 1619. An emissary sent to the Netherlands took counsel with the Collegiants, and then returned to England where he and a fellow elder baptized the sending congregations. It is likely that the baptizer, Richard Blunt, himself received baptism from the Collegiants, although the primary source is ambiguous.[53]

The last group to be considered are the Quakers or Society of Friends who, as did the Baptists, emerged from the left wing of Puritanism, and in many cases were formerly Baptists themselves. The Quakers, in the minds of some interpreters, represented the extension of the Anabaptist ideal. They took the fellowship of the spirit, the informality of liturgy and the rejection of churchly patterns to their logical conclusion. There has been a vigorous debate about the antecedents of the Quakers, some stressing Continental connections and, more recently, some scholars contending for the Puritan derivation alone. The early Quakers considered themselves to represent a recovery of primitive Christianity.[54]

Part 1   The Anabaptists

1

Answers to a List of Questions

Editor's note

It was the common practice of the governmental authorities to question captured Anabaptists, under the threat and actual use of torture. They hoped to find confirmation of their fears of rebellion and heresy and to learn the names of other radicals, especially leaders, so that they could be hunted down as well. The records of these questions and the answers given by the prisoners provide much of the detailed information still preserved about the movement, although the circumstances must always be kept in mind in evaluating the information thus provided.

Some revealing excerpts from an examination of the Austrian Anabaptist, Ambrose Spittelmaier, provide insight into the method and beliefs of Anabaptist missioners. Appended to the excerpts is a brief note composed by government officials as a partial basis for questioning and as a repudiation of Spittelmaier's position.

Ambrose Spittelmaier (ca. 1497–1528) was a university student with a good command of Latin, a thorough knowledge of the bible, and a ready pen. He was baptized in Linz, Upper Austria, in July, 1527, by the itinerant apostle of the Anabaptists, John Hut. Forced to flee Linz within a month of his baptism, Spittelmaier travelled through southern Germany briefly before his arrest and imprisonment in September, 1527. During his arduous captivity, he answered the lengthy questionnaires of his captors in considerable detail. His replies provide a glimpse of the views of Austrian and South German Anabaptism under Hut's influence.

The judicial decision of February 6, 1528, demanded the death penalty by beheading because of his seditious activity. Spittelmaier's teachings on community of goods, mentioned several times in the judgment, raised the specter of another peasants' war in the minds of the authorities. The excerpt and the note are translated from the source collection of Anabaptist records from Bavaria.

9. Our teaching is nothing other than the eternal pure word of God. Thus, when I or someone else meet a person not of our faith, I first ask him if he is a Christian, what his christian conduct is like, how he treats his brethren, whether he holds everything in common with his brethren and his brethren with him, whether any among them suffer from lack of clothing or food, whether they practice brotherly discipline among themselves, what they consider the use of all creation is before God, and how they acknowledge God and Christ in this, etc.

If it turns out that one or more of them are ignorant of these matters, and if someone desires to learn more, then we show him the will of God quite plainly through the creation [Mark 16:15]. Each is shown, according to his trade, by means of his tools as Christ taught (Job 12[:7–12]; John 15[:1–8]; Matt. 4[:18–22]; Luke 9[:57–62]; Matt. 21[:28–43]) that a man can learn through his trade, as from a book given to him by God to learn his will. Thus, a woman learns from her flax which she spins or from any other kind of housework that she performs daily. In sum, our teaching is nothing other than that we help everyone clearly to recognize the will of God through the creation, as a visible demonstration of invisible things. This is why God has placed the creation before the eyes of man. Even the apostles of Christ taught in just this way, for all of history is nothing but a creation.

As for the covenant and brotherhood which we hold one with another, through which we bind ourselves together, this is nothing other than this: when we are together we try to practice brotherly discipline if one of us sees and finds another in wrongdoing, as Christ has commanded us; we do not want to part one from the other at all despite our antagonisms; none intends to annoy another; no one keeps his possessions from the others, but rather all hold everything in common, be they spiritual or material gifts; we do not cause one another sorrow, and therefore desire to keep the covenant between God and man as long as life and body remain. This covenant is renewed when we hold communion.

It is certainly neither our intention to betray or to abandon the country and the people nor to create an uproar. The uproar which is to engulf all men will come from God because of the sins which are committed daily before God in great numbers. [49] I say to you: Beware! Beware! Abstain from your sins and Christ will be your light. Everyone bears a dead soul in a living body, but he ought to bear a living soul in a dead body.

10. There are seven decrees [*Urtl*] in the scriptures which, though scattered throughout the bible, completely comprise the will of God. They are:

The first decree is about the covenant of God which God makes with those whom he receives as his children. This covenant is made in spirit, in baptism, and in the drinking of the chalice which Christ called the baptism with blood (Matt. 20[:22]; Matt. 26[:27–29]; Luke 22[:17–18]; 1 Cor. 11[:25–30]), that we may covenant ourselves with God in one love, spirit, faith, and baptism to remain with him (Eph. 2[:13ff.]). In return God covenants to be our father and to support us in all of our tribulations. The entire bible is full of this covenant.

The second decree is about the kingdom of God, which God will give only to those who are poor in spirit (Matt. 5[:3]; Luke 6:50 [20]). No one can inherit this kingdom except those who on earth are poor with Christ. A Christian calls nothing his own, not even a place to lay his head. A real Christian should not own more on earth than he can cover with one foot. This does not mean that he should have no trade, or sleep in the woods, that he should own no fields or pastures, or that he should not work; rather, that he should use nothing for himself alone, saying: "This house is mine, this field is mine, this money is mine." Instead, he should say: "Everything is ours," just as we pray: "Our Father."

In sum, a Christian should not call anything his own, but hold all things in common with his brother and not allow him to suffer want. I should not work so that my house be filled, and my bowl be full of meat, but rather I should see that my brother has enough. A Christian is more concerned about his neighbor than about himself (1 Cor. 13). Whoever wants to be rich on this earth and lack absolutely nothing for his body or in possessions so that he might be respected and feared by all men, and refuses to lie at the feet of the Lord as did Mary Magdalene, or the king of Nineveh before King David—he will be humbled in heaven (Luke 22[:24ff.]; Luke 18 [:9ff.]; 1 Pet. 5[:5–6]). The kingdom of God will come here on earth (Matt. 5) but heaven and earth will first be renewed by fire (Isa. 66[:15–16]). . . .

Arguments against Ambrose
Spittelmaier (1527)

[66] If a true Christian cannot call anything his own, who then
would want to plough the fields; who would want to work?

Also, how would one maintain law, peace, and order if everyone
ran around haphazardly, like untended cattle?

When an honest man saves something, he is obligated to share it
with lazy, drunken bums, who do not want to work. Also, if everyone were supposed to share things, all the lazy ones would say that
the others were not real Christians because they owned something
for themselves [and would cry]: "Let us all beat them and take
their possessions away from them!"

Thus, the irresponsible, drunken bums would count for more and
be esteemed higher than pious Christians, who have earned their
bread in the sweat of their brows, according to the commandment
and teaching of almighty God, that he gave to Adam in the Garden
of Eden.

Editor's note

Dr. Balthasar Hubmaier (ca. 1481–1528) was thought by many contemporaries to be the chief instigator and spokesman for the Anabaptists. His oratorical skills and his prolific writing placed him quickly in the front ranks of the radical movement, although his views on government and war separated him from other Anabaptists. When the Index of Prohibited Books was created by Rome, Hubmaier was listed along with Luther, Calvin, Zwingli, and Schwenckfeld, as the foremost heretics.

Born in Friedberg near Augsburg, Hubmaier experienced a meteoric academic career as a protégé of Dr. John Eck, Luther's chief Catholic opponent. He earned a doctorate in theology at Ingolstadt (1512) and then combined a professorship there with pastoral responsibilities. In 1515 he was named pro-rector of the university. A year later he moved to Regensburg where he further developed his talent and fame as a popular preacher.

It was as a priest in the small border city of Waldshut near Switzerland after 1523 that Hubmaier began to reform his congregation along Protestant lines. Though first favored by the Swiss Reformer Ulrich Zwingli, he aligned himself with those of Zwingli's circle who formed the first Anabaptist church in 1524–25. Hubmaier put their views into practice in Waldshut in the spring of 1525, with more than 300 of his congregation following him in adult baptism. The Austrian authorities intervened at this point to suppress the radical activity in their territory. Hubmaier fled in late 1525 to Zürich, where he was forced by Zwingli to recant under torture some of his beliefs as the price of freedom.

Nicolsburg in Moravia became his place of refuge, and Hubmaier soon made it into an outstanding center of Anabaptist life. It is said that over 12,000 became Anabaptists there, including the local lords of Liechtenstein. Because of the great influx, Hubmaier spent much effort in guiding the young congregation, including the introduction of church order. The following treatise on church discipline was probably written in late 1526 and published in 1527. The present translation was made from the standard edition of Hubmaier's works edited by the Swedish scholars Gunnar Westin and Torsten Bergsten.

Dr. Balthasar Hubmaier
of Friedberg

On Brotherly Discipline

Where this is absent, there is indeed no church even though water baptism and the Lord's supper are there observed.

"Truth is immortal."
Nicolsburg, 1527.

The people, having heard and accepted the word of God, gave [themselves] in faith. They have, according to Christ's command, before the church publicly covenanted with and promised God in water baptism to live henceforth in accord with it. They have submitted themselves to the power of God the Father, Son, and Holy Spirit in work and suffering, in happiness and sorrow, in joy and pain, in life and death, whichever God may send (Matt. 28[:19]; Mark 16 [:15ff.]; Acts 2[:38]). They are willing to accept all of these things and to suffer, die, and be buried with Christ in the hope and certainty of being raised from the dead with him, by the glory of the father, to walk in the newness of life (Rom. 6[:4]). From now on they will not let sin govern their mortal flesh, neither will they obey the lusts of the flesh. Instead, in obedience to the Lord God they deliver their bodies as weapons in [339] the service of justice, that they may be sanctified and attain the goal, which is eternal life and a gift of God in Christ Jesus our Lord. Thus, they may be able to shout and sing "holy, holy, holy" to his praise, laud and glory.

To do and complete this, the people made public confession of the christian faith, and by receiving water baptism, were registered, listed, and incorporated into the community of the holy, universal, and christian church, outside of which there is no salvation, just as there was none outside of Noah's ark (Rev. 4[:8]; Matt. 16[:16]; Acts 8[:38]; Gen. 6[:7]; 1 Pet. 3[:21]). Now these people have become a separate and visible church. A new daughter has been born to the mother, that is to the universal christian church. It is only proper that the daughter should do the will of her mother, just as the mother (the universal christian church) does the will of her spouse and bridegroom, who is Christ Jesus, son of the living God, whose will he in turn obeyed to the death. Thus, the will of God the father will be done equally by his beloved son, mother and daughter on earth as in heaven (Matt. 16[:16]; Matt. 26[:63]; Matt. 6[:10]; Luke 11[:2]).

Oh, devout Christians, since men are by nature children of wrath, of an evil and sinful disposition, it is always necessary to treat them with healing medicine. Sometimes, it is even necessary to cut off the gangrenous and stinking flesh together with the poisoned and unclean members, lest the entire body be deformed, desecrated and spoiled by them (Eph. 2[:13]; Psalm 13, [14:3]; 1 Cor. 15[:35]). This is so Christians might continue and persevere in their newly begun, fresh and christian life and not fall again under the wrath of God like a filthy sow into the cesspool of sin (2 Pet. 2[:22]). The only way this is possible is by the brotherly discipline initiated and ordained by Christ (Matt. 18[:15ff.]).

Yes, God lives and witnesses himself that I speak the truth. Unless brotherly discipline is again upheld, accepted and practiced according to the earnest commandments of Christ nothing will be right or in good order among Christians on earth. Though all of us proclaim, write about and listen to the gospel until we are hoarse and tired, all of this noise, effort, and work is unavailing and useless. In fact, even water baptism and the breaking of bread are in vain, useless, and fruitless if brotherly discipline and the christian ban do not accompany them—brotherly discipline with water baptism, and the ban with communion and fellowship. We have witnessed and experienced all of this for some years in many places. During all this time, the people learned but two things, without, however, any improvement in conduct. The first is that they say: "We believe; we are justified by faith." The second: "We can do no good thing by ourselves." Now, both of these are true. But under the cover [340] of these two half-truths, all manner of wickedness, unfaithfulness, and injustice completely gained the upper hand. During the same time, brotherly love has become more extinguished in more hearts than previously in many thousand years (Matt. 24[:12]).

Yes, the well-known proverb is all too true and is being fulfilled: "The older, the more wicked. Things will get worse before they get better. The older, the colder. The longer the world lasts, the worse it gets." [*Ye elter, ye böser. Es bessert sich nit, es bösert sich wol. Ye ölter, ye költer. Ye lennger die welt steet, ye böser sy wird.*] We even have to suffer this slap in the face from the godless. Sad to say, we must confess before God that we have only ourselves to blame. We all want to be Christians and good Protestants [*gütt Euangelisch*] by taking wives, by eating meat, and by dropping the mass, fasting, and praying. Yet, nothing is seen in their place but boozing, swilling, blaspheming, taking usury, lying, cheating, tormenting, exploiting, compelling, forcing, stealing, looting, burning, gambling, dancing, courting, loafing, whoring, adultering, raping, tyrannizing, strangling, and killing. Every frivolity and looseness of the flesh is rampant in the highest degree. Worldly voluptuousness takes the highest seat, reigning, rejoicing, and triumphing in all things. No christian work is seen to shine among men. Fraternal love and faithfulness are completely extinguished. Sorry to say, all of this is still being done under the guise of the gospel.

As soon as you say to such a Protestant: "Brother, the bible says 'Refrain from doing evil and do good,'" he answers right back: "The bible says that we are unable to do good. All things are done through God's providence and are therefore necessary." (What they mean by this is that they are allowed to commit sin.) If you say further: "The bible says that those who do evil will be condemned to the eternal fire" they immediately find a bunch of fig leaves to cover their vices and say: "But the bible says that faith alone justifies us and not our works" (John 5[:29]; Gen. 3[:7]). It is possible with such hair-splitting talk to remain a good Protestant and to quote scripture like the friends of Job or even the Devil (Matt. 4) to defend our reckless freedom, and in a well-mannered and masterful way to cite, embellish, and refine the vulgarity of our flesh. If brotherly discipline were to be reintroduced among us, such excuses and artful concealing of our sins and vices would soon be discovered and terminated. Therefore, let us with the aid of God begin such brotherly discipline not only in teaching but also in act and deed. May God grant us his grace and power to complete this task.

[341] Then, the old Adam will really begin to prick his ears, complain, leap about, snort, and kick front and rear. He just cannot stand this discipline. He wants to be a Christian and yet be undisciplined [unstrefflich]. We wish to show him by the authority of holy scripture something quite different and to beg his innate pride to grant us a gracious audience. If he does not care to permit this here and now, then he will have to on judgment day. Thus, we would herein have preserved our honor and conscience against many.

Christ Jesus, our Lord and Savior, has always applied great diligence and zeal to rout out and subdue vices among his people by which many men are seduced, made wicked, and robbed of their eternal life. He speaks: "Woe to the world for temptations to sin! Woe to the man by whom the temptation comes! It would be better for him if a millstone were hung round his neck and he were cast into the sea, than that he should cause one of these little ones to sin. Take heed to yourselves (Luke 17[:1–3]; Matt. 18[:7]). If your brother sins against you, go and tell him his fault, between you and him alone. If he listens to you, you have gained your brother. But if he does not listen, take one or two others along with you, that every word may be confirmed by the evidence of two or three witnesses. If he refuses to listen to them, tell it to the church; and if he refuses to listen even to the church, let him be to you as a Gentile and a tax collector. Truly, I say to you, whatever you bind on earth shall be bound in heaven, and whatever you loose on earth shall be loosed in heaven" (Matt. 18[:15–18]).

Here, christian reader, in this brief phrase "against you" it may be seen that there are two kinds of sin—public and private. Public sins are those that are committed shamelessly before men. Such sins should be punished publicly and immediately lest good and simple people be seduced or made wicked and perhaps be led to say: "If he can do it, so can I." For example, the people began to live promiscuously when they saw that this was what priests and officials were doing. Again, when the pope allowed the unspiritual mob [of clerics] and the monasteries to keep five guilders or more for every hundred [as interest] against the clear and honest word of Christ (Luke 6[:34–35]), other people began to practice the same and even made an "honest" business out of this [usury]. A wicked sin is temptation, for it spreads like a cancer and leprosy unless it is cut out at once by brotherly discipline.

For this reason Paul teaches us, saying: "As for those who persist in sin, rebuke them in the presence of all, so that the rest may stand in fear" (1 Tim. 5[:20]). [342] In the same way Christ rebuked Peter, when the latter out of humane and well-meaning motives urged him with but a few words to spare himself and, to avoid suffering, not go up to Jerusalem. At that time Christ said to him: "Get behind me, Satan! You are a hindrance to me, for you are not on the side of God but of men" (Matt. 16[:23]). Again, Peter rebuked Simon [the magician] who wanted to purchase the Holy Spirit from the apostles, and said: "Your silver perish with you, because you thought you could obtain the gift of God with money! You have neither part nor lot in this matter, for your heart is not right before God. Repent, therefore, of this wickedness of yours, and pray to the Lord that, if possible, the intent of your heart may be forgiven you" (Acts 8[:20–22]).

Yet every honest Christian must take care that this discipline and sharpness of speech flow from love and not from envy, hatred, or anger, as can be seen in the words of Peter when he desired the betterment of Simon, saying: "Repent, etc." In the same way Paul rebuked Peter when he realized that Peter did not behave according to gospel truth. He said: "If you, though a Jew, live like a Gentile and not like a Jew, how can you compel the Gentiles to live like Jews?" (Gal. 2[:14]). Indeed, Paul criticized Peter in public face to face, because he was in error.

Some sins, however, are private and are committed secretly and quietly. Such sins should be dealt with in private, according to Christ's commandment. Nathan the prophet rebuked King David thus, and Christ the traitor Judas—though in front of the disciples, it was with hidden meaning (2 Sam. 12[:7]; Matt. 26[:24]). If your brother listens to you, accepts your admonition, and refrains from the sin, then you have won by this more than all the Venetian merchants in their lifetimes. If he does not listen to you, then take one or two along with you in order to have witnesses. If he does not listen to them either, then tell it to the church, for in this you are obeying the will and earnest commandment of Christ, who combined in one commandment two saving ordinances. That is, he commanded you to admonish your brother or otherwise participate in his sin. In the same words he has admonished your brother to accept brotherly discipline from you in a peaceable and polite manner. If he does this, it is for his salvation; if not, you are before God then innocent of his sin.

Here, however, mortal wisdom (for which all of God's word is poison and gall) protests, saying: "It does not seem right to me that my brother should reveal my secret sin. He would not like for me to do it to him. Therefore, it is only fair that he should leave me alone, or rather, should help me hide my sin." Answer: He only admonished you in private so that your sin might not be revealed. As you did not listen to him, he had, in accordance with Christ's commandment, to bring two or three with him in his attempt to save your soul, lest you be embarrassed before the entire church. [343] When you refused that also, he had no choice but to bring it before the entire church. He was more concerned for the commandment of Christ and the salvation of your soul than for your secular, false and hypocritical honor and piety, for your being considered pious when you are the opposite. It would be far preferable for you to be shamed before your particular congregation than before the church universal and all the heavenly choirs of angels on judgment day. No matter how secret you try to keep it, it is bound to be revealed and your sin especially is bound to be punished (Matt. 10[:26]).

Since you refused to listen even to the church, what could have been more beneficial for you than to be expelled and considered a heathen? Better this, than that you should have defiled the entire church with evil, and perhaps have involved many more members in sin and eternal ruin along with yourself. It was also more beneficial for you in that it might cause you to repent, realize your sinfulness, refrain from sinning, and then be received again with great rejoicing into the church and be permitted again within the christian fellowship.

Now you see, devout Christian, how useful and beneficial brotherly discipline is to him who recognizes its salutary nature and accepts it. Yet, neither flesh, blood, nor [un]spiritual man can understand it (1 Cor. 2[:14]). He always wants to be thought of as pious, and not be disciplined by anyone. But the spiritual man judges all things. This discipline and ban are beneficial to man from an objective point of view. But it would also be better for him that a millstone be tied around his neck and that he be cast into the sea, than that he should cause the least reproach or annoyance in the church and compound his sins (Matt. 18[:66]).

Since brotherly discipline and the christian ban flow from such an inward, heartfelt, and zealous love (as a Christian should bear for another in true faithfulness), he would be an ignorant, vile, and godless monster—indeed, a veritable Herod—who would not accept this discipline in an amicable, peaceable manner and with thanksgiving from his brother (Mark 6[:14ff.]; Matt. 14[:11ff.]).

Another thing should be mentioned here, devout reader. This is that there are two kinds of commandments. The first constrains each Christian to discipline his brother according to Christ's ordinance (Matt. 18[:15ff.]). The other commands the one who does the disciplining to remove first the log from his eye before he sets about removing the speck from the eye of the brother. This is indeed a true ordinance of Christ which must be obeyed (Matt. 7[:4ff.]; Luke 6[:42]). Nevertheless, the first commandment is not revoked by the second. To the contrary, it is better to observe one commandment than to neglect both. [344] Accordingly, no one will be excused from disciplining his brother on the ground that he is himself a sinner, because otherwise all brotherly discipline would break down. Even the greatest sinner is obligated to discipline his brother, lest by his silence he make himself liable for the other's sins.

This is what Isaiah meant by consorting with thieves (Isa. 1[:23]). David calls it being a friend of thieves and keeping company with adulterers (Psalm 49[50:18]). For this reason I have written all of this, because under the excuse that we are all sinners, no one has wanted to discipline the other any more or to accept discipline. In this way the practice of brotherly discipline has been completely extinguished and turned to ashes.

How One Should Discipline
Another

According to the scriptures, it should take place in this way: "Brother, the bible says that on judgment day men shall render account for every careless word they utter (Matt. 12[:36]). Now, dear brother, you have given a baptismal pledge to Christ Jesus our Lord, publicly covenanting and pledging before the church that you will conduct and govern your life henceforth according to his holy word (which is witnessed to in the holy scriptures). Failing in this, you promised to submit yourself willingly to discipline, according to Christ's commandment, upon which you received water baptism and thus you were enrolled in the membership of christian fellowship."

"Now, however, you use many careless and frivolous words, whereby good morals are considerably harmed, which hardly befits a Christian (1 Cor. 15[:33]). Therefore, I remind you, my very dear brother, of your baptismal covenant, that you may recall your promise to God. I beg of you, for the sake of God and the salvation of your soul, to avoid this useless drivel and to improve your life. If you do this, you do the will of God."

If thereupon your brother abandons his sin, you will have gained a precious jewel. If he does not, then take two or three witnesses with you and try again, using the same words. If he does not listen to them, then tell it to the congregation, who will know how to handle things. Deal with other sins in the same way.

Further, dear christian reader, if you notice that a brother is not in harmony with another, be it from envy, hatred, or another form of enmity, bring the two together. Confront them with the teachings of Christ, who says: "So if you are offering your gift at the altar, and there remember that your brother has something against you, leave your gift there before the altar and go; first be reconciled to your brother and then come and offer your gift" (Matt. 5[:23–24]). God is not pleased to receive anything from us as long as we bear enmity toward our neighbor.

Therefore reconcile [345] them [your brethren] with yourself and each other. If they will not listen to you, then follow the instructions given above about brotherly discipline. Truly, truly, where this is done God will undergird his word so powerfully and wonderfully that christian brethren and their congregations will be able to reconcile and unite difficulties and differences which could not otherwise be brought about in many years with great costs and damages. Whichever party is not willing to be reconciled will be punished by God to such extent that he will lose one hundred guilders for every ten, even life and limb. So powerful is God that he is at peace with the peaceful and contends with the contentious. That is, he can repay in kind.

This admonition and discipline, christian brother, can only be practiced through the introduction of the divine word, that is the ten commandments and other christian teachings (Ex. 20[:1–17]; Deut. 5[:6–21]; Matt. 5–7; Rom. 12). "Now these things," says Paul, "are written for our instruction, upon whom the end of the ages has come." And in another place: "All scripture is inspired by God and profitable for teaching, for reproof, for correction, and for training in righteousness that the man of God may be complete, equipped for every good work" (1 Cor. 10[:11]; 2 Tim. 3[:16–17]).

From this may clearly be seen whence comes the authority for one brother to have the privilege and right to admonish another. It derives from the baptismal covenant which the brother made before receiving water baptism, when he submitted himself to the church and all its members according to Christ's ordinance. This, however, the Antichrist and his cohorts will not tolerate. He wants nothing less than to be infallible, free, and blameless, though he daily leads large numbers of souls to hell. Yet, he wants no one to ask him: "Why are you doing this?" For this reason he overthrew the true baptismal covenant along with water baptism because they could not be made compatible with his pride, pomp, and greed. Nevertheless he wants to be counted among the baptized Christians, indeed, as a pillar of the church.

Despite this, he would not tolerate being told: "Brother pope, brother bishop, brother emperor, king, prince or lord—you sin and err before God!" This is why the Antichrist has worked with such great industry night and day to cast out Christ's water baptism and to replace it with his fictitious, miserable, and antichristian infant baptism. He did this so that if he were reminded and reproached because of his sacramental baptismal vow and promise of faithfulness, he might be able to excuse himself readily by saying: "I was a child then; I did not understand the Latin; I neither promised anything nor did I even know then what covenant, faith, Christ, baptism or brotherly discipline were." Nonetheless, you antichristian pack, this sort of excuse will not help you, for the gospel has been preached throughout the world as a testimony to all the nations! (Matt. 24[:14]) No one may excuse himself by saying he has not heard it.

Whoever discards the least of Christ's commandments will be ranked the least in heaven. Woe, woe, woe to all those who [346] have rejected the water baptism of Christ, brotherly discipline, the Lord's supper, and the christian ban and have practiced something else instead! (Matt. 5[:19]) Blessed, blessed, blessed are they, however, who rightly perform and teach Christ's commandments, for they will be ranked high, high in heaven!

This must be said to all those who cry: "What is there to water baptism? What is there to the Lord's supper? These are only outward symbols. They are nothing other than water, bread, and wine. Why quarrel about them?" Those people have in all their lives never learned even to understand why these symbols were ordained by Christ, what their purpose is, or to what end they are to be practiced. The end is the gathering of a church, the covenanting publicly to live according to Christ's word in faith and brotherly love, and the submitting of themselves in brotherly discipline and the christian ban because of their sins. All this they pledge publicly with a sacramental oath before the christian church and all of her members (be they present in person or in spirit) by the power of God the Father, Son, and Holy Spirit and by the power of our Lord Jesus Christ, which is the same, and seal this with a handclasp. This is the important thing, dear brother, and not the water, bread, or wine. Our water baptism and breaking of bread have become but empty illusions, indeed, nothing better than the futile infant baptism and spoonfeeding of children in communion has been where brotherly discipline and the christian ban are not also present.

In summary, where water baptism is not administered according to Christ's ordinance, it is impossible for brotherly discipline to be accepted in good spirit. For no one knows who is inside or outside the church. No one has power over anyone else. We are scattered like sheep without a shepherd, without pasture, without marking. Furthermore, we do not know or recognize who has been marked as a sheep of Christ, or who chooses to remain a goat outside of Christ's sheepfold (John 10[:2]). God help us all that we might go through the right door into the sheepfold of Christ and not attempt to climb in elsewhere, against the express commandment of Jesus Christ. Amen.

Truth is immortal.

1527.

Editor's note

Wolfgang Brandhuber (d. 1529) was a representative leader of
Austrian Anabaptism. He was originally a tailor from St. Niclas near
Passau, where he was baptized in 1527, and became an elder in Linz,
Upper Austria. He helped found congregations throughout the Austrian
crown lands. That his influence extended farther as well is indicated by
the fact that he baptized the leader of the Anabaptists in Thuringia,
who came to Wels (near Linz) for this purpose.

Shortly after writing the present letter of exhortation and admonition
to the threatened congregation at Rattenberg on the Inn, he was
himself taken by the authorities (as the postscript to the letter states).
He was burned at the stake along with a fellow minister. Peter
Riedemann, later to become the outstanding Hutterite leader, succeeded
Brandhuber as elder of the Upper Austrian Anabaptists.

These dissenters, endangered as they were by imminent capture and
sudden death, were more ready than some of their fellows—especially in
Switzerland and South Germany—to pool their goods communally. It is
not surprising that the early communitarian Hutterite colonies were
largely peopled by refugees from Austria. Yet Brandhuber's exhortation
to a community of goods should not be thought of as a call for
complete community of production and consumption, but rather as an
extensive sharing of material as well as spiritual gifts. He taught that
each should devote himself to honest labor, which would result in an
abundance to be given to others as need arose.

Hand in hand with this sharing was a puritan-like criticism of a fancy
style of life. Such conspicuous consumption was thought to be evidence
of a self-centered and secular frame of mind. Those who refused
fraternal discipline on such matters in this life would need to face a
sterner trial on judgment day.

The epistle is translated from the collection of Anabaptist testimonies
of faith (*Glaubenszeugnisse*) edited by Lydia Müller.

Wolfgang Brandhuber   An Epistle from Our Dear
Brother and Servant of Jesus
Christ, Wolfgang Brandhuber,
to the Church of God at
Rattenberg on the Inn (1529)

Wolfgang, an unworthy servant of Christ called by the grace of God
which God has granted me, to the church at Rattenberg on the Inn
together with all the saints who with us and you have become par-
ticipants in the faith of Christ. Grace be with you and peace in
God our father and our Lord Jesus Christ. Blessed be God the father
of our Lord Jesus Christ, the father of mercies and God of all solace,
who comforts us in all our affliction, so that we may be able to
comfort those who are in any affliction, with the solace with which
we ourselves are comforted by God the father. For as we share
abundantly in Christ's suffering, so through Christ we share abundantly in comfort too [2 Cor. 1:4–5]. Amen, so be it.

Much beloved brethren in the Lord and my fellow-members, you
are well informed how powerfully and wonderfully the merciful God
works among you in Rattenberg and how he chastises and admonishes you with so much paternal discipline as his dearly beloved
children, which is for your own good. Every child accepted by the
father is chastised by him. Notice then the great love, goodness,
and mercy which he has shown you after you had fallen into sin
and the father rescued you from it again. Therefore I and all the
fellow-members praise and magnify his holy name, that he has preserved you so many times and even now is preserving some of you.
Be patient in bearing all that comes to you for the sake of the word
of God, for you know what good effect patience brings. Therefore
examine yourselves well in the Lord that you might recognize the
false spirits. Many of these now spread among the people of God,
after the false prophets, yes, the ravening wolves, have gathered
the selfish and the deniers of truth. They see and hear that they are
told to begin living in accordance with the ordinance or commandment of the Lord.

In the church of God not every person is to be treasurer, for only
he who is elected to that office disburses the possessions of the rich
and the poor. The actions of irresponsible people have caused irregular conduct, annoyance, and offense [138] even in the christian

church contrary to the word of God. They go about hypocritically, contradicting the life of Christ in his christian church, even the order which the dear apostle taught and observed. These are the very people of whom John said that they have gone out from us [1 John 2:19]. Paul, Peter, and Jude also mention the same kind in their epistles.

They say that it is wrong to hold all things in common or to reveal to another in love the extent of one's property. They do not care to have deacons or elders who minister to the needy. Rather, they say that charity should be with the knowledge of the church officials or that each person should be his own steward. This I say is wrong. If God wills it and the state permits it, all things should be held in common to the greater glory of God, for since we have become partakers of Christ in the greatest things (that is in the power of God), then why not even more so in the least, that is in the material realm?

That is not to say that all goods should be piled together, for conditions are not the same in all places. But every head of a household together with all those living there who are united with him in the faith should pool their earnings, be they master, servant, wife, maid, or other fellow-believers. Though every worker should be given his daily wages, according to the words of Christ that every laborer deserves his wages [Matt. 10:10; Luke 10:7], love should compel each person to place faithfully his wages in the common purse. Indeed, it should be done from love!

Further, all members should be faithfully observed so that they might be admonished and corrected according to biblical command until the witness of their lives and their confession of faith is thoroughly known. At this point the commandment of the Lord should be followed by having the men presented to the congregation in the word, that the order of the spiritual body of Christ be furthered and the work completed, just as the Lord says: "How beautiful . . . are the feet of him who brings good tidings, who publishes peace" [Isa. 52:7].

In the same way how lovely are the eyes of those who take note of the needs of their neighbors. Blessed is the hand which nourishes itself with its work and prospers honestly, so that it has something to give to the needy and can thus preserve the whole body.

You well know how Paul described the natural body as an example and said that no part can be concerned for itself alone, but rather that all parts are responsible for the entire body; none can take precedence over the other [1 Cor. 12:14–26]. I do not write this as to those who are ignorant of it but as to those who already know it! I exhort you, my brethren and fellow-anointed in the Lord, that you earnestly take notice of all things which are expected of us, for the Lord has not told us in vain through the power of the spirit what we should do or not do. For it is through the scriptures and the law in our hearts that he has told us to do the things which are pleasing in his sight. [139] He also told us in many places to cast off the weapons of unrighteousness, admonishing us to act in love and humility. Thus he sets about preparing us for the last day of his wrath.

If we have not paid attention and discarded whatever displeases him, then, he says, he will remove it himself on that day. That is: the beautiful buckles, the precious bonnets, the golden pins, collars, bracelets, ribbons the lovely full dresses, musk apples, clasps, rings, diadems, holiday clothes, and the hats, cloaks, veils, and clasps, the mirrors, shirts, scarves and summer gowns, etc. Eventually there will be a stench instead of fine fragrance, a loincloth instead of trousers, plainness instead of fancy stuff, sackcloths instead of scarves, black hues instead of beautiful colors. Therefore, pierce your hearts instead of your garments. Discipline the idol-makers and those who honor and worship them, even those who merely cast their eyes upon them.

God also raises a loud cry of woe upon all merchants with no exceptions, whether small or important, even upon those who once were merchants and whored with the great whore of Babylon. The Lord speaks powerfully: "Innocent blood cries out to me without ceasing, in deed the blood of the sorrowful." He says: "Even though I have forgiven everything else, I will not allow the innocent blood to remain unavenged."

Take care then, my brethren, that all of those things are put away in the love of God and chastisement will be light for you, but for the disobedient it—that is, the correction—will be heavy. Further, I want to be sure to admonish you not to allow Christ to be made into a Moses, as some are now doing who want to preserve the sword on the basis of the Mosaic law. They contradict the teachings and life of Christ, as mentioned above. They even want Christians to judge and condemn others to death, which, however, the long-suffering lamb Christ never taught us.

Dear brethren, remember, if all scriptures are overturned for you, withdraw to the innermost recesses of your hearts, recall what the power of the Holy Spirit has taught and promised us, saying: "He who overcomes as I have overcome, to him will I give the heathens as an inheritance; he shall lead them to pasture with a scepter and smash them as a potter's crockery" [Isa. 14:5–6]. Paul also says: What do those outside matter to you? [1 Cor. 5:12–13]. Therefore look alone at our example, the prince of our faith, and upon him who fulfilled the faith, Jesus, who divested himself of all such things, even though judgment and righteousness are his alone. Nevertheless, he despised these things and told us to follow him, etc.

Let us also remember that every person who judges himself will not be judged by the father but rather be chastised, and he will thereafter [140] himself judge the world, even the angels. In sum, take heed lest you fail in the trial which comes from those who wield the sword on the basis of the law of Moses, for they have already published a booklet dealing with this. They esteem the servant higher than the son. It is not that I despise Moses for being a loyal servant of God, but he was still in the shadow. The curtain had not been rent yet through which the light has shone for us. Oh brethren, the kind of trial that this is or shall be you will soon have occasion to discover. Whoever so perseveres in this furnace that his faith is not damaged, will find the sight of the Lord beloved and pleasing.

In the second place, take care also in relation to warfare, lest you mistakenly defend your bodies, as if you were obeying the authorities in this matter. This is against God. Otherwise, however, the authorities should be obeyed in all things which are not against God's will as far as life and property are concerned. Yes, this matter of war is not the least of your trials. I sometimes think that in this will be revealed the name of the beast of which John writes [Rev. 13:16]. Its signs have already been partly revealed to us, namely the dead elements—the meaningless sign of confirmation on the forehead of children and the dead element of the bread in the mass. If anyone, contrary to the correct knowledge of truth, considers these important in his life, then he denies in this the will of the Lord outwardly before men, and he also has the sign on his right hand, that is, eternal damnation.

In the same way infant baptism is an abomination and word of blasphemy of our God, which John only mentions in his revelation but which will be further revealed to us if we only seek the Lord and remain in his truth and word, persevering to the end. He will reveal it to us, for to him alone belongs the interpretation.

Dearly beloved in the Lord, I admonish you with much sighing in divine and brotherly love that everyone from the bottom of his heart should seek and look to the Lord and his righteousness. The Adversary has already assumed the appearance of an angel, and men are almost everywhere saying: "Lo, here is the Christ" or "There he is" [Matt. 24:23]. They disguise and conceal this fact, but it is still true.

They also believe that Christianity is to be found in the outward appearance among those who can orate and speak in beautiful words about it, who conduct themselves decorously while listening and gather politely from time to time, exchanging greetings, even the peace of the Lord. It is the secret Adversary who hides behind this deceptive appearance and vain ways, who is always pleased with himself. Indeed, many are of the opinion that this really pleases God; they consider themselves better than others, thus truly erecting a golden calf [141] in Israel, upon which must be put gold and jewels. He who is wise should remember not to worship the work of his hands lest he lose sight of his true goal and build on hay and stubble which will be consumed in the fire.

Therefore, dearly beloved brethren in the Lord, be not deceived. The Lord says that the kingdom of God will not come in outward appearances and gestures, neither is it to be found in words, food, or drink, but rather in the power and witness of the Holy Spirit. Since God is a spirit, he wants to have spiritual servants, for the carnal is opposed to the spiritual. Therefore, we will not be able to seek or find the spiritual word in those dead elements, for the kingdom of God is justice, joy, life, and peace in the Holy Spirit who is the true life. Realizing then, beloved in God, that God is a spirit we must worship him in spirit and in truth.

The worship of God must be conducted in spirit and truth—not outside but inside the truth. You must listen, like David, to God speaking within you. The image of God within you and his likeness accuse you, that is, accuse your flesh. That is why the two adversaries rise up in your soul. If you want to go to God, then you have to enter by the gate through which Adam was expelled. That means you will have to subdue your flesh, will, lusts, and love and follow the law which is in your heart; you must follow the loud voices of John [the Baptist] and Isaiah in the wilderness to prepare the way of the Lord [Matt. 3:3; Isa. 40:3].

[If you do this] then the weaker will have to give way to the stronger, that is to the spirit of Christ. Nevertheless, such a person will always experience the strife and conflict of the flesh within himself, which will compel him with a greatly troubled and fearful heart to appear before the countenance of the Lord in true humility and lowliness. To such persons John reveals in the innermost recesses of their hearts the true lamb of God, who has taken unto himself the sins of all men, but especially of those who are his own. To these he shows his salvation and permits his power to be revealed in them. However, this does not happen in a physical way, for he has risen to be with the father and will only come again some day to judge the living and the dead, etc. Yet he remains in power, truth and spirit with those who are his own until the end of the world. Flesh and spirit must always struggle against each other within that person who has chosen what is good, which of course he cannot achieve and attain through his own power and strength. Since he does not spare his efforts, the anointing of the Holy Spirit follows, which signifies the unspeakable grace of the goodness and mercy of God. Yet it really troubles this person that he cannot be freed and rid of his flesh, which constantly attempts to prevent him from contemplating God's goodness and power and causes him all kinds of tribulation. This battle goes on unceasingly.

[142] A godfearing man continually looks to God and walks with great care for he knows that the victory is not his but God's. For this reason he prays without ceasing for deliverance from evil. No one desires to be delivered from evil until he truly recognizes what is good. This, then, is the beginning of a christian life. At that point a person is careful not to mistreat any of God's creatures even if they are distrustful of him. He rejects riches and luxury, for they are dangerous [allies] of his enemy, his flesh. Even though all may be well with him, he does not trust his flesh, for he is searching for something else, namely, the creator of all created.

This man remains constantly in the fear of the Lord as did Job, and also fears all of [God's] works. He does not think highly of himself, does not accept that which he in fact is, but rather considers himself unworthy. He accepts the lowest place at the wedding banquet, looks only at the true light, and subjects all thoughts, words, and deeds to this light, which is Christ through whom the will of the father was revealed. He has prepared the way for us through true humanity, so that no man will have an excuse on that day. It is his will according to which all of our actions and life should be patterned, for "I and the Father are one," says the Lord [John

10:30]. If we also wish to be one with him, we must do his will;
that is when we realize our misery and love him in return. If we
love him, we keep his commandments, for if there is to be love, it
has to be in our hearts. How else should love express its intent and
purpose than by unceasingly desiring that which it so dearly loves,
just as the bride in the Song of Solomon disregards everything else
and sings and speaks only of her love.

False Christianity does not do this, for there is found only much
frivolous chatter, etc. True Christianity has only love. She needs no
law, for she fulfills the law of God from sheer love, practicing this
day and night, discarding everything else, despising everything else.
Why? She seeks because she loves. The more she loves, the more
she desires to love. She rejoices in her love. When she sees her
beloved in the distance beyond the lattice, resting in the shadow
of faith, she does not care that others mock her.

Oh brethren, where love is absent what use is great knowledge,
talk, and teaching without love? What does the Adversary do? He
also erects and builds a love of God, but this one—like the other
which comes from the law—must have properly prescribed words,
set laws and rules, and must be visible, for otherwise one could not
tell that they were Christians. Therefore, they have to sound the
trumpets. That which the spirit worked among the former and which
they did from sheer love and from the bottom of their hearts, must
—like the mimicry of apes—be done similarly for the sake of propriety. Oh brethren, let every one be concerned with the truth of his
heart before the countenance of God because God rejects the outward appearance. May the father of all grace grant the true bread
to all those who hunger that they might preach the scriptures [143]
with unadulterated understanding and without strings attached, for
the spirit of God will not be bound.

Read this epistle diligently and carefully, and pray to God for
understanding. He will give great wisdom to all those who attend
his school and accept his discipline. Thus I commend you to the
powerful hand, protection, and care of the almighty king. Amen.

All brothers and sisters in Linz greet you in the Lord. I ask you
to pray for them and for us all that the Lord might not let us succumb to temptation. We will do the same for you. Greet one another
with the kiss of love. Depart from your Sodoms and Gomorrahs,
you children of Lot, that you may not, like them, be destroyed and
share in their wicked deeds.

I understand that you would very much like to have the booklet about baptism.* I cannot send this to you now, for the copying would be too much work, but if you do not have it, let me know in writing and it will be sent to you. Yet, the true foundation is the letter of the heart, which can alone be judged by God. The end.

[P.S.] Through the hatred and envy of the old serpent this dear brother, servant and witness of Jesus Christ has given up his ghost in fire to God his heavenly father for the sake of the divine truth, in Linz, Upper Austria, and has thus also been made a sacrifice.

In the year of our Lord 1529.

---

*Possibly the booklet by John Hut, *Vom Geheimnis der Tauf* (ca. 1527) is meant.

Editor's note

An early church order or discipline comes from the ranks of the South
German Anabaptists, thought by some scholars to represent a different
grouping of Anabaptism from the Swiss Brethren. Although there are
some different emphases in doctrine, both the Swiss Brethren and the
South German Anabaptists shared the same foundation principles.

The author of the church order was Leopold Scharnschlager (d. 1563),
who was an associate of Pilgram Marpeck, a leading figure among
Anabaptists. Like Marpeck a native of the Tyrol, Scharnschlager was a
man of considerable property, which he lost when he joined the
outlawed movement. For a time he lived in Strassburg, until he was
expelled for his nonconformity in religion. He pointed out in an eloquent
appeal for religious liberty to the Reformed city fathers that they had
asked for tolerance themselves when they were still a persecuted
minority, but now when they had control refused to tolerate other
evangelicals. At that, Strassburg followed a milder policy of punishment
than other important cities, using expulsion rather than execution to
rid themselves of dissent.

For several years after 1534 nothing specific is known about
Scharnschlager, but it is assumed that he was located somewhere near
Marpeck, who lived at this time in Augsburg. The latter period of his
life Scharnschlager spent in the Grisons (Graubünden) in present-day
Switzerland, earning his living as a school teacher. He was one of the
few leading figures of Anabaptism to experience a natural death, dying at
Ilanz (Grisons) in 1563.

The church order which follows is found in the significant manuscript
collection of Anabaptist data known as the *Kunstbuch*, now located in
the state library in Berne, Switzerland. This translation is made from
the first publication of the church order in the source book on the
left wing of the Reformation edited by Heinold Fast (who
rediscovered the *Kunstbuch* in 1955).

Leopold Scharnschlager

Communal Rules for the
Members of Christ, Arranged
in Seven Articles (ca. 1540)

Yesterday:
"Children, let all your works be done in order with good intent in the
fear of God, and do nothing disorderly in scorn or out of its due season"
*(Testament of Naphtali 11:9).**
Today:
Paul says in 1 Corinthians 14:40: "All things should be done decently
and in order." Likewise in Colossians 2:5: "[I rejoice] to see your good
order and the firmness of your faith in Christ."

Preface

[131] Our heavenly father, to whom be given praise, honor, and
thanksgiving forever, has called us in these latter days from the
darkness of the world into his wonderful light through the knowledge of his holy truth. We have all been baptized and have agreed
to become one body in Jesus Christ, regardless of where we happen
to be in the world. Therefore, in order that we may be faithful to
our calling not only with words but also with deeds and in truth,
it is necessary that we observe an order through which in love we
can exist, be admonished, and be corrected, for all things exist
through order. Such an order is drawn up in several articles in the
following. Nevertheless, adaptations will have to be made daily
according to the nature and opportunity of the time, but always
for the sake of improvement.

The first article

In the first place: Because of the various kinds of temptations
spreading everywhere, it is necessary that the called, pledged, and
committed members of Jesus Christ should not, as far as they are
able, abandon the meetings, wherever they may be in the world
and in distress (Heb. 10:25). Rather, wherever and however they
can—depending on the place and the extent of persecution—they
should gather for the sake of the love of Christ, be they few or
many—2, 3, 4, 6, 10, 15, or 20—more or less. This should be done
with wisdom, humility, reason, discipline, amity, and discretion, the
more so as we realize that the day of the Lord is near. The Lord

---

*The Testament of Naphtali is part of the *Testament of the Twelve*
Patriarchs, among the so-called Pseudepigrapha, included in biblical
manuscripts in the middle ages.

says: "Where two or three are gathered in my name, there am I in the midst of them" (Matt. 18:20).

The second article

[132] In the next place: When they meet they shall, in the absence of a regular elder [*Vorsteher*], invite in a friendly and loving manner one of their number (whom they think capable) to read or preach to them according to the gift he has received from God. Or, someone shall volunteer his service out of love. Then one after another —according to the gifts they have received as Paul teaches (1 Cor. 14[:26–33])—they shall speak and exercise their gifts for the edification of the members. This is so that our church might not be like the falsely praised [congregations], where only one person and no one else is allowed to speak.

Before they begin to speak, however, they shall fall on their knees and sincerely call upon the Lord that he might endow them with the gift of preaching in a profitable manner (1 Tim. 2:1). At the conclusion they shall diligently exhort one another to walk in the ways of the Lord and to remain constant with him, faithfully watching until he comes (Matt. 24:42, 26:41; Luke 12:35ff.). Then we may be found without blemish by him (Phil. 2:15) and may be with one another, not only here but also much more so in the next world, rejoicing eternally in the Lord (Isa. 4:2ff.). Likewise, before parting again, they shall call upon the Lord and pray for all members, also for their material needs, and for all mankind according to the direction of our dear brother Paul (1 Tim. 2:1ff.). They shall also give thanks for all gifts and blessings received from God (1 Thess. 5:17ff.). And, as has been said, from time to time, as opportunity [133] offers, they shall break bread one with the other before parting as a memorial to the death of the Lord (1 Cor. 11:24).

The third article

In the third place: Where they meet in this manner, a minister or, if none is present, another elder (1 Cor. 14) shall remember the poor members with such wise, warm, mild, and sweet words— not in a demanding but yet in an earnest and emphatic way—that their hearts may be stirred to selflessness and mercy, and a truly godpleasing manner and power of love may grow. Above all, a brother should always be at hand with a collection box or purse, and this fact be known to the members of the church, so that every member may know where to place the freewill offering and [gift of] thanksgiving either during or after the meeting, if he is urged by the Lord to do so. Thus it will be possible at any time to minister to the poor according to what is available and what is the need of each one. These funds should then always be distributed (by the brother with whom they were deposited) conscientiously and in the fear of God—indeed with the greatest care, not as the world does with its poor without examining and inquiring into their conduct and life, whether needy or not, whether greedy or not—for this is a holy office (Acts 6:1ff.).

The fourth article

In the fourth place: There is a scarcity of faithful workers in the vineyard of the Lord, who faithfully search and labor on his behalf in the proper manner, with wisdom and good conscience (1 Thess. 5:12ff.), which daily causes much error, dissension, [134] and anger. It is therefore extremely important that when such a faithful worker has been found great care be taken of him. He should be respected (Heb. 13:7), obeyed, and paid double the usual honor, according to the words of Paul (1 Tim. 5:17). Share with him every good thing (Gal. 6:9ff.) and service, as far as possible and according to his needs beyond what he can himself supply. This is so that we may not treat the messengers and laborers of the Lord, whom we are daily praying for, in an unworthy manner (Luke 10:2), lest the Lord permit us at last to be scattered without shepherds. This is said not only for the sake of those who recognize the truth but also for the sake of the weak, the milk drinkers and vegetarians (1 Cor. 3:2; Heb. 5:12; Rom. 14:2) and for the sake of those who are yet to be gathered to the Lord.

The fifth article

In the fifth place: The example [community of goods] of the early church at Jerusalem (Acts 4:32–5:11) has been misunderstood by many; this has caused error, contempt, schisms, and the like to rise. Some have made of it a law, compulsion, bonds, almost a carnal [works-]righteousness, demand and the like. Therefore, we should realize that in this first church at Jerusalem everything was done

voluntarily and that after the scattering of this church conditions
there and elsewhere were such that Paul also taught about assistance
and community of goods (Rom. 15:25ff.; 1 Cor. 16:1ff.; 2 Cor.
9:1ff.). We should, therefore, in true apostolic fashion also strive
to do this, so that the bride and flock of Christ may not be coerced
but rather follow and go voluntarily to pasture.

For this reason a treasurer [*Steuersammler*] should be mindful to
receive the smallest gift as well as the larger one without discrimina-
tion (Luke 21:1–4), [135] from the rich as from the poor, and
sincerely thank God and the giver. After that, leave it to the Lord.
Even though someone might say with a worldly understanding: "But
such person has already promised to give and has pledged himself;
why not speak up and demand what is necessary?" To this the
answer is: The order of the Holy Spirit does not permit it. The work
is not that of men, just as it was not the flesh which originally made
the promise. Therefore, it should not be secured in a secular way
but in a spiritual way. Otherwise we destroy the voluntary principle
of the people of God.

The sixth article

In the sixth place: If a brother or sister is found to be burdened
with the vices of the flesh, false beliefs, irregular conduct and character, or other similar snares, be it in word or deed, there shall
always be forthcoming from the elders moderate, discreet, and warm-
hearted admonition and correction, in fear and trembling before
God and in love (Gal. 6:1; Matt. 18:15ff.). The greatest care should
be taken in the case of every trespass—be it in private or in public,
small or large, whether after being admonished once or more often
—about the manner in which the correction is done, as to mildness
or severity, forbearance or immediate action. A difference must be
made between disciplining and banning according to the facts of the
case and the witness of the scripture, so that everything is done in
the spirit of love and not after the manner of the flesh (Titus 3:13;
1 Cor. 5:1ff.; Rom. 2:1ff.; Eph. 5:11; 1 Cor. 6:5). The authority
of Christ is not an authority to destroy or to tyrannize but one of
improvement, so that the bride of Christ is kept pure for him everywhere, both in relation to those inside the church as well as those
outside. This is so [136] that a respectable and irreproachable way
of life is led and the way and road to Christ and his kingdom is not
blocked or made suspicious for anyone.

The seventh article

In the seventh place: Concerning the doctrines, baptism, and
Lord's supper, these are to be observed by and through us according
to the command and custom of the Lord and his apostles. Nothing
should be distorted or changed; neither should anything be added
to or taken away (Deut. 4:2, 12:32; Prov. 30:6) as is the case with
the Antichristians and the falsely praised. Each brother and sister
shall at all times live according to the secrets of the way of christian
faith. Whatever the Lord entrusts him with is to be borne in good
conscience before the world in order to prevent blasphemy of Christ's
name, word, and honor. All other everyday issues or errors that
occur are to be dealt with in the fear of God and acted upon in
accordance with the gospel of Christ (Phil. 1:27) and the faith, and
so as to serve the improvement and edification of each person. We
are to observe this in all faithfulness, and avoid all unrighteousness
in words, deeds, and gestures. We should flee from these, shun them,
and be separate from them (2 Cor. 6:17) to the glory of God and
our bridegroom Jesus Christ. Then, when he comes we may joyfully
appear before him with holy adornment and graced with the Holy
Spirit (Matt. 24) and we may receive what he has earned for us
and prepared by the blood of his mercy (John 14).

To this end we pray to our heavenly father that he might grant
us to attain and achieve this through Jesus Christ, his dearly beloved
son, [137] our Lord, to whom be praise, honor, and glory in the
Holy Spirit, from eternity to eternity. Amen.

In Christ the Lord, by a brother through grace and servant of the
truth, also a companion in that tribulation, which is in Christ, Leopold Scharnschlager.

Part 2   The Münsterites

5

**A Restitution or a Restoration
of True and Wholesome
Christian Doctrine, Faith,
and Life**

Editor's note

During the exciting events in the Westphalian city of Münster from 1533
to 1535 the leading theologian and publicist for the revolutionary
"New Jerusalem" was Bernard Rothmann (ca. 1495–1535). Originally a
Roman Catholic priest, he turned to Lutheranism, then Zwinglianism,
then Anabaptism, and finally to the millenarian revolt led by John
Mathijs of Haarlem and John Beukels of Leiden.

Born in Stadtlohn in the bishopric of Münster, Rothmann was first a
teacher and then became a preacher in a monastery at the gates of
Münster. When he preached some Lutheran tenets, the canons sent him
to the University of Cologne, then a citadel of scholasticism, expecting
that study there would cure him of his incipient heresy. But on his
return he spoke even more openly about his Protestant beliefs so that a
group of Lutheran-inclined guildsmen raised money to send him in 1531
to the centers of German Protestantism. In Wittenberg and Strassburg
he spoke with Melanchthon and Capito. This visit was to confirm
Rothmann's evangelical sympathies.

Defying an order from the bishop of Münster to cease his preaching,
Rothmann moved into the city and found enthusiastic support from
the citizens, who were in open revolt against their Catholic ruler. As the
religious complexion of the city changed, Rothmann changed with it and
helped in part to bring about the revolution by his fiery sermons. During
the siege of the city he busied himself writing theological and biblical
justifications for the Davidic kingdom. His most important work was
the *Restitution*, which he wrote in one month's time in the autumn of
1534. It combined some passages which could be accepted by all
Anabaptists with Old Testament apologies for armed resistance and
polygamy, which they condemned. The treatise found broad distribution
in the Germanies and the Netherlands and was even shot over the walls
into the ranks of the besiegers as an early form of psychological warfare.

The present selections include those bearing most directly on the
themes of mutual aid and the nature of the church. The translation is
from the original Low German, most recently published in a critical
edition by Robert Stupperich.

Bernard Rothmann

A Restitution or a Restoration of True and Wholesome Christian Doctrine, Faith, and Life, Made Public Through the Grace of God by the Church of Christ in Münster (1534)

Chapter Eight
On the Holy Church or
Congregation of Christ

The first man, whom God had created to his own praise as his bodily and spiritual creation, rebelled and abandoned God's word, by obedience to which he was to have praised God (Prov. 8). Through this, the most merciful God—so that he might be honored by men because of his goodness—again established and willed that from then on there should be a people on earth from generation to generation [240] who would keep these things in mind and praise him, that he might bestow the more mercy upon them at all times. For it is his desire to be present with the children of men. As they were unfortunately very careless in this matter, God himself taught and instructed them for a long time, until the wickedness of men became predominant. Therefore, God (who is the sole and perfect God) could no longer tolerate them. Indeed, you can read how he through his own mouth instructed Adam, Cain, and the rest, in that which is good.

And although he has [now] ceased to do this, he persisted in sending one messenger and prophet after another, who were to teach mankind what was good and to admonish them that men should acknowledge and praise his goodness and be saved. However, none of this availed, for in the end all of them were disobedient and despised God's voice and word. This was not all, for they also mocked and murdered all the prophets and servants of God.

Therefore, God from the very beginning has always sought a people who would obey his judgment, honor his holy name, and be saved. He awakened various patriarchs and prophets—Moses and other prophets, priests and judges, dukes and queens, and all kinds of other servants of his. Yet none of them succeeded. They all went astray, became corrupt, and there was none that did good (Psalm 14[:3]).

When in the end God realized that these efforts and labors were completely wasted upon mankind and that they would listen to no prophets, God, the most gracious lover of men, nevertheless resolved not to abandon mankind. Even though they were so very ungrateful, he again, with unspeakable love, sent his only begotten son to see if perhaps mankind would honor him. He also wished to gather a new people who would praise his name in holiness and righteousness. Indeed, he gave his son to the heathens for this purpose and placed him as a king on the holy hill of Zion, that he should proclaim his will to them and to prepare them to become a people pleasing to his father (Psalm 2[:6]).

Now the son of God did come and deliver with all diligence the message and will of his father. He sought the lost sheep and carried it on his shoulders again to the father. Yet he was not esteemed on earth according to his worth and honor but he was killed by the ungrateful, just like all of the other messengers of God. Despite this, he did gather a flock, even though it was a very small one, who accepted his word and were willing to live according to his will. Consequently, after he had taught them this and proclaimed everything which he had received from his heavenly father, he was taken from them and raised to heaven. In order that they might be capable in all things, [241] he sent them the Holy Spirit as a comforter and master of truth. Behold, this small flock whom Christ gathered and whom he endowed with a spirit, was the congregation of Christ and the beginning of the holy church.

In this way the holy church began, that is, as a congregation of such people—gathered from Jews and Gentiles and from all peoples of the earth—who have received the teaching of Christ and persisted therein according to the will of Christ to the glory of God the father. From that time on, this church has truly and solely been the people of God. And although the Jews also claim to be God's people because of Abraham and the law, since they rejected Christ, the son of God, and refused to accept him, God also rejected them and graciously revealed himself to the Gentiles who had accepted Christ his son.

Again, this is to be known about the holy church of Christ. As she had been so miserably devastated and destroyed after the time of the apostles that nothing healthy was left in her, it is now necessary to define fully the nature of the holy christian church and that which goes with her. Not everyone who is called christian is truly

a Christian, but only those are Christians who abide and live stead-
fastly in Christ (Matt. 7[:21]).

Now this is the nature of the true christian church: a gathering
large or small who, in the true confession of Christ, are founded
upon Christ in such a manner that they obey his word and obey
his will and commandments. Such a gathering is truly a church of
Christ. Those lacking anything herein, even if they bear his name a
hundred times over, are in truth no church of Christ. That this is true
and that this is the true knowledge of Christ and of whence he
comes, and that he alone is the savior and messiah, the foundation
of the christian church—this is abundantly testified throughout the
scriptures: Isaiah 28[:16]: "Behold, I am laying in Zion (for) a
foundation a stone"; "He who believes in him will not be put to
shame" (1 Pet. 2[:6]). In Matthew 16[:13–16], Christ expressed
this clearly. In that passage he spoke to his disciples: "Who do men
say that the son of man is?" etc. and he further spoke to them: "But
who do you say that I am?" Simon Peter then replied: "You are
the Christ, the son of the living God" (John 7[:41]; John 15).

And when again you read that it is necessary to stand fast on this
foundation, namely, that we obey only the teaching of Christ and
do his will, this he himself revealed publicly to his disciples when
he said: "If you continue in my word, you are truly my disciples."
And again: "You are my friends if you do what I command you"
[John 8:31, 15:14].

But those who follow other teachings and commandments can
neither be disciples nor friends of Christ, and consequently cannot
be part of the church of Christ (Matt. 27). For no one can belong
but the disciples and friends of Christ who obey his teaching and
commandments. Therefore, when Christ sent out his apostles in
order to gather his church, he spoke, [242] giving them this command: "Go therefore and make disciples of all nations, baptizing
them in the name of the Father and of the Son and of the Holy
Spirit, teaching them to observe all that I have commanded you"
(Matt. 28[:18–20].

In the first place they were to proclaim to them God's will in
Christ and teach it to them from the beginning. If they desired to
accept this and to become Christ's disciples, they [the apostles] were
to baptize them, so that they might put on Christ and be incorporated into his holy church (Gal. 3[:2]; 1 Cor. 12[:33]. After this
and lastly, in order that they might remain friends of Christ, they
were to teach the baptized persons to obey all that Christ has com-

manded. This you clearly learn throughout the apostolic scriptures. Behold, this has been the true church of Christ from the beginning until now. Even though many others often claim to be the christian church, as does the thoroughly antichristian band of the Papists, this is all idle and worthless. Not all that glitters is gold.

From what has been said here it can easily be understood that two things are needed most for belonging to the true christian church, namely: to believe in Christ in the true knowledge of Christ and to listen only to his words and obey all that he has commanded. Unfortunately, for over fourteen hundred years this truth has been so completely obscured, hindered, and suppressed—mostly by the pope and his cohorts—that it is virtually impossible to find a trace of the true christian church upon earth. And now in these latter days, through the light of the second coming of Christ, who wants to build up his church and make it glorious notwithstanding the gates of hell, the light of truth and the teachings of the holy gospel have broken forth again. Oh, dear friend, could we have said: "Behold, there is a true Christian," and denied the existence of a church of Christ? Then all would have left so that we might have said with the prophets and with Paul: "If the Lord of hosts had not left us children, we would have fared like Sodom and been made like Gomorrah" (Rom. 9[:29]).

When someone wants to question this he usually denies that this has actually happened. Well then, it is easy enough for us to prove a few of these things. In the first place, concerning the true knowledge of Christ, that he is said to be the eternal and living son of God, and that the word had become flesh, etc. Have we not received knowledge of this, and such knowledge as John and the old writers witnessed to? John is the one who punished lies, the writers those whom he corroborated (1 John 4[:6]).

He [Christ] began to be obscured in the time of the apostles. The same holds true for the salvation of Christ, that he alone is our mediator and savior, and that men are to put their trust in him alone. Is it not obvious that this has been obscured through silver and gold, stone and wood, water and bread and that the dead saints and papal bulls were put in his place and salvation was sought in them? This is too well known for us to consider it necessary to write much about it.

God might well say to us as he spoke to Judah and Jerusalem [243] through Jeremiah: "For your gods have become as many as your cities, O Judah; and as many as the streets of Jerusalem are

the altars you have set up to shame, altars to burn incense to Baal"
(Jer. 2[:28], 11[13]). Again, that men have not persisted in the
wholesome teaching of Christ and have not obeyed his commandments but rather have bandied about idle human teachings, is sufficiently witnessed to by decree and decretal, synodical councils and
statutes. This is proved as well by that most horrible idolatrous
worship which is still customary in the Roman church and, to some
extent, still tarnishes the Protestants, which is a shame indeed. For
as the Lord says: "Would that you were cold or hot! So, because
you are lukewarm . . . , I will spew you out of my mouth" [Rev.
3:15–16].

Thus it would be better for them to remain papal altogether than
to deal with half-truths, since half-truths are certainly not truths.
The example of the foolish virgins, who dealt in half-truths (Matt.
25[:1–13]) shows and confirms that they will be locked out. In the
same vein are the Lutherans who oppose the papal Latin masses,
condemn them so heartily and replace them with their own chosen
German masses just as if it were worse to celebrate in Latin than in
German! Take this to heart, dear reader, and ponder it. Then you
will give praise to the Lord without doubts and confess the truth
along with us. It would become too lengthy if we were to discuss
all this in print.

Now, after having stated what the true holy church is and who
belongs to it, and also where it has deteriorated so that it could
scarcely regain its proper state, we now finally wish to say how—
through God's grace—it has been restored among us, and how it is
daily increased. In the beginning, after we had understood the true
and proper teaching of Christ through God's grace from God's word
and after much effort and labor, we desired to conduct ourselves in
accordance with it. Then God awakened those who baptized us after
we had become believers in the name of God. Thus through his
spirit we became one body, one faith, and one brotherly love [in the
one] hope [Eph. 4:4–6]. Consequently we have endeavored since
then to obey God's word and commandments through christian
community with each other. Yes, and what we can daily discover
to be God's will, we shall do it, cost it what it may. We do not say
this to praise ourselves, for to God alone be the glory who has
created us anew for such love and set his son Christ over us to be
our head.

But enough of this now, for this ought to be said yet that where
there is true forgiveness of sin in the christian church and an open

path to salvation, there is likewise but a narrow gate to it. Therefore: "Strive to enter by the narrow door, for many, I tell you," says
Christ, "will seek to enter and will not be able" (Matt. 7[:14]; Luke
13[:24ff.]). That is from the time on when the householder has risen
up and shut the door.

Chapter Nine
On Obeying the Commandments
of Christ and on Good Works

[244] We have written above about the holy church and said—which
is true—that whoever enters the church and desires to remain therein
as a friend of Christ must do everything which Christ has commanded. Therefore, we wish to continue by treating the obedience
to God's commandments and good works. The reason for this is that
we notice that there are various feelings on these matters, both
among the scholars as well as among the common folk. There are
some three opinions on good works and the obedience to the commandments of God.

In the first place, the Papists consider their fictitious hypocrisy
as the true good works and say hardly anything about God's commandments and words. They believe that in this way they can
achieve salvation. But their covering is so insufficient that their
shame can plainly be seen, the Lord be praised! and there is no need
for us to uncover it.

In the second place, there are the common Protestants who boast
so much of their faith. They cling to this with such lack of understanding that they very rarely pay attention to obeying the commandments of God and [doing] good works. They say publicly that good
works do not assist toward salvation, etc. Furthermore, the Devil
has persuaded them that if they practiced the obeying of God's
commands and good works they would be called hypocrites and pre-
tenders. Unfortunately this opinion has caused the gospel great
damage and scandal. It is to be feared that it has led many people
to damnation who accepted the faith of the gospel along with hatred
for the Papists and their ilk. The power of the faith and of the
gospel had been forgotten because of such false opinions and therefore such workers of wickedness will eventually become guilty, as
Christ said about those who claimed to have prophesied and worked
miracles in his name (Matt. 7[:22]).

In the third place, there are also some who say: "Obeying the
commandments of God and practicing good works are indeed useful

and necessary, but a man is unable to keep and observe them." This opinion discourages many a sincere-hearted person so that he does not dare to begin the struggle and work of overcoming evil and bringing about good. In this regard it is most important that a Christian be well instructed. Therefore [we will see] how the three above opinions are wrong and wicked, and we will discuss the last two with the aid of the holy scriptures. Let us then with God's aid and mercy uncover the true understanding of the commandments of God and good works. We hope that in this way the errors in such matters will be sufficiently and irrefutably made known and hence avoided.

There can be no argument about the fact that God from the beginning has given man [245] a commandment intending that he should obey it and conduct his life in accordance with it. Thus you can read both in the Old and the New Testament that God will promise and eventually give his eternal blessing and kingdom to those who in time obey his will, not failing by an iota or dot insofar as they are able, cost it their life or whatever. Deuteronomy 6[:3]: "Hear therefore, O Israel, and be careful to do them [God's commandments]; that it may go well with you, and that you may multiply greatly, as the Lord, the God of your fathers, has promised you, in a land flowing with milk and honey" etc. Likewise, Christ speaks in the New Testament: "Not every one who says to me, 'Lord, Lord' shall enter the kingdom of heaven, but he who does the will of my Father who is in heaven" (Matt. 7[:21]). If you will read the whole bible with this point in mind, you will find that God's will must be done and his commandments obeyed, and that with all carefulness and zeal if we are to enter into the life and the kingdom of God. Christ says in Matthew 19[:17]: "If you would enter life, keep the commandments." Paul says the same (Phil. 2[:12]): "Work out your own salvation with fear and trembling" etc. Thus if you view the scriptures with innocent and proper eyes you will clearly find that not only is obedience to the commandments of God and the practice of good works beneficial and necessary, but also that no one may enter God's kingdom unless he, so far as he is able, has in time fulfilled God's will and commandment.

As mentioned above, we do not consider it worthwhile to respond to the opinion of the Papists, for what they do is idle hypocrisy and idolatry. Now, the opinion of the common Protestants is that obedience to God's commandments and the practice of good works are not necessary for salvation, and justification is by faith alone, etc. To this we respond and say with the entire scriptures a loud

"No"! This is a great and scandalous misinterpretation, for where good works are thus despised, such an opinion becomes the cause of carnal license for the common man, so that you can find more license, or at least as much, in Protestants as in Papists or others. We have already demonstrated on the basis of the scriptures that God's will and commandments must be obeyed in a scrupulous manner through deeds. Therefore, so that the errors of the foolish Protestants may be avoided and the saving truth may be known, we will here show brieflly how this must be done.

First of all, you must consider that there are two different kinds of people on earth, namely the unbelievers and the believers. We know about the unbelievers that they are without Christ and separated from the children of Israel. They are in the dominion of the prince of this world, in the lusts of the flesh; they obey the desires of their flesh and senses, and are children of wrath (Eph. 2[:3]). In the same way they have no knowledge of God or at least only a little, and consequently [246] care nothing at all about his commandments. It is not necessary to write any more about this.

Secondly, about the believers: These, then are the believers who, after they have heard about Christ and attained a true understanding of him, have believed in his name. They have so completely united themselves with Christ that they consider everything outside of Christ as filth and dirt. These, then, are the righteous Christians and believers for whom Christ gave himself and whom he redeemed from all iniquity, whom he purified to be his own people zealous for good deeds (Titus 2[:14]).

Behold, that is then a true believer who hears the gospel of Christ, believes it, and accepts Christ. Such a person will be forgiven all of his previous sins and evil deeds through his faith in Christ. This is also certain that if he remains steadfast to the end in obedience to the commandments of Christ, he will be saved. On the other hand, even if he has promised it a dozen times over, if he does not do God's will and neglects his commandment, yes, if he still obeys the lusts of the flesh, he must still die and will not remain in God's grace. Thus spoke Paul to the faithful in Rome (Rom. 8[:13]): "For if you live according to the flesh you will die, but if by the Spirit you put to death the deeds of the body you will live." Again, Christ says (John 5[:29]): "Those who have done good [will come forth] to the resurrection of life, and those who have done evil, to the resurrection of judgment." To this end Christ commanded his disciples that after they had baptized the believers they should teach them to observe all that he had commanded them (Matt. 28[:19–20]).

Thus the truth is that it is not faith alone but also the fulfillment of all of God's commandments through deeds which are necessary for salvation. Therefore those err badly who insist that obeying God's commandments and practicing good works are not needed for salvation. They have and praise a dead faith; they preach freedom while they are themselves slaves of corruption (2 Pet. 2[:18–20]; James 2[:24]).

It will easily be understood by now that of those who accept the faith there are two different kinds. In sum, as we have already said, there are those who indeed believe that Christ died for them and are content that he washed them with his blood. But here the matter rests as far as they are concerned. To follow in his footsteps and fulfill his will by deeds, they consider unnecessary for salvation. But these are false believers, waterless springs, who know many proud words without foundation, as 2 Peter 2[:17] and Jude [16] testify.

In the second place, there are some who mean well. They realize that if it is necessary for salvation to believe in Christ with the right understanding, one must also obey all of his commandments, for as the prophet Habakkuk says [2:4]: "The righteous shall live by his faith," and John says: "He who does right [247] is righteous, as he is righteous. He who commits sin is of the devil" (1 John 3[:7–8]; Acts 2[:38–39]). That the Lutherans interpret righteousness only as belief and sin as unbelief and therefore ignore good works, is a sophistical hairsplitting. For to fulfill righteousness is to do God's will in deeds out of true faith. To commit sin is to do deeds contrary to God's will out of unbelief. Here, consider those who accept the faith and say they know Christ but are neglectful and careless. They sin, that is, they act contrary to Christ's commandments and allow themselves to be seduced by the lusts of the world. John says in chapter nine [verse 41]: "If you were blind, you would have no guilt; but now that you say, 'We see,' your guilt remains."

In final summation, God wants obedience and the fulfillment of his will. Therefore two things make for a true Christian. That is, that he truly believes in Christ and follows as one sanctified in all of his commandments. Christ says about the former (John 6[:29]): "This is the work (will) of God, that you believe in him whom he has sent." About the latter Christ says (John 15[:14]): "You are my friends if you do what I command you." Further, Paul (2 [1] Thess. 4[:3]): "For this is the will of God, your sanctification."

You can read about the nature of true sanctification in James, chapter one.

Therefore, in brief, you may cover yourself with as many sackcloths and [fig] leaves as you wish, nothing will be accepted before God other than doing his will with earnestness.

"Yes," the well-intentioned people may say, "dear God, we would very much like to do your will, but we are simply not able to." Answer: It is true that we are not able to do this alone, and as long as we are unbelieving and ignorant, we have neither inclination nor power to do it. But after we have become believers, witnessed to the truth, and accepted Christ, we will then have the power to do his will. Not for ourselves, but Christ gives this to us, said John 1 [:12]: "To all who receive him, who believe in his name, he gave power to become children of God."

As in Adam's fall we fell into the captivity of the Devil without our own fault, we shall likewise be redeemed and freed again by Christ without our own merit. If therefore we are set free by Christ, we are truly free and liberated (Rom. 5[:6ff.]). That is, we may turn and move wherever we wish. Christ says this in John, chapter 8 [verse 36]: "So if the Son makes you free, you will be free indeed." God wishes no coerced worship. Therefore, to those who have become his servants through Christ he gives freedom that they may serve him from their own free will and be crowned, even if they are [here] condemned and despised.

"Yes," you say, "but a man does not have this in himself." Answer: We do not say that he does. God anticipates him and gives it to him, and when he has given it to him then he does indeed have it. The Lord gives [243] to everyone his pound and commands that he increase it; he gives him power so that he may employ it. Those who are faithful and take their pound to the exchange will be accepted and rewarded. But those who refuse to do this and bury their pounds in the ground will be punished (Matt. 25[:14–30]; Luke 19[:12–27]; Isa. 18). In sum, God gives each person so much that he is not guilty of anyone's damnation, for God takes no pleasure in the death of the sinner. He gives each person the power to be converted. Unfortunately most refuse it, as Christ said: "How often would I have gathered your children together as a hen gathers her brood under her wing, and you would not!" (Matt. 23[:37]).

Therefore, no one can say that he cannot do God's will if he is called a believer, for to such a person the power is given after all. In brief, whomever God wants to be reached by this word and command, to him he also gives the power that he may accept and obey, or ignore it. Whatever other reason or pretext you may voice will not excuse you before God (John 16[:13]).

Furthermore, the well-intentioned say: "I am indeed willing, inclined and ready to do all of God's will and strive constantly to achieve this. But I just cannot achieve it in the manner that I would like, and I am sincerely sorry." Answer: It is evident from the scriptures that those well-intentioned servants of God must resist the attacks of the Devil, who through prodding the lusts of the flesh is forever trying to unseat and vanquish the knight of Christ. It is true that he is sometimes weakened against his will so that he wished that it were better, and he cannot conquer as quickly as he wishes. But for all of this he is not powerless to do God's will, for God wants him to fight such battles. And he who fights courageously and like a man will be crowned, and he who conquers shall have dominion over all (2 Tim. 2[:5]; Rev. 2[:26]). All of us want to be victorious when we go into battle, but this takes work and it has its costs. If we remain in Christ and do not willfully turn away from him and succumb to the Devil but hold fast to Christ, he has promised us the victory (John 16[:8]; Phil. 2[:12]). We will be able to do all things in him who makes us strong.

Thus, in conclusion, if God wants us to do his will he also wants us to struggle against the Devil's lusts and schemes until we conquer. Then we shall have dominion over all. But if we are subdued by the Devil and are captured by him, alas, all will be lost! Therefore, let everyone stop arguing with and accusing God, as if he did not give us the power to do good, and as if it were his fault that we do evil. But let everyone strengthen himself in the Lord, and in the strength of his might, put on the armor of God that he may withstand the subtle wiles of the Devil (Eph. 6[:11]).

Chapter Twelve
On the Loving Fellowship
of the Saints

[255] It is not necessary to recount how the fellowship of saints, which began in the time of the apostles, has been corrupted since then, and how selfishness and egotism have taken its place. This is amply proven for the whole world witnesses this sufficiently. The Lord be eternally praised and magnified, this fellowship has been restored by God among us (Heb. 13[:1ff.]) as it was in the begin-

ning and is pleasing to God's holy will, as described in Acts 2[:44]
and 4[:32ff.]. We also hope that our fellowship may be as strong
and splendid and kept with pure hearts through God's grace as it
may have been before. For not only have we in a body turned our
goods and possessions over to the deacons as communal property
and live on it according to our need, but we also praise God through
Christ with one heart and mouth. We are willing to prefer one
another with all kinds of services.

There are many things that have served selfishness and property,
such as buying and selling, working for money, taking of interest,
even with the unbelievers. Likewise, eating and drinking by the
sweat of the poor, which is to praise one's own self and use our
neighbors in such a way that they should have to labor so that we
may gorge ourselves, and other things like that which are detrimen-
tal to love. Therefore we have done away with all those things in
the power of love and fellowship. And as we do know that God
wants to do away with such monstrous things, we would rather begin
this than that we should again turn to these things.

We know that God is pleased with such an offering from man.
Indeed, no Christian or saint can please God who does not belong
to such a fellowship, or at least does not feel an inclination in his
heart towards such. The dragon and beast still hinder some well-
intentioned persons from joining such a fellowship (Rev. 13[:1–10]).
May the Lord deliver them and raise up a pure fellowship for his
saints. Amen.

Part 3   The Mennonites

6

Exhortation to a Church in Prussia

Editor's note

Menno Simons (ca. 1496–1561), although not in the first generation of leaders in the Radical Reformation, was one of its most influential personalities. He entered the scene during the troubled 1530's, when the events at Münster brought more notoriety to the Anabaptist movement. By rallying misguided dissenters in the Low Countries and northern Germany, as well as those who had never accepted the idea of violence, he, with other leaders, made possible the continuation of Anabaptism in these areas.

His birthplace was the village of Witmarsum in Friesland. At the age of twenty-eight he was ordained a Catholic priest and served in a neighboring village. His reading of the bible and some of Luther's tracts confirmed his suspicion that what he had been taught about baptism and the sacraments was in error. Although he became increasingly convinced of this and spoke to others of it, he was put off by the turn to coercion among some of the Anabaptists. The débacle of Münster brought on a crisis for Menno, for he felt that he shared responsibility for the tragedy. He had not done all that he could have done to prevent some from being led astray. "The blood of these people, although misled, fell so hot upon my heart that I could not stand it, nor find rest in my soul," he wrote later.

In early 1536 he left home and position to begin an underground existence as an Anabaptist; some time later he was ordained an elder. From 1536 to 1554 he led the dangerous life of an Anabaptist missioner, traveling secretly to hold meetings, give counsel, and baptize, for much of the time with a price on his head. After 1554 he found a relatively secure home in the German province of Holstein. During the later period of his life he had to devote a great part of his energies to dealing with the question of church discipline, about which there was much disunity.

The following example of Menno's teaching is directed to an unknown congregation in Prussia that he had visited shortly before. It is taken (as are the other two selections of this section) from the English translation by Leonard Verduin, edited by John C. Wenger.

Menno Simons Exhortation to a Church in
Prussia (1549)

To the elect, holy children of God in the land of Prussia, grace and
peace. You know, my dear brethren and sisters in Christ Jesus,
what grievous solicitude, care, trouble, labor, and sorrow we experienced in your midst this past summer, as well as how it ended; a
matter that still at times causes us to be greatly troubled at heart on
your behalf, fearing lest the disturber of all peace and christian love,
that is, that ancient coiled serpent which never ceases his ragings,
might by means of the past transaction once more sow his seed
among many, and by means of all that follows, these might fail in
God's sight and come to shame and our services of some weeks
expended in your behalf be lost again; a thing which even though I
write thus, I nevertheless hope not.

Nor do we cease in all our prayers to God our heavenly father
in the name of our Lord Jesus Christ to remember you, requesting
him according to his great goodness to have mercy on you all, to
give you to drink of his Holy Spirit, and watch and keep you all
together with an eternal, uninterrupted peace, love, and unity, according to your good intention and unto his eternal praise and glory.
And since we are called to be members of one body in Christ Jesus,
therefore brotherly faithfulness requires us at all times to be solicitous for each other's welfare. Therefore I have taken it upon myself
with this my brief admonition and to the extent that the Lord gives
me grace, fraternally to quicken your God-given faith, love, and
obedience, and to serve you according to the humble gift that is mine.

[1031] In the first place, I admonish and pray you as my precious
brethren and companions in Christ Jesus with faithful hearts to
observe and realize that Christ Jesus (blessed forever, in whose
word we believe and to whom we have voluntarily committed ourselves with body and soul) is called by the prophet Isaiah a prince
of peace [Isa. 9:6] and by Paul, a lord of peace (2 Thess. 3:16):
yes, such a Lord and prince who has left and taught to his own an
abundant peace, as he says: "Peace I leave with you; my peace I
give to you" (John 14:27); "Peace be with you" (John 20:19).
In like manner Paul, his faithful messenger and servant: "And let
the peace of Christ rule in your hearts to which indeed you were
called" (Col. 3:15). "Strive for peace . . . and for the holiness without which no one will see the Lord" (Heb. 12:14). "So far as it
depends upon you, live peaceably with all" (Rom. 12:18). "Seek

Fig. 1. The ordinance of foot-washing performed by Dutch Mennonites, by Hendrik de Winter (1717–ca. 1782). Source: H. Schijn and G. Maatschoen, *Geschiedenis der Christenen, welke in de Vereenigde Nederlanden onder de Protestanten Mennoniten genaamd worden* (Amsterdam, 1743–45).

peace and pursue it" (Psalm 34:14; 1 Pet. 3:11). "For God has called us to peace" (1 Cor. 7:15).

Nor was the entire life of Christ anything but love and peace. For although he came to his own and his own received him not, but thrust him forth from the vineyard and desired him not; and although (oh, the shame of it!) he was reviled and blasphemed by them because of the lovely fruits and services of his divine love bestowed on them, was pursued to the death, and at last was reviled by them and blasphemously called an evildoer; and although he was finally nailed by them to the cross as a malefactor, yet his holy peace remained unbroken, his blessed heart did not become bitter nor cruel, but rather he prayed to his father for his enemies in pity for their blindness, for they knew not what they did (Luke 23). Moreover, his bitter death is become to us poor sinners a certain peace and life, even as Paul says: By his cross he has reconciled him that is in heaven and those that are on earth (Col. 1:20).

Seeing then that Christ Jesus is the prince and the lord of eternal peace, and since his entire doctrine and life, as also his death has represented, portrayed, and implied nothing but peace, as was said, therefore none can be the recipient of his honor and good will, or be given a place in his kingdom except those who have the holy peace of God in their hearts. For his kingdom is the kingdom of peace; it knows no strife, even as it is written in the prophets that in the kingdom of Christ and in his church they beat their swords into plowshares and sit under their fig tree and vine, and no more raise up their hands to warfare (Isa. 2[:4]; Mic. 4[:3–4]).

Since no one can be in the kingdom and church of Christ who does not dwell there through love and peace, as the scriptures testify, therefore all those who are quarrelsome, tumultuous, slanderous, defaming, bitter, wrathful, and cruel of heart may well rouse themselves, be sorry, and repent, for they show in deeds that they do not possess peace, do not heed Christ Jesus the true prince of peace, nor are they in his kingdom, even though they do carry the external appearance of being Christians, and are greeted as brethren. [1032] Brother, let each man beware, for the Lord Christ does not judge according to externals as do men, but according to the hidden reality of the heart, which is altogether naked and open before his blessed eyes.

Since then for a long time, alas, a severe quarrel has existed among you; and since you have now again received one another with a kiss of peace and have saluted each other as brethren, therefore I now admonish you as in Christ Jesus to try yourselves rightly as to whether you love your brother with a genuine brotherly love, such as the scriptures teach, and whether you also in the spirit of Christ say to your brother: "Brother, the peace of the Lord be with you." Oh, brethren, I do greatly fear that in the case of some among you peace is usually heard upon the lips rather than found in the heart. Let each one be careful to have heart and mouth agree, for he that does in fact express peace toward his brother but carries hostility toward him in his heart is to my mind a make-believe rather than a true Christian. Therefore, let each person take care when he says or does anything toward his neighbor to say or to do it as in the presence of God who knows and sees all things.

Dearest brethren and sisters in Christ Jesus, I admonish you in love, and that with the word of the Lord, that if there are still among you some who are at variance with others—a thing which I, however, do not hope—that such might leave their sacrifice before the altar [Matt. 5:24] (that is, their fasting, prayers, and alms), so long as they are not reconciled and have not agreed. Let the unclean hypocritical heart be far from you.

Let no one have any complaint or grievance concerning his brother even if your poor companion through ignorance or transgression has sinned against you and in that way owes you ten or twenty pence. Do not assail your erring brother so vehemently, but by all means remember how your own account stands before God, namely, that you owe so many thousand pounds and have not a penny with which to pay. If you are to escape your Lord's punishment, prison, and judicial severity, then it must be graciously forgiven, and the crimson blood of Christ must stand in your place. If you now seek to receive gracious pardon for your sins from the Lord, then forgive also your brother if he has transgressed against you in some matter. If you do not forgive now, you will likewise not be forgiven, as Christ himself says in Matthew 18[:35]. Therefore, I admonish you with the holy Paul to be kind to one another, gentle and merciful, and to forgive one another even as God has forgiven you in Christ Jesus [Rom. 14:10ff.].

Worthy brethren and sisters in the Lord, consider the word of God. Have you not heard and read that he who is angry with his brother is guilty of the judgment, and he who says to his brother: "Raca,"* is in danger of the council, and he who says: "You fool," is guilty of hellfire? [Matt. 5:22]. Do you not know that John says: "He who does not love (his brother) remains in death" (1 John 3[:14])? "He that takes vengeance," says Sirach, "will suffer vengeance from the Lord, [1033] and he will firmly establish his sins. Forgive your neighbor the wrong he has done, and then your sins will be pardoned when you pray. Does a man harbor anger against another, and yet seek for healing from the Lord? Does he have no mercy toward a man like himself, and yet pray for his own sins? If he himself, being flesh, maintains wrath, who will make expiation for his sins? Remember the end of your life, and cease from enmity" (Ecclus. 28[:1–6]).

Dearest brethren, do not think that I have written this admonition

---

*"Raca" is an obscure Greek term of abuse.

with a certain brother's person in mind; not at all. But I have seen
with my eyes and heard with my ears the heathen impurity of many
a heart; the wicked pride and slander, yes, the cruel and bitter fruits
that come forth out of a quarrel. Therefore, I admonish you all
together herewith in general, and that with this intention: that all the
pious who now with a pure heart and in true christian peace have
reached an agreement with their brethren might continue in it forever; and if then there are still some in whose heart the poisonous
fang of bitterness still sticks fast, these may, without delay, rouse
themselves, do penance, pray God for his grace, [and] thus desire,
seek, and practice the very desirable christian unity, love, and peace
with their brethren who have, with them, been called to the way of
the cross.

In the second place, I admonish you as my fellow soldiers in the
struggle and in the patience of Christ that if you desire to live this
above-mentioned peace with faithful hearts, even as I do not doubt,
then promote the genuine christian love among yourselves, for un-
doubtedly you know how it behaves itself in all things and what is
its nature and disposition. Yes, if you would bend your shoulders
to its scepter, and voluntarily join its administration and government,
then the holy peace of God would surely constantly abide with you,
and grow and increase in you from day to day.

For love conducts and behaves itself without reproach, and is
careful of its words and works lest it sin against God and give
offense to a brother, trouble or sadden him. It is always diligent
and eager to go before its neighbor in all righteousness, to teach and
instruct him. It gives to no one an incentive to evil, being of a divine
nature, and hating all unrighteousness, willfulness, and trickery. If it
is wronged, whether in words or deeds, it bears it with patience and
knows no vengeance. It is gracious and loves the truth; and therefore
none can be wronged or cheated by it. It is kind and gentle, and
therefore it treats others in humility and reasonableness, also those
who are its enemies and foes, so as by such readiness to lead and
attract many to the truth and in that way to win the hearts of the
hostile to it and to reconcile them in Christ Jesus. Nor does it think
any evil. Therefore it conducts itself before all, privately as well as
publicly, with pious and honest heart without any subtlety or deceit,
even as before God in Christ Jesus.

Moreover, this love is not bitter; therefore it does not reproach
a poor brother for his fault, neither does it talk behind his back nor
defame him, for it covers a multitude of his sins, even as James and

Peter teach and instruct the pious [James 5:20; 1 Pet. 4:8]. This love is of God and therefore at all times it behaves according [1034] to its divine nature and disposition. It admonishes its neighbor in pure love, comforts those of little faith, raises the weak, teaches the foolish, rebukes the delinquent, bears all that may properly be borne; it receives the destitute, clothes the naked, feeds the hungry, and gives the thirsty drink, visits the sick; in a word, its resources are ready to serve all men. If by chance it happens, as happen it does, that a pious Christian impelled by his love errs in human fashion, then this very same love is prepared at all times to receive fraternal rebuke and instruction; it does not puff itself up, but receives it with much thanksgiving, even as it becomes the wise, as Solomon says: "Reprove a wise man, and he will love you" [Prov. 9:8]. For he acknowledges in what spirit and with what intention it is done, and that in it nothing is sought and desired but the praise of God and their own salvation.

Faithful brethren in the Lord, I think this love is indeed a well-paved road to all brotherly unity and peace. Oh, if only this above-mentioned love had held the helm of your ship, never would it have collided so violently with the shore! My brethren, understand what I am driving at. It is still today, rise up and delay not. And be diligent henceforth in this pure and genuine love, and that with all your power and ability. So that you may in this way deal with each other in all prudence and considerateness, politeness, fidelity, and piety; may avoid all offense; may flee and avoid all useless bickering and disputations; so that the genuine, evangelical christian peace may not depart from you in such fashion, but may rather in all happiness take root, repose, and dwell among you as in the congregation of the saints.

Holy and beloved brethren in the Lord, this I would ask of you at this time and admonish you: With deeply serious hearts do consider how you together with all Christians are received and called by the God of peace, under the prince of peace, by the messengers of peace, to the body of peace, with the word of peace, unto the kingdom of peace, out of simple love and grace. Therefore walk in this same peace, so that on that day you may in his grace be able to stand before your God with a confident and happy conscience when body and soul must part. Oh, my brethren and sisters, fear your God with all your heart, and purify yourselves in one another's presence as before God in Christ Jesus, in order that just as many brethren and congregations may have been saddened because of your contentions they may now once more be refreshed and gladdened in Christ Jesus by your lovely reconciliation and christian peace.

Behold, worthy brethren in the Lord, this my little admonition and exhortation to peace I have written out of an upright heart and intention to you all as to such as are desirous of the genuine christian peace and who at all times gladly [seek] the best and the most blessed in my dear brethren and companions. For I hope that I may say with the holy Paul, and that according to the testimony of conscience, that it is my life if you abide in the Lord [Phil. 2:16]. Therefore receive it in such a spirit as I have written you. Therefore I [1035] desire for the Lord's sake that you read it, and understand it correctly, and judge it in the light of the word and spirit of the Lord, so that I may not have labored in vain, and you may find in it instruction, profit, and joy.

The merciful Father grant his grace to that end. Amen.

I commend you to the most high and to the word of his eternal peace. Wait for his appearance, for he will come as a thief in the night, in the hour when we do not expect it. Happy that man who will not be surprised by him. I hope after this to hear much happiness concerning you and no sadness. The Lord of peace grant you his peace in all places and in every manner. May that very same peace keep your hearts and minds in Christ Jesus. Amen.

All the saints that are with us greet you. And so you greet one another with your hearts, with a holy kiss of love. Peace be with you forever. Amen.

Written by Menno Simons to the church in Prussia, October 7, 1549.

7

A Sorrowful and Christian
Apology and Justification

Editor's note

As seen in the cases of other Anabaptists, communism was a persistent charge leveled by opponents of the movement. Not only would community of goods associate them in the popular mind with the medieval sectarians, it also tended to link the movement with recently suppressed peasant uprisings. For both the landed and the rising middle classes, the thought of losing property elicited no little fear.

Along with the accusation of holding and using goods communally went the suspicion of polygamy—a community of women. With the memories of actual multiple marriage at Münster fresh in their minds, established authorities found it easy to conclude that Menno and his followers accepted the same practice. Menno wrote, in repudiating the charge that they supposedly said to each other: "Sister, my spirit desires your flesh," that the faithful followed no other arrangement than that established by Adam and Eve, namely "one husband and one wife." They would rather die "ten deaths than commit such abominations" as those with which their opponents taxed them.

The stance of the Dutch and North German Anabaptists on property exactly parallelled that taken by other Anabaptists. Goods were to be held privately, but always were to be at the disposal of needy members of the household of faith and others in need. Menno agreed that the early Christians did in fact practice community of goods but averred that this was transitory and not to be taken as binding for all time.

This attitude brought criticism from the Hutterites, who characterized the Lowlands leader under the title "How near one may be to the light and not completely dare it." "The truth," they wrote, "is the more dangerous the nearer one approaches to it." While praising Menno's attacks on greed and his presentation of christian essentials, they found that he "slid past very carefully a little to one side of truth." He was close to the kingdom but did not reach their goal—complete community.

This selection is an excerpt.

A Sorrowful and Christian
Apology and Justification
(1551)

IV. In the fourth place, some of them charge that we have our
property in common.
Answer: This charge is false and without truth. We do not teach
and practice community of goods. But we teach and maintain by
the word of the Lord that all truly believing Christians are members
of one body and are baptized by one spirit into one body (1 Cor.
12:13); they are partakers of one bread (1 Cor. 10:18); they have
one Lord and one God (Eph. 4[:5–6]).

Inasmuch as then they are one, therefore it is christian and reasonable that they piously love one another, and that the one member
is solicitous for the welfare of the other, for this both the scripture
and nature teach. The whole scripture speaks of mercifulness and
love, and it is the only sign whereby a true Christian may be known
—that is "that you are my disciples, if you have love for one another" (John 13[:35]).

Beloved reader, it is not customary that an intelligent person
clothes and cares for one part of his body and leaves the rest destitute and naked. Oh, no! The intelligent person is solicitous for all
his members. Thus it should be with those who are the Lord's church
and body. All those who are born of God, who are gifted with the
spirit of the Lord, who are, according to the scriptures, called into
one body and love in Christ Jesus, are prepared by such love to
serve their neighbors, not only with money and goods, but also after
the example of their Lord and head, Jesus Christ, in an evangelical
manner with life and blood. They show mercy and love, as much
as they can. No one among them is allowed to beg. They take to
heart the need of the saints. They entertain those in distress. They
take the stranger into their houses. They comfort the afflicted; assist
the needy; clothe the naked; feed the hungry; do not turn their face
from the poor; do not despise their own flesh (Isa. 85:8 [58:7]).

Behold, such a community we teach. And not that any one should
take and possess the land and property of the other, as many falsely
charge. Thus Moses says: "If there is among you a poor man, one
of your brethren, in any of your towns within your land which the
Lord your God gives you, you shall not harden your heart or shut
your hand against your poor brother" (Deut. 15:7). Tobias says:
"Give of your bread to the hungry, and of your clothing to the

naked" (Tob. 45[4:16]). Christ says: "Be merciful, even as your
Father is merciful" (Luke 6:36). "Blessed are the merciful, for they
shall obtain mercy" (Matt. 5:7). Paul says: "Put on then, as God's
chosen ones, holy and beloved, compassion etc." (Col. 3:12). "For
judgment is without mercy, to one who has shown no mercy; yet
mercy triumphs over judgment" (James 2:13; Matt. 18:33).

Again, this mercy, love, and community we teach and practice,
and have taught and practiced these seventeen years. God be thanked
forever that although our property has to a great extent been taken
away from us, and is still daily taken, and many a pious father and
mother are put to the sword or fire, and although we are not allowed
the free enjoyment of our homes as is manifest [559], and besides
the times are hard, yet none of those who have joined us nor any
of their orphaned children have been forced to beg. If this is not
christian practice, then we may well abandon the whole gospel of
our Lord Jesus Christ, his holy sacraments, and the christian name,
and say that the precious, merciful life of all saints is fantasy and
dream. Oh, no! "God is love; and he who abides in love abides in
God and God abides in him" (1 John 4[:16]).

This I write to shame our backbiters because of their envy. They
are so blinded that they are not ashamed thus shamefully to slander
us and wickedly to convert good into evil. For although we in accordance with all scripture teach mercy and love, and serve the
god-fearing poor by the sweat of our brow, and would not let them
suffer for want, yet we must hear that we teach community of goods,
and that every person should beware of us; for we would like to
reach into the chests and pockets of others! Full well they know that
it is written "He shall have judgment without mercy, who has shown
no mercy" (James 2[:13]); and "He who does not love his brother,
remains in death" (1 John 3:14). They also see plainly that we
daily and freely sacrifice our goods for the testimony of Jesus Christ
and our consciences.

Oh reader, it would be well for your soul that you would take
notice, and learn to know your preachers. For how can they teach
you that which is good while they hear no mercy?

Is it not sad and intolerable hypocrisy that these poor people
boast of having the word of God, of being the true, christian church,
never remembering that they have entirely lost their sign of true
Christianity? For although many of them have plenty of everything,
go about in silk and velvet, gold and silver, and in all manner of
pomp and splendor; ornament their houses with all manner of costly

furniture; have their coffers filled, and live in luxury and splendor, yet they suffer many of their own poor, afflicted members (notwithstanding their fellow believers have received one baptism and partaken of the same bread with them) to ask alms; and poor, hungry, suffering, old, lame, blind, and sick people to beg their bread at their doors.

Oh preachers, dear preachers, where is the power of the gospel you preach? Where is the thing signified in the supper you administer? Where are the fruits of the spirit you have received? And where is the righteousness of your faith which you dress up so beautifully before the poor, ignorant people? Is it not all hypocrisy that you preach, maintain, and assert? Shame on you for the easygoing gospel and barren bread-breaking, you who have in so many years been unable to effect enough with your gospel and sacraments so as to remove your needy and distressed members from the streets, even though the scripture plainly teaches and says: "If any one has the world's goods and sees his brother in need, yet closes his heart against him, how does God's love abide in him?" (1 John 3[:17]). Also Moses: "There will be no poor (beggars) among you" (Deut. 15[:4]).

You see, reader, this charge is as false as are the rest. For although we know that the apostolic churches from the beginning have practiced it, [560] as may be seen from the Acts of the Apostles, yet we may notice from their epistles that it went down in their time and (perhaps not without cause) was no longer practiced. Since we find that it was not permanent with the apostles, therefore we leave things as they are and have never taught nor practiced community of goods. But we diligently and earnestly teach and admonish assistance, love, and mercy, as the apostolic scriptures abundantly teach. Behold, in Christ we tell you the truth and do not lie.

And even if we did teach and practice community of goods as is falsely reported we would be but doing that which the holy apostles full of the Holy Spirit did in the previous church at Jerusalem, although as was said they discontinued it.

But the reason why our opponents lay this to our charge may be easily guessed. Often their hearts are filled with avarice, as Peter says [2 Pet. 2:3], and they know also that their disciples are intent upon the lusts of the flesh, money, and goods. They are all covetous, as the prophet says [Jer. 6:13]. And therefore they make the charge that thus the precious gospel, the pure truth of our Lord Jesus Christ, which, God be praised, now springs up in many places, may become

Fig. 2. The oldest portrait of
Menno Simons, by Christoffel van
Sichem (1546–1624). Source:
*Het Tooneel der Hooft-Ketteren
. . . in't Koper gesneden door C. v.
Sichem* (Middelburg, 1677).

a stench and abomination to all men. Behold the arts and cleverness of the serpent.

Reader, beware; let not such liars deceive you. Adam and Eve believed the deceiver and thereby so wickedly sinned against their God. Israel was miserably deceived by the false prophets. And what "good things" they have done in the New Testament and still do their deeds and fruits openly show.

Editor's note

The longest of Menno Simons' publications was his *Clear Reply to Gellius Faber*, issued from the undercover print shop at Lübeck in 1554. The work is best known for the section (often separately printed) in which Menno describes his "Renunciation of the Church of Rome" and the process by which he came to join the Anabaptists.

Faber was, like Menno, formerly a priest in the Roman Catholic church in Friesland. He served as a pastor for the Reformed congregation at Emden, where he participated in 1544 in an important public debate between Menno and several spokesmen for the Reformed faith. Faber had attacked the Mennonites in print in 1552 with a booklet (no longer extant), which Menno thought deserved a reply. Its point-by-point refutation covered virtually all of the controversial doctrines which separated the larger Protestant body from its radical brethren. Menno proceeded by listing the accusations made by Faber, which he refuted in a detailed defense of his position, buttressed by a great many biblical citations. The style of writing is sharp and polemical.

An important section dealt with the distinction between a true and a false church. Menno's first two points, as mentioned in the Introduction, parallel the Lutheran notes of the church—proper preaching of the gospel and proper sacraments, although there were differences as to what form this preaching and these sacraments should take. Moreover, Menno listed four additional points. The true signs, said Menno, through which the church of Christ may be known are: "(1) By an unadulterated, pure doctrine; (2) by a scriptural use of the sacraments; (3) by obedience to the word; (4) by unfeigned brotherly love; (5) by a bold confession of God and Christ; and (6) by oppression and tribulation for the sake of the Lord's word." The church of the Antichrist could not measure up to these standards. Rather, the opposite was to be seen by intelligent observers, Menno concluded.

This selection is an excerpt.

85

The Signs by Which
Both Churches May Be Known

Although I surmise, good reader, that the difference between both
churches [the church of Christ and the church of the Antichrist]
may be fully grasped in the foregoing comparison, I will, nevertheless, for the sake of greater clarity, briefly present the following
signs by which the one church may be known from the other so that
the truth may be fully declared and known.

In the first place, the sign by which the church of Christ may be
known is the salutary and unadulterated doctrine of his holy and
divine word. God commanded Israel to abide in the doctrine of the
law and not to deviate therefrom, neither to the right hand nor to
the left (Deut. 5:32). Isaiah admonished Israel to conform themselves to the law and its testimony or they would have no dawn
(Isa. 8:20). Christ commanded his disciples, saying: "Go into all
the world and preach the gospel to the whole creation" (Mark
16:15), "teaching them to observe all that I have commanded you"
(Matt. 28:20). The prophets testify on every hand that they spoke
the word of God. Thus saith the Lord of hosts, they say. Again, the
mouth of the Lord says. Again, thus speaketh the Lord God who
has led you out of the land of Egypt—and other like testimonies.
Paul also says: "But even if we, or an angel from heaven, should
preach to you a gospel contrary to that which we preached to you,
let him be accursed" (Gal. 1:8). In short, where the church of
Christ is, there his word is preached purely and rightly.

But where the church of Antichrist is, there the word of God is
falsified. [740] There we are pointed to an earthly and unclean
Christ and to foreign means of salvation which the scriptures do
not know. There we are taught a broad and easy way. There the
great are coddled, and truth is perverted into falsehood. There easy
things are taught, such as the poor, ignorant people gladly hear. In
short, there they are consoled in their predicament so that they may
underrate it, and say: "Peace, peace, when there is no peace" (Jer.
8:11). They promise life to the impenitent, whereas the scriptures
say that they shall not inherit the kingdom of God (Rom. 1:32;
1 Cor. 6:10; Gal. 5:21; Eph. 5:5).

The second sign is the right and scriptural use of the sacraments
of Christ, namely, the baptism of those who, by faith, are born of

God (Titus 3:5), who sincerely repent, who bury their sins in Christ's death, and arise with him in newness of life (Rom. 6:4), who circumcise the foreskin of their hearts with the circumcision of Christ, done without hands (Col. 3:11), who put on Christ (Gal. 3:27), and have a clear conscience (1 Pet. 3:21): moreover the participation in the Lord's holy supper by the penitent, who are flesh of Christ's flesh, and expect grace, reconciliation, and the remission of their sins in the merits of the death and blood of the Lord, who walk with their brethren in love, peace, and unity, who are led by the spirit of the Lord into all truth and righteousness, and who prove by their fruits that they are the church and people of Christ.

But where they baptize without the command and word of God, as they do who do not only baptize without faith, but also without reason and intelligence; where the power and thing signified in baptism, namely, dying unto sin, the new life, the circumcision of the heart, are not only not practiced but also hated by those who come to years of discretion; and where the bread and wine are dispensed to the avaricious, the showy, and impenient persons; where salvation is sought in mere elements, words, and ceremonies, and where a life is led contrary to all love, there is the church of Antichrist. This all intelligent persons must admit. For it is manifest that they reject Christ, the son of God, his word and ordinance, and place in its stead their own ordinance and performed works, and so establish an abomination and an idolatry.

The third sign is obedience to the holy word, of the pious, christian life which is of God. The Lord says: "You shall be holy; for I, the Lord your God, am holy" (Lev. 19:1). Christ says: "Let your light shine before men" (Matt. 5:16), Paul says: "Be blameless and innocent, children of God without blemish, in the midst of a crooked and perverse generation, among whom you shine as lights in the world" (Phil. 2:15). John says: "He who says he abides in him ought to walk in the same way in which he walked" (1 John 2:6).

But how holy the church of Antichrist is, how her light shines, how unblamably and purely they walk, and how their life agrees with Christ's life, may, alas, be seen from their words and works on every hand.

The fourth sign is the sincere and unfeigned love of one's neighbor. For Christ says: "By this all men will know that you are my disciples, if you have love for one another" (John 13:35). Yes, reader, wherever sincere, brotherly love is found without hypocrisy, with its fruits, there we find the church of Christ. [741] John says:

"He who loves is born of God and knows God . . . for God is love"
(1 John 4:7–8).

But where brotherly love is rejected, where they hate, defame,
strike, and beat each other, where everyone seeks his own interests,
where they treat each other deceitfully and faithlessly, where they
curse, swear, and vituperate, where they defile their neighbors' maids,
daughters, and wives; deprive each other of honor, possessions, and
life; commit all manner of willfulness, abomination, and malice
against each other, as may, alas, be seen on every hand; all intelligent persons may judge according to the scriptures, whether there
is not the church of Antichrist.

The fifth sign is that the name, will, word, and ordinance of
Christ are confidently confessed in the face of all cruelty, tyranny,
tumult, fire, sword, and violence of the world, and sustained unto
the end. Christ says: "So everyone who acknowledges me before
men, I will also acknowledge before my Father who is in heaven"
(Matt. 10:32). "For whoever is ashamed of me and of my words
in this adulterous and sinful generation, of him will the Son of man
also be ashamed, when he comes in the glory of his Father, with
the holy angels" (Mark 8:38). Paul also says: "For man believes
with his heart and so is justified, and he confesses with his lips and
so is saved" (Rom. 10:10).

But where the Papists stick with the Papists, Lutherans with the
Lutherans, Interimists with the Interimists,* etc., now build up, and
then demolish and act the hypocrite in keeping with the magistracy's
wishes, everyone who is enlightened by the truth and taught by the
spirit may judge what kind of church that is.

The sixth sign is the pressing cross of Christ, which is borne for
the sake of his testimony and word. Christ says unto all his disciples:
"You will be hated by all nations for my name's sake" (Matt. 24:9).
"Indeed all who desire to live a godly life in Christ Jesus will be
persecuted" (2 Tim. 3:12). Sirach says: "My son, if you come
forward to serve the Lord, prepare yourself for temptation. Set your
heart right, and be steadfast, and do not be hasty in time of calam-
ity. Cleave to him, and do not depart, that you may be honored at
the end of your life. Accept whatever is brought upon you, and on
changes that humble you be patient. For gold is tested in the fire,

---

*Interimists were those holding to the religious settlement ("Augsburg
Interim") imposed in 1548 by Charles V as part of his campaign to
recatholicize the empire.

and acceptable men in the furnace of humiliation" (Ecclus. 2:1–5). Read also Matthew 5:10, 10:23, 16:4; Mark 13:13; Luke 6:22; John 16:2; Acts 14:8; 2 Timothy 2; Hebrews 11:37, 12:2.

[742] This very cross is a sure indicator of the church of Christ, and has been testified not only in olden times by the scriptures, but also by the example of Jesus Christ, of the holy apostles and prophets, the first and unfalsified church, and also by the present, pious, faithful children especially in these our Netherlands.

On the other hand, the ungodly, heathen lying; the hating, envying, reviling, blaspheming; the unmerciful arresting; the exiling, confiscating, and murdering, and the sentencing to water, fire, sword, and stake, seen in various localities, are plain signs of the church of Antichrist. For John says that the Babylonian woman was drunken with the blood of the saints, and with the blood of the martyrs of Jesus (Rev. 17:6). He also saw that to the beast which arose from the sea, a mouth was given, speaking great things, and blaspheming against God and his holy name, and his tabernacle or church, and those that dwell in heaven. And it was given unto him to make war with the saints, and to overcome them (Rev. 13:5–6). Yes, my reader, this is the very way and work of the church of Antichrist, to hate, persecute, and put to the sword those whom she cannot enchant with the golden cup of her abomination.

Oh Lord! Dear Lord! Grant that the wrathful dragon may not entirely devour thy poor little flock, but that we, by thy grace, may in patience conquer by the sword of thy mouth; and may leave an abiding seed, which shall keep thy commandments, preserve thy testimony, and eternally praise thy great and glorious name. Amen, dear Lord. Amen.

Part 4

The Hutterian Brethren

Editor's note

The nonconformist legacy of the Hussite wars and a long tradition of
political independence made it possible for Moravia to become a center
of religious toleration in the sixteenth century. One of the most
interesting developments was the formation of the Christian communistic
settlements (*Bruderhöfe*) of the Hutterite Brethren. The Hutterites
resulted from a split within the Anabaptist community of Nicolsburg,
the center of a large ingathering of religious dissenters.

In 1528 a group of Anapabtists left Nicolsburg because of differences
with the lord of Liechtenstein over the social order, pacifism, and the
care of the refugees. On their way to an unknown destination, the party
of two hundred decided to pool their goods: "At that time these men
spread a cloak before the people, and every man did lay his substancc
down upon it, with a willing heart and without constraint, for the
sustenance of those in necessity, according to the doctrine of the prophets
and the apostles." They were given shelter at Austerlitz and attempted
communal living.

Dissension threatened to disrupt them completely but the advice of a
respected visitor from the Tyrol, Jacob Hutter (d. 1536) helped to
arbitrate the differences. In 1533 Hutter came for a longer period and
took the leadership upon himself, placing the community on its
permanent basis. Although pressure from the Margrave Ferdinand I
resulted in repeated expulsion and harrassment, the Hutterites survived,
thanks equally to their persistence and to the desire of the Moravian
lords for skilled artisans and farmers. After the death of Ferdinand in
1563 the Hutterites experienced a "golden period" of relatively
undisturbed life until 1592.

The best description of the manner of life of the Hutterites of this
period is found in their *Chronicle*, a basic source for all Anabaptist
history. The author was the elder John Kräl (d. 1583), aided by his
scribe Hauptrecht Zapff (d. 1630). At this period there were more
than 128 colonies with perhaps 20,000 members. The Counter
Reformation caused the final expulsion from Moravia of the Hutterites
in 1622 and the despoiling of their once flourishing settlements.

This selection is an excerpt.

The Oldest Chronicle of the
Hutterian Brethren (1569)
[A Description of the
Community]

[During] all these years and this time also God has given his people
a quiet time. First, the Lord purified his community [*Gmain*] in
different ways and sent her much tribulation and diverse sorrow,
trials, misery, and poverty for a long period of years (as may be
seen and learned in this book). Then God—this we cannot help
but describe particularly in honor of his memory—decided to give
his people also a time of quiet and rich blessing, as came to Job
after his temptation. This was to see how they would conduct themselves during such a period. It was also for the purpose of making
his work and ordinances known to all men and publishing them
abroad by having them publicly practiced and observed. This God
did and he granted his people, against the intent and assaults of the
entire world, a good and tranquil time where there was no general
tribulation or persecution for almost twenty years or more—as can
be read later in this book—except for what from time to time occurred here and there.

It is true that during this time there were many plans and decisions made by emperor and king at the imperial diets [*Reichstage*]
and also at the provincial diets [*Landtage*], where all classes and
faiths (even though otherwise completely disunited) were united in
this one thing, that our people must be rooted out, annihilated, and
[431] tolerated no longer. But the Lord prevented this often and in
various ways. For example, he occupied their hands with something
else or perhaps discouraged them from it. The Lord knows how to
temper the wind for the shorn lamb (Acts 4; Isa. 8, 19; Psalm 33).

Many stepped forward who undertook not to rest easy until they
had driven them out and annihilated them, and even had received
the authority to do so (but not from God). Yet, the Lord annihilated them [the oppressors] before they began. Many often intended
to harm them but they were the ones to suffer disappointment
(Jer. 2).

There was much taking of counsel. One advised that the brethren
should be hanged, another wanted to burn them, a third to seize
their elders and tear them out by their roots. The fourth, for example, wished he had power over them for he knew how to make
them disappear from this earth. Many of these, however, lived only

Fig. 3. Hutterite family and
dwelling, by an unknown sixteenth-
century artist. Source: C. Erhard,
*Gründliche kurtz verfaste Historia
von Münsterischen Widertauffern*
. . . (Munich, 1589).

a short time thereafter. Death prevented them from attaining any
or many new years of life, as we experienced and could substantiate
with names.

The class [*geschlecht*] of priests continually and in many ways
agitated with the authorities wherever they could, and still do so.
But only the Lord our God stood in the way, the grand prince
Michael, who stood by the children of his people, for otherwise they
would long ago have been swallowed and devoured like bread (Dan.
12; Psalm 124; 2 Esdr. 1). But as a mother hen gathers her chicks
under her feathers and holds her wings over them, pecking and
biting at anything that tries to attack her brood (Matt. 23[:37]),
even as an eagle hovers over his young, in the same way and to a
much greater extent does God act on behalf of his people. Consequently, even the unbelievers had many times to acknowledge and
admit that God would not permit anyone to root out or drive away
his people (Deut. 32).

Thus they dwelled in the land which God had especially ordained
and provided for them. They were given wings from the eagle to

fly there as the place which God had prepared for them, to be nourished and edified there as long as it pleased God (Rev. 12). Therefore, they gathered in peace and unity, taught and preached the gospel and the word of God in public. Twice a week, and sometimes more often, such meetings were held for the word of God. There united prayers were also offered to God for all of the needs of the community, and [432] glorious thanksgiving was given for all the good things they had enjoyed. Likewise, they offered intercessory prayer for emperor, king, princes, and the secular rulers, that God might grant them earnestness in the office to which they had been ordained, to conduct it rightly for the protection of the godly and for a peaceful government (Heb. 10; 2 [1] Tim. 2).

Along with this they practiced the christian ban of the vice-ridden, insofar as they belonged to the community. They were expelled, separated, and disciplined, each according to his guilt. Those, however, who truly repented, were accepted again and reincorporated.

According to the commandment of the Lord and the apostles, christian baptism was conducted for those who were of adult and accountable age, who were able to hear God's word, understand it by themselves, believe it on their own, and accept it by themselves. In all aspects infant baptism is contrary to this and wrong (Matt. 28; Mark 16; Acts 2, 8, 10, 16, 19).

They met together and held the Lord's supper as a memorial and renewal in holy remembrance of the suffering and death of Jesus Christ who, through his death, redeemed us, who would otherwise have been lost. He reconciled us and made us of one mind with him, even members of his body. This was held as a feast of thanksgiving for his love and unspeakable goodness in what he had done on our behalf and what we should do [in return] out of gratitude for his sake (Matt. 26; Luke 22; Acts 2, 20; 1 Cor. 10, 11). (The idolatrous sacrament of the priests is quite the opposite of this Lord's supper.)

Christian community of goods was practiced as Jesus had taught and practiced with his disciples, and as the early church had also done. Other-minded persons were not accepted. Those who had previously been poor or rich now had one purse, one house, and one table in common, healthy as healthy, sick as sick, and children as children [i.e., all were treated the same] (Matt. 19; Luke 14; John 13; Acts 2, 4, 5).

Swords and spears were forged into and used as pruning hooks and saws and other useful tools. There were no muskets, swords, or pikes—not a single weapon made for fighting was to be found at all. Each was completely the brother of the other. It was purely a peace-loving people who contributed nothing toward war or bloody conflict with their taxes, let alone participated in it themselves. [433] They took no revenge. Patience was their weapon in all conflicts (Matt. 5, 23; Rom. 12).

They submitted themselves to and obeyed the secular authorities in all good things which were not opposed to God, faith, or conscience. They paid them their due on behalf of the office given to them by God, which is as necessary in this wicked world as daily bread (Rom. 13; [1] Pet. 2). In sum, all twelve articles of the christian apostolic faith* were proclaimed and practiced as well as everything founded in the holy scriptures.

Christian missions were instituted as the Lord had commanded (Matt. 10, 28; Mark 16) and said: "As the Father has sent me, even so I send you" (John 20[:21]). Again: "I chose you and appointed you that you should go and bear fruit" (John 15[:16]). Therefore each year servants of the gospel with their aides were sent out to those lands where there was need. They visited those who wished to improve their lives, who strove and sought for the truth. These people were led out from there by day and night, if they so wished, despite the executioners and hangmen. Many of them risked and lost life and limb for this. Thus, the people of the Lord were gathered as is appropriate for good shepherds.

Separation from and denial of the world and its wicked, unjust life were observed, especially the shunning of false prophets and false brethren (2 Cor. 6; Rev. 18; 2 Cor. 5; 2 John 1).

Among these people was heard no cursing or blasphemy, without which the world cannot speak. There was no oathtaking or swearing of vows. There were never seen any dances or gambling, no boozing or toast-drinking. No more slit and lowcut, vain and indecent clothes were seen. All of these things have been done away with. There was no singing of scandalous whore-songs, of which the world is full, but rather of christian and spiritual as well as biblical songs (Matt. 5; James 5; Eph. 5; Col. 3).

The offices were held by elders, men set aside to lead with God's word, who persevered in reading, teaching, and admonishing. They only administered, practiced the office of reconciliation, spoke judg-

---

*The creeds of the ancient church were customarily divided into twelve sections.

ment, and settled cases, [434] and did the overseeing (Titus 1; Acts 6; 1 Tim. 4).

There were specially appointed men [*Diener der Notdurfft*] who directed the temporal economy. They accounted for receipts and expenditures, cared for the necessities of food, placed orders, and made purchases. Other men were selected to organize the people for their labor, and direct each to what he knew and was able to do well, in the fields and wherever there was need. These were stewards.

Other men served at the tables. Everyone went to meals with prayer and thanksgiving to God and again to work with thanksgiving. With thanksgiving and prayer one went to bed in the evening and again in the morning to work with thanksgiving and prayer, each to his task. Other men were set aside for the direction of the school, to aid the sisters in the discipline of the children and to supervise everything.

There were no usurers or traders but only honest earning. Everyone earned his bread with daily manual labor (Eph. 4; 2 Thess. 3), with masonry and farm work, in the vineyards, fields, meadows, pastures, and gardens. There were quite a few carpenters and construction workers who worked especially in Moravia and also in Austria, Hungary, and Bohemia. They constructed for low wages many beautiful, efficient, and sturdy mills, breweries, and other buildings for princes, nobles, burghers, and others. There was for them an especially appointed brother and foreman who supervised the carpenters everywhere, accepted work, hired and made contracts with the people on behalf of his brethren and the community.

There were also quite a few millers, and the mills in the country (upon the requests and desires of the lords and others) were taken over and leased by them [for the community]. As far as the mill work was concerned, they made a fair contract for the third or the fourth share, as was customary and fair in that country. There was also one miller who, on behalf of the community with the advice of the elders, accepted this millwork, made the agreements and contracts with the mill owners, and generally supervised the millers and saw to it that the mills were occupied and cared for.

[435] Also, they supplied for a long time many rulers (especially in the lands where they lived) and noblemen with people for their estates and other farms. Some received a third [share], others wages, depending upon what seemed just and acceptable to both parties. In addition, sometimes, there was also one brother appointed who, upon request and sometimes after long insistence on the part of the

lords, took over the general supervision on behalf of the community
of those estates which they felt confident and able to handle. Therefore, he made honest contracts and agreements with the lords and
saw to it that the estates were staffed and supplied from time to
time with necessary persons.

In sum, no one went idle. Each person did that which he was
asked to do and which he was capable of and knew how to do. No
matter if a person had previously been a noble, rich or poor, he
learned to work and labor, even former priests.

There were also many other kinds of honorable, useful trades
such as: mason, blacksmith, scythesmith, sicklesmith, coppersmith,
locksmith, clockmaker, cutler, metalworker, tanner, leatherdresser,
furrier, shoemaker, saddler, harnessmaker, bagmaker, cartwright,
cooper, cabinetmaker, turner, hatmaker, clothmaker, clothcutter,
tailor, blanketmaker, weaver, ropemaker, sievemaker, glazier, potter,
brewer, surgeon, barber, and physician. For each of these trades
there was a foreman in the shop who accepted the work, gave
orders, assigned it again, sold it according to its worth, and faithfully gave the proceeds to the community.

Everyone, wherever he might be, worked for the common and
equal good, need, aid, and service where there was necessity. This
was nothing less than a perfect body which had and used only active,
living members serving one another.

It was like a well-constructed clock where one wheel and piece
always turned another, moved and helped it along, making it func-
tion for its purpose. Yes, it was like a collection of those useful little
animals, the bees, who work together in their common beehive,
some making wax, others honey, others carrying and bringing water,
others doing other work, until their tasty work of sweet honey [436]
is completed. They do not only produce what they need for their
own nourishment, dwelling and need, but enough to share with men
and the people for their benefit and use. The same was true there
[in the community]. There must be order and discipline in this and
all other things because it is in order that every good thing consists
and can thus be carried out and preserved. This is especially so in
the household of God where the Lord is himself the foreman and
proper supervisor. Where there is no order there is disorder [and]
confusion, in which God is not present, and the undertaking soon
disintegrates.

Besides this the community became well known and famous everywhere partly through those who were imprisoned from time to time

for witnessing to Jesus Christ and his truth. These were servants [of the word] and other brethren, the foundations of whose faith (as may be seen in this book in many places) were diligently looked into and examined. This was done in many ways and in many places in the German lands, wherever brethren were imprisoned—often for long periods of time—who testified through their word and deed, life and death, that their faith was the truth.

In part, the community became well known also by emperor, kings, princes, lords, and their courts, but especially everywhere in the German lands—their religion, deeds, teaching, and conduct, what they believed and practiced—because princes, lords, nobility, and commoners, and those who were at the courts of the emperor, king, and princes very often came to see and to inquire for themselves. Even apart from this they found out for certain that the community was innocent of the many lies and rumors spread about them. Consequently, many of them were convinced and praised them as a devout people and said that this must be an institution of God. Otherwise, [they said] it would be impossible for so many people to dwell together in unity in one place. [This was] because in their own case even where but two, three, or four housed together, they quarreled with one another daily and were very discontented until they ran away from each other.

Many of them liked the brethren best as servants and workers. They preferred them in this to all other people. For this reason, although it was considered (because of their religion) that there were too many brethren in the country, when it came to the availability of loyal servants, then there were far too few, for they were widely sought after.

[437] It was a curious situation. Some lords were angry at them because of their religion and did not want them to be tolerated in the country. Others were angry when the community did not give them more brethren as servants and laborers, for whom they often had to ask and wait for many years. In brief, some wanted very much to keep them, others wanted to drive them out. Some spoke of them in the highest terms, others in the worst.

The whole world did not want to tolerate the community, but had to. God guided the oceans (that is to say, the furious nations of this world) so that the brethren could come here from all lands. After a multitude had gathered they fearlessly carried out the work of the Lord, which was in opposition to the Devil and the world. Yes, if you ponder it, it was a miraculous work of God. Some people con-

sidered it to be right and proper for those who could do it. Some
wished that they could also do it. Others, however, and this was the
great mass, considered it, in their blindness, to be an error and
seduction or a slavish undertaking (Isa. 11, 29).

But the whole world hated and envied them, so that they could
say with David: "More in number than the hairs of my head are
those who hate me without cause" (Psalm 69[:4]). As soon as the
brethren stepped outside their door, they were called names and
blasphemed as "Anabaptists," "Twice-baptists," "New Baptists,"
"sectarians," "rabble-rousers," and many other evil names of shame.
Everyone was in an uproar about them, despised and mocked them,
spreading cruel lies and rumors, for example, that they devoured
children and many similar monstrous accusations. Such things we
would have been loath to dream or imagine, let alone do. Indeed,
many strange accusations were raised against the community, which
were inhuman, not to say unchristian, with the intent of making
them suspicious and hated (Matt. 5; Luke 6; 2 Cor. 6; 1 Pet. 4).

This hatred and enmity of the world came to us solely for the
sake of Christ and his truth and because we followed him, and not
because of any other guilt. Take this as sure proof, that if any person
came along with only a staff in his hand, with no intent to harm, or
gave thanks before he ate, he was considered an Anabaptist, heretic,
this or that. (So gross is the Devil!) But as soon as someone de-
fected [from the community] and went about in heathen manner
with a sword at his side and musket on his shoulder, he was [438]
at once welcomed and again considered a good Christian by the
world.

If anyone happened by without a frill around his neck or any
other sign or mark of vanity on his clothes and said that gambling,
pride, vanity, swilling, guzzling, and toasting [of drinks] were sinful,
wrong, and against God, and if, at the same time, he had a quiet
manner, was graced with patience and other traits appropriate for
a disciple of Christ, in the eyes of the world he had to be a heretic,
sectary, seducer, scoundrel, and who knows what else. Then he was
engulfed by the world's universal hatred and shame, even though
they had never seen him before in all their lives and knew no wrong
to accuse him of, neither had he ever done any of them any wrong
nor intended to do so. To this extremity has the world now come.

He, however, who abandons [the right way] again and returns to
the world, frequents the inns, and calls: "Comrade John, I'll buy
you one!" starts to sing drinking and whore-songs, drinks himself

blind drunk with them, sticks a bundle of feathers—the sign of the fool—in his hat, frequents the gambling and dance halls, wears large frills and ruffles around his neck, wears wide trousers or fancily slit and cut clothes, who also makes much of their most worthy and innumerable sacraments, curses and swears, finds again words to blaspheme and curse God—such a person is from that moment on received by the universal love and friendship of the world. She claims him again as her own. She is pleased with him; she praises him saying: "Oh, you were right in leaving your brethren, repenting, and becoming a true Christian. Now you have the true faith. Just don't let yourself be seduced again from the christian church. Indeed, you have done well to part from this sect" (as they call it).

He may travel where he will, he will generally find good friends and people who like him and find him pleasing, even though they may have never seen or known him before in their whole lives. Though they are aware of his wickedness and vices, nevertheless, he is dear to the world because he has left the truth of God. Thus, it can be clearly seen from this that they hate and persecute us only because we strive after God. This hatred comes from the envy of the old serpent solely for the sake of God's truth. [439]. Although no one wants to grant this, it is still true.

Finally, the hatred of the neighbors in the land was not slight. They envied us as Esau did Jacob because of the blessing which God granted us, so that, along with our diligence, effort, and labor, we enjoyed a sufficiency in buildings, dwellings, and food, God be praised. [The neighbors] however, generally lived in scarcity and misery because they spent everything for wine, were always found drinking, and often drank up their money before it was earned. They loved laziness and idleness.

What are we to say about the false brethren and communities, who criticized, complained, and talked about the community more than any one else? They never found anything good in it but had contempt for it. Their hatred and enmity is so rampant because we chastized the faults and errors into which they had fallen. This sufficiently proved the truth of Christ's saying to his followers: "You will be hated by all for my name's sake" (Matt. 10:24[22]). Because the words of the Lord really have been borne out among us, all of this strengthened and quickened us the more.

Also, the Lord has strengthened his community and given to us a great testimony in that many of those who fell away from the truth and returned to the world could find neither peace nor rest in their hearts, year in, year out, no matter how long they have lived outside. Whether they arose or retired, whatever they undertook, their conscience always tormented them, and they always carried fear in their hearts because of their apostasy. Those who returned, with much pleading, crying, and shedding of tears, repenting and confessing of sins, seeking peace with God and his community, would henceforth rather lose their lives than renounce or give up the truth.

Indeed, this also gave us great certainty, as we have often experienced, heard and seen for ourselves the great fear and sorrow, indeed, the despair, of those who have fallen away, who had once acknowledged and accepted this truth of God but later rejected it. When God seized them and cast them into illness, and when they faced death (at which time all is revealed to men) [440] they began to wail pitifully and experienced a futile, belated repentance that they had been apostate from the truth of God and must now die in their apostasy.

Some who had foreseen their fate and penalty carried on frightfully, cried woe over themselves as those for whom there was no redemption. Others said that they had kicked the doors of heaven shut with their own feet. Others claimed that if they were brethren again and had repented they would be quite happy to die and leave this life. Many pleaded and prayed in their great fear that if God would let them recover this once they would do penance and return to what they had left. Many who recovered actually kept their promise and did not delay. Many others, however, could no longer attain or live to see this but, as was said previously, died and departed with heavy consciences and great fear as those who had defied God. For when God called them, they did not wish to listen. Now when they called upon God, the Lord would not hear them (Jer. 7; Prov. 2; Psalm 81). Herewith we wish to let these matters rest and return to the narration of other things.

Editor's note

The outstanding spokesman for the Hutterian Brethren was Peter
Riedemann or Ridemann (1506–56). A native of Silesia, he is first
noticed in the records of Anabaptism as an elder in Upper Austria,
where he was imprisoned for three years in Gmunden. While in prison
he wrote a long *Account of Our Faith* (*Rechenschaft*) which
circulated in manuscript.

After escaping this captivity he traveled to Moravia and joined the
Hutterites, who sent him as a missioner on several trips. On one of these
he was arrested in Nuremberg and held for over four years (1533–37).
Upon his promise never to return there, he was released, but went on
further mission trips to other parts of Germany. He was seized by the
authorities in Marburg in the summer of 1540. After a first severe
imprisonment he was transferred to the castle of Wolkersdorf north of
Marburg where he was treated more leniently.

He used his enforced stay in Hesse to write another extensive *Account*,
this one meant for the eyes of Landgrave Philip. Riedemann's treatise
became the accepted doctrinal confession for the Hutterian Brethren,
and was one of the few of their many writings to be published in
printed form, first in 1545 and then in 1565. It is divided into two
unequal parts, the longer first section dealing with important points of
doctrine and ethics, the second dealing with characteristic practices of the
Brethren. Riedemann's volume is still considered by the Hutterites as
their basic confessional statement.

In 1542 Peter Riedemann returned to Moravia when the community
called him to be their spiritual leader. During the bitter persecution of
1547–51, when they survived only by going underground in elaborate
caves, his pastoral leadership was of immense aid in preserving morale.

As with much Hutterite preaching and writing, the *Account* consists
largely of carefully linked biblical quotations. The translation from
which the following excerpts were taken was made by the Society of
Brothers in 1950 and is taken from the latest edition (1970).

Community of Saints

Every good and perfect gift comes down from above from the father of lights, with whom is no variableness nor change to darkness (James 1:17). He gives and shares all things with us who believe in him, as Paul said: "If God is for us, who is against us? He who did not spare his own Son but gave him up for us all, will he not also give us all things with him?" (Rom. 8:31–32). Thus the father desires to pour out all good things upon those who believe his word and walk justly and faithfully before him; as his promise also shows when he said to Abraham: "I am God almighty," that is, one with authority and might, [with] fullness to overflowing and sufficiency of all good things. "Walk before me, and be blameless (devout, and faithful unto me). And I will make my covenant between me and you, and will multiply you exceedingly. . . . And I will establish . . . an everlasting covenant, to be God to you and to your descendants after you" (Gen. 17:1–6). It is as though he said: "If you hold to me and do and keep my will, you shall have all good things in me, yes, I shall give you all that is useful and lovely" (Gen. 17:1–9). Even as the father is the fullness of all good things, he has given it to the son to be so likewise, as it is written: "For in him all the fullness of God was pleased to dwell" (Col. 1:19), and again: "The Word became flesh and dwelt among us, full of grace and truth; we have beheld his glory, glory as of the only Son from the Father" (John 1:14), [43] and again: "For in him the whole fullness of deity dwells bodily, and you have come to fullness of life in him" (Col. 2:9–10).

We, however, become partakers of this grace of Christ through faith in the truth, as Paul said: "And Christ may dwell in your hearts through faith" (Eph. 3:17). Such faith, however, comes from the preaching of the gospel (Rom. 10:17). Thus through attentive hearing and observing of the gospel we become partakers of the community of Christ, as may be recognized from the words of John, when he said: "That which we have seen and heard we proclaim also to you, so that you may have fellowship with us, and our fellowship is with the Father and with his son Jesus Christ" (1 John 1:3), "for all that I have heard and received from my Father I have made known to you" (John 15:15).

Community, however, is nothing else than that those who have fellowship have all things in common, none having anything, but each having all things with the others (Acts 2:42–46, 4:32–37), even as the father has nothing for himself, but all that he has he has with the son (John 17), and again, the son has nothing for himself, but all that he has, he has with the father and all who have fellowship with him (Rom. 8:10–11; 1 John 1:2–3).

Thus all those who have fellowship with him likewise have nothing for themselves, but have all things with their master and with all those who have fellowship with them (Eph. 4:1–16) that they might be one in the son as the son is in the father (John 16:13–15).

It is called the community of saints because they have fellowship in holy things, yes, in those things whereby they are sanctified, that is in the father and the son, who himself sanctifies them with all that he has given them (1 John 1:5–7). Thus everything serves to the betterment and building up of one's neighbor and to the praise and glory of God the father (1 Cor. 14:26–33).

Concerning the Supper of Christ

[85] The Lord Christ, the salvation of the world (Isa. 62:11), was sent by the father that those who believe in his name might have eternal life (John 6:29–40, 20:30–31) and be renewed into the divine likeness (Eph. 4:20–24; Col. 3:1–10) and grafted into his nature (2 Pet. 1:2–4); which access to the father and his grace he won through his death for us, who bear the likeness of his death (Eph. 2:17–22). Therefore when he desired to go again to the father from whom he had come (John 14:1–3), he wanted to show this to the disciples whom he had chosen from the world and to impress it on their inner being, so that after he had gone from them they might remember his grace and know for what purpose they had been chosen and accepted by God (John 15:1–11), that they might not be without hope like the rest, who know nothing of God (1 Thess. 4:13).

Therefore he took a loaf of bread, thanked his father, broke it and gave it to his disciples and said: "Take, eat: this is my body, which is broken for you. This do, as often as you do it, in remembrance of me." He took the cup in the same way and said: "Drink of it, all of you" (Matt. 26:26–29; Mark 14:22–25; Luke 22:14–20; 1 Cor. 11:23–26). "This cup which is poured out for you is the new covenant in my blood, for the forgiveness of sins do this in remembrance of me" (Luke 22:20ff.).

Now, in taking the bread and giving it to his [86] disciples, Christ desired to show and explain the community of his body to his disciples, that they had become one body, one plant, one living organism, and one nature with him (John 15:1–9), as Paul interpreted it: "Because there is one bread, we who are many are one body, for we all partake of the one bread" (1 Cor. 10:17). He, however, in saying this, did not give them his body, his flesh and blood to eat (John 6:29–37), as it has been twisted by the deceiver and made into idolatry; but, as we have said, he taught them that they are members of his body, and as the bread is made a loaf by the bringing together of many grains (1 Cor. 10:1–4, 12:12–20; Rom. 12:4–5), even so we, many human beings who were scattered and divided, of many minds and purposes are led by faith into one, and have become one plant (Rom. 11:17–24), one living organism and body of Christ (1 Cor. 6:15–20), cleaving to him in one spirit (Rom. 12:1–3; Phil. 2:1–5), as the Lord pictured more clearly for them in still another parable, when he said: "I am the vine, you are the branches" (John 15:1–8). Here he showed once more distinctly and clearly that they are one plant, organism, matter, substance, and body with him. Therefore it is sufficiently clear that nothing other than this alone is Christ's meaning.

In that he broke the loaf for them, however, and commanded them to eat (Matt. 26:26; Luke 22:19), he showed that they must bear the likeness of his death, be ready to die like him, if they would partake of his grace and become heirs of God. As Paul also said: "We are . . . heirs of God and fellow heirs with Christ, provided we suffer with him in order that we may also be glorified with him" (Rom. 8:16–17).

That it has the above-mentioned meaning, and that this is truly what Christ meant, is proved by his own words, in that he said: "This cup which is poured out for you is the new covenant in my blood" (Luke 22:20ff.). Here he does not say: "This is my blood. Drink of it, all of you," but: "This is the new covenant." What is then the [87] new covenant? Is it to eat the body of Christ and drink his blood? On the contrary, show where that is anywhere promised! Oh, what great folly—that one does not want to see and know!

We find indeed that God has promised a new covenant, not of the body or of eating flesh and blood, but of the knowledge of God, as the word says: "This is the covenant that I will make with [them]: I will put my laws into their minds, and write them on their hearts . . . for all shall know me" (Jer. 31:33; Heb. 8:10). Through this knowledge, however, man is led to God (Wisd. 7, 18:1–4), is grafted into and becomes a fellow-member of his nature and character (2 Pet. 1:2–4), whereby we are also all led into the one mind and will of Christ (Rom. 12:1–2; 1 Cor. 2).

For this reason he gave them wine, since many grapes have become one drink, and said: "This is the new covenant in my blood" (Luke 22:20ff.), as though he meant to say: That is ratified or made strong and confirmed by my blood. For I have led you into such a covenant of grace and made you partakers of it (Heb. 9:14–15), that you now have become one bread and one body with me through faith (1 Cor. 10:16–17), that henceforth, led by one spirit, you should be of one mind and purpose (Acts 2:42–47, 4:32) to prove that you are my disciples (John 13:35).

Thus, the meal, or the partaking of the bread and wine of the Lord, is a sign of the community of his body, in that each and every member thereby declares himself to be of the one mind, heart, and spirit of Christ (1 Cor. 10:16–31). Therefore said Paul: "Let a man examine himself, and so eat of the bread and drink of the cup. For any one who eats and drinks without discerning the body eats and drinks judgment upon himself" (1 Cor. 11:28–32), as though he would say: Let the man consider, examine, and search himself well to see if he is partaking of this grace of Christ (John 14, 16:13–20; Acts 2:22–23) and is a true member of Christ, as he declares himself to be. For where this is not so he brings judgment upon himself in eating and drinking (1 Cor. 6:12–20, 10:11–24; Rom. 12:1–5).

Concerning Community of Goods

[88] Now, since all the saints have fellowship in holy things, that is in God (1 John 1:1–3), who also has given to them all things in his son Christ Jesus (Rom. 1:16–17)—which gift none should have for himself, but each for the other; as Christ also had nothing for himself, but has everything for us, even so all the members of his body have nothing for themselves, but for the whole body, for all the members (Phil. 2:1–8). For his gifts are not sanctified and given

to one member alone, or for one member's sake, but for the whole body with its members (1 Cor. 12:12–27).

Now, since all God's gifts—not only spiritual, but also material things—are given to man, not that he should have them for himself or alone but with all his fellows, therefore the communion of saints itself must show itself not only in spiritual but also in temporal things (Acts 2:42–47, 4:32–37); that as Paul said, one might not have abundance and another suffer want, but that there may be equality (2 Cor. 8:7–15). This he showed from the law touching manna, in that he who gathered little had no less, since each was given what he needed according to the measure (Ex. 16:16–18).

Furthermore, one sees in all things created, which testify to us still today, that God from the beginning ordained nothing private for man, but all things to be common (Gen. 1:26–29). But through wrong-taking, since man took what he should not and forsook what he should take (Gen. 3:2–12), he drew such things to himself and made them his property, and so grew and became hardened therein. Through such wrong-taking and collecting of created things he has been led so far from God that he has even forgotten the creator (Rom. 1:18–25), and has even raised up and honored as god the created things which had been put under and made subject to him (Wisd. 13:1–3, 15:14–19). And such is still the case if one steps out of God's order and forsakes the same.

[89] Now, however, as has been said, created things which are too high for man to draw within his grasp or collect, such as the sun with the whole course of the heavens, day, air, and such like, show that not they alone, but all other created things are likewise made common to man (Gen. 1:25–31). That they have thus remained and are not possessed by man is due to their being too high for him to bring under his power, otherwise—so evil has he become through wrong-taking—he would draw them to himself as well as the rest and make them his property (Gen. 3:2–6; 2 Esdr. 3:4–7, 7:21–25; Rom. 5:12–14).

That is so, however, and that the rest is just as little made by God for man's private possession, is shown in that man must forsake all other created things as well as this when he dies, and can carry nothing with him to use as his own (1 Tim. 6:6–9). For which reason Christ also called temporal all things foreign to man's essential nature, and said: "If you have not been faithful in that which is another's, who will give you that which is your own?" (Luke

16:11). Now, because what is temporal does not belong to us, but is foreign to our true nature, the law commands that none covet strange possessions (Ex. 20:17, Deut. 5:21), that is, set his heart upon and cleave to what is temporal and alien (Luke 16:11–12). Therefore whosoever will cleave to Christ and follow him must forsake such taking of created things and property (Matt. 10:32–39; Luke 9:23–26; Mark 8:34–38), as he himself has said: "Whoever of you does not renounce all that he has cannot be my disciple" (Luke 14:33). For if a man is to be renewed into the likeness of God, he must put off all that leads him from him—that is the grasping and drawing to himself of created things—for he cannot otherwise attain God's likeness (Eph. 4:20–32; Col. 3:1–11). Therefore Christ said: "Whoever does not receive the kingdom of God like a child shall not enter it" (Mark 10:15; Luke 18:17), or "Unless you turn and become like children, you will never enter the kingdom of heaven" (Matt. 18:1–4).

[90] Now, he who thus becomes free from created things can then grasp what is true and divine; and when he grasps it and it becomes his treasure, he turns his heart towards it, empties himself of all else (Luke 12:33–40) and takes nothing as his, and regards it no longer as his but as of all God's children (Acts 2:44–45, 4:32–37). Therefore we say that as all the saints have community in spiritual gifts (1 John 1:3), still much more should they show this in material things, and not ascribe the same to and covet them for themselves, for they are not their own; but regard them as of all God's children (Luke 16:11–13), that they may thereby show that they are partakers in the community of Christ (1 Cor. 10:16) and are renewed into God's likeness (Eph. 4:22–24; Col. 3:1–10). For the more man yet cleaves to created things, appropriates and ascribes such to himself, the farther does he show himself to be from the likeness of God and the community of Christ (Gen. 1:25–27).

For this reason the Holy Spirit also at the beginning of the church began such community right gloriously again, so that none said that any of the things that he possessed were his own, but they had all things in common (Acts 2:44–45, 4:32–37); and it is his will that this might still be kept, as Paul said: "Do nothing from selfishness or conceit, but in humility count others better than yourselves," or: "Let each of you look not only to his own interests, but also to the interests of others" (Phil. 2:3–4). Where this is not the case it is a blemish upon the church which ought verily to be corrected. If one should say, it was so nowhere except in Jerusalem, therefore it is

now not necessary, we say: Even if it were nowhere but in Jerusalem, it does not follow that it ought not to be so now. For neither
apostles nor churches were lacking, but rather the opportunity, manner, and time (Acts 2:38–45, 4:32–37).*

Therefore this should be no cause for us to hesitate, but rather
should it move us to more and better zeal and diligence, for the
Lord now gives us both time and cause so to do. That there was no
lack of [91] either apostles or churches is shown by the zeal of both.
For the apostles have pointed the people thereto with all diligence
and most faithfully prescribed true surrender, as all their epistles
still prove today (Phil. 2:1–11; Rom. 14:7–18). And the people
obeyed with zeal, as Paul bears witness—especially of those of
Macedonia—saying: "We want you to know, brethren, about the
grace of God which has been shown in the churches of Macedonia,
for in a severe test of affliction, their abundance of joy and their
extreme poverty have overflowed in a wealth of liberality on their
part. For they gave according to their means, as I can testify, and
beyond their means, of their own free will, begging us earnestly for
the favor of taking part in the relief of the saints—and this, not as
we expected, but first they gave themselves to the Lord and to us by
the will of God" (2 Cor. 8:1–5).

Here one can well see with what inclined and willing hearts the
churches were ready to keep community not only in spiritual but
also in material things, for they desired to follow the master Christ,
and become like him and one with him (Phil. 2:5–8), who himself
went before us in such a way, and commanded us to follow him
(Matt. 10:22–25; Luke 14:33).

---

*This is in answer to the criticism of some Anabaptists that the example of
the church at Jerusalem was an isolated case. See the comments by
Menno Simons in *Sorrowful and Christian Apology and Justification.*

11

The Five Articles of the Greatest Strife Between Us and the World

Editor's note

Of all the Anabaptist groups it is primarily the Hutterian Brethren who created an extensive doctrinal literature. The latter half of the sixteenth century provided the outward conditions enabling such writing, and the aggressive Hutterian mission outreach supplied the motivation.

In the Hutterite *Chronicle* is found an extended passage under the year 1547. This reflects a debate held two years earlier with the Gabrielite Brethren (the name derives from Gabriel Ascherham of Silesia), which resulted in the eventual union of the two church bodies. Along with the other themes of adult baptism, the Lord's supper, warfare and nonresistance, and divorce, a major chapter was devoted to the foundation of community. The Hutterite exposition was primarily given over to a listing and paraphrase of biblical passages. It stressed the importance of *Gelassenheit*, a term of medieval mystical origin. It has the meaning of yielding, surrendering, abandoning of self-will. For the Hutterites, it was interpreted as the necessity of giving up all material possessions.

This *Book of Five Articles,* as it was called, was revised, expanded, and published separately in 1577, most likely by Peter Walpot (1521–78), the spiritual leader of the Hutterites at that period and one of the ablest of all their elders. Several lengthy excerpts from this publication were made and circulated in Europe. It won a special refutation (of 265 pages) as late as 1659, from the hand of a German pastor. In 1680 another version of the Walpot edition was printed in the Netherlands, but under the name of John Denck, sixteenth-century Anabaptist. It was reprinted in 1967 in the series of Anabaptist sources.

This is the first English translation of the original chapter three, taken from the critical edition of the *Chronicle.*

| *Hutterite Elders* | The Five Articles of the Greatest Strife Between Us and the World (1547) |

On True Self-Surrender and
Christian Community
of Goods

Exodus 16: When the Lord God had led the children of Israel out of Egypt and they had come into the wilderness of Sin, he gave them bread from heaven, the manna. This they gathered, some more, some less. When they had measured it with an omer, he who had gathered much had nothing in excess and he who gathered little had no lack. But whoever kept some until morning found that it had bred worms and become foul. Since God has in this day led the christian church out of the contemporary Egypt, they are to conduct themselves also in the wilderness of this world so that the rich man has no more than the poor, and the poor man no more than the rich. Rather, they should place everything in common and equal use, as has been prefigured for us. This has been interpreted in the same way by the apostle Paul as well (2 Cor. 8[:15]).

Leviticus 25; Deuteronomy 15: In Israel each man was allowed to gather the fruits of his fields for six years. But the seventh year was a year of release and it was proclaimed that the land should observe [this year as] a sabbatical for the Lord. The yield of the seventh year was to be common for all, the householder and his [286] servant, and maids and daylaborers, the members of the household and the sojourners, the cattle and beasts of the field. In the same way, he who had loaned something to his neighbor or brother was not allowed to exact it during the seventh year, but rather had to forgive it. For, he says, it is a glorious and most festive proclamation of the year of release of the Lord. This year of release was to be a prefiguration of the New Testament in Christ when the true year of release was the acceptable year of the Lord, as the prophet interpreted it (Isa. 61).

Therefore, all property which God has bestowed on us in our time is to be held and enjoyed in common with our brethren, our neighbors, and their households out of christian love. No more—as in the preceding six years—are we to hoard or gather these for ourselves. For now is a much more glorious and more highly festive proclamation of the year of the Lord, even the year of grace, than was the case in the Old Testament.

Deuteronomy 15[:4]: The Lord commanded Israel that there were to be no poor among them. We should fulfill this much more perfectly in the [time of the] New Testament through christian community.

Numbers 18; Deuteronomy 11; Joshua 13; Ezechiel 44: The Lord speaks to Israel that the priests are to have an inheritance: "Yes, I shall be their inheritance; otherwise they should have no possessions among the people, for I am their portion." This is a parallel [*concordantia*] to the entire people in Christ Jesus who are a royal priesthood of God and belong to Christ as well (1 Pet. 2[:9]; Rev. 1[:6]). Those priests supported one another with the sacrifice which, after it was offered, was no longer his who had sacrificed it. It is the same today with the christian churches.

Isaiah 23[:18]: The prophet says how God would punish the city of Tyre: "[All] her merchandise and her hire will be dedicated to the Lord; it will not be stored or hoarded, but her merchandise will supply abundant food (for the hungry) and fine clothing (for the aged and) for those who dwell before the Lord." This is a prophecy of the gathered church in Christ.

[287] Isaiah 60[:8–9]: The Lord indicated the same when he spoke through the prophet: Even the islands (that is the heathen) will be gathered to me and especially the ships of the sea, that from afar they may bring you sons together with their silver and gold to (the glory of) the name of the Lord your God, the holy one of Israel, who exalts you.

Zecharia 14[:21]: The prophet says that at that time, that is of the New Testament, there will be no longer in the house of the Lord any Canaanites, traders, or merchants, as several translations have it.

Luke 3[:11]: John the Baptist said to the people who asked what they should do: "He who has two coats, let him share with him who has none; and he who has food, let him do likewise." Behold, how clear!

Matthew 5[:3]: Christ says: "Blessed are the poor in spirit, for theirs is the kingdom of heaven." This also means those who renounce things temporal and give them up for the sake of Christ. They no longer have any property. Those whom the spirit drives to this poverty and self-surrender are the poor in spirit who may expect the heavenly goods and to be called blessed (2 Cor. 6[:10]). Those, however, who persist in the opposite will not be blessed.

Matthew 6[:24]; Luke 6[16:13]: Christ says: "No one can serve two masters; for either he will hate the one and love the other, or

he will be devoted to the one and despise the other. You cannot
serve God and mammon." The latter is one's temporal goods, money
and riches. Christ says here that it is impossible to cling to and care
for both. Therefore, no one should say that it *is* possible. Whoever
is a servant of mammon is certainly not a servant of Christ. Therefore, whoever wants to have the one must abandon the other.

Again, it is a main article of the christian faith to confess [288]
one holy christian church and one fellowship of saints. This is not
a half-way community, but both a community of spiritual and temporal goods and gifts. Whoever then confesses a community of the
saints with his mouth but does not hold true community, he is false
and not a true member of the church.

Matthew 8[:20]: "The birds of the air have nests," said Christ
to him who offered to follow him and become his disciple, "and
the foxes have holes, but the Son of man has nowhere to lay his
head."* This is as much as to say: "You must completely surrender
yourself and deny your possessions and stand free of them, if you
wish to be my disciple."

Matthew 13[:22]: Christ says: "As for what was sown among
thorns, this is he who hears the word, but the cares of the world
and the delight in riches choke the word, and it proves unfruitful."
Therefore, both cannot exist side by side. It is a fraud if someone
wants to retain and possess both.

Matthew 14–15; John 6: Christ also taught the christian community by example when he twice—first with five thousand (not count-
ing women and children), again with four thousand who came to
him in the wilderness—fed [multitudes] with bread and fish. The
disciples were asked to share gladly what little they had with the
others, to give each according to his needs and to distribute everything in common. This teaches us that we (who like them have left
our home, fatherland, and friends) should also do this today for
the sake of God's word, which we hold on to and follow in this
wilderness. We do this by holding our temporal food and goods in
common and by using them, indeed, out of love for the neighbor
to the equal benefit of all.

Matthew 13[:44–45]: "The kingdom of heaven is like treasure
hidden in a field, which a man found and covered up; then in his
joy he goes [289] and sells all (note, all) that he has and buys that

---

*The Revised Standard Version has the sentence in different order: "Foxes
have holes, and birds of the air have nests. . . . "

field." The same should be done by those who find the treasure of divine truth, and they should also do it joyously.

"The kingdom of heaven is like a merchant in search of fine pearls, who, on finding one pearl of great value, went and sold all (note, all) that he had and bought it." Again, in the same way all those to whom God shows his truth should gladly give up temporal things.

Matthew 19[:21ff.]; Mark 10[:21ff.]; Luke 18[:22ff.]: To the rich young ruler who asked what he still lacked, Christ said: "You lack one thing; if you would be perfect, go, sell what you have, and give it to the poor, and you will have treasure in heaven; and come, follow me." You see, he called it perfection to sell everything (note, everything) and give it to the poor. Love is a band of perfection. Where it dwells it does not effect halfway but full and complete community. Giving to the poor, however (this means the poor in spirit), does not mean that the poor bring about his salvation, but rather that following Christ and his commandments makes him saved (Matt. 5[:3]; James 2[:5]).

Again, "How hard it will be for those who have riches to enter the kingdom of God! Again I tell you, it is easier for a camel to go through the eye of a needle, than for a rich man to enter the kingdom of God." If Christ did not demand self-surrender and community of goods in his church from all those who wish to enter eternal life and inherit together the heavenly goods, then it would not be hard for the rich to enter the kingdom of God but rather easy as for the poor.

Again, Peter said (and each devout person should be able to say the same): "Lo, we have left everything (note, everything), and followed you." The Lord said: "Everyone who has left houses or brothers or sisters or father or mother (or wife) or children or lands, for my name's sake will receive a hundredfold, and inherit eternal life." [290] That does not mean to stay at home with your house, farm, and goods.

Matthew 20[21:12ff.]; Mark 11[:15–17]; Luke 19[:45–46]; John 2[:13–17]: Jesus went into the temple of God and drove out all who sold and bought in the temple, and he overturned the tables of the money changers and the seats of those who sold pigeons. He said to them: "It is written: 'My house shall be called a house of prayer,' but you have made it a den of robbers." For this reason,

Christ will not tolerate trading, selling, or buying in his house, but rather [only] a christian community. Such buying and selling is a sign whereby everyone can recognize the false churches in that he sees what Christ once drove out with a good whip.

Matthew 22[:35–40]; Mark 12[:28–34]; Luke 10[:25–28]: "You shall love the Lord your God with all your heart, and with all your soul . . . ." This is the foremost commandment. The second which flows from it is equal to it: "You shall love your neighbor as yourself." Whoever wants to do this must share at all times with his brother and neighbor and hold all things in common. Otherwise, it is not loving as he loves himself, but only a pharisaical, heathen and despicable love.

Matthew 25[:35ff.]: Christ will say to his own on the day of judgment and last verdict: "You gave me food, you gave me drink, you clothed me" and not yourselves only. He will say: "As you did it to one of the least of these my brethren you did it to me. Enter into eternal life." The others, however, who had not done this, will be placed on the left hand and be condemned eternally.

Luke 12[:33]: "Sell your possessions, and give alms; provide yourselves with purses that do not grow old, with a treasure in the heavens that does not fail, where no thief approaches" but rather remains for ever. He does not mean alms as the world [291] gives. For if one gives and shares with one of the beggars in the streets— who has by gambling, fighting, drinking, and squandering lost his means or who has ruined himself otherwise or who has nothing because of laziness, and even though he is poor is yet as full of vice as anyone else—it cannot be said that it was done unto Christ. For such persons are not his members, although it is not wrong and shows human mercy and pity [to give to them]. But Christ speaks here about perfect alms in the community of the saints with all that one has and is able to do.

Luke 14[:33]: "Whoever of you does not renounce all (note, all) that he has cannot be my disciple." Therefore, no one can and should ever keep or possess or remain with his own, to be himself its master, steward, and ruler. That would not be renunciation.

Luke 16[:9–12]: "Make friends for yourselves by means of unrighteous mammon, so that when it fails they may receive you into the eternal habitations." (This habitation is the true church of God which will always aid those in need in brotherly love and take care of them in spiritual and temporal matters—Rev. 22.) Those then are true friends who thus pool their property equally out of christian love.

"He who is faithful in a very little is faithful also in much and he who is dishonest in a very little is dishonest also in much." The least is the temporal; whoever is not honest in this and does not prove himself in christian community in the church of God does not count before God in the greater, that is in the spiritual. "If you have not been faithful in the unrighteous mammon, who will trust you with true riches? And if you have not been faithful in that which is another's, who will give you that which is your own?" He calls the temporal "another's" because whoever presumes to possess and own it is unrighteous and deals unjustly.

[292] Luke 21[:1–4]; Mark 11[12:41–44]: Christ "looked up and saw the rich putting their gifts into the treasury; and he saw a poor widow put in two copper coins. And he said: 'Truly, I tell you, this poor widow has put in more than all of them; for they all contributed out of their abundance, but she out of her poverty put in all the living that she had'" (note, all her living). Therefore, the Lord demands the total capability and the entire heart for a christian community (Matt. 19[:16ff.]). He said about the rich to the rich young ruler that they should offer their gifts, and lest the poor say: "I have little," he taught them to do the same. Thus, we must all practice christian community.

John 13[:34–35]: "A new commandment I give to you, that you love one another; even as I have loved you . . . . By this all men will know that you are my disciples, if you have love for one another." Christ thus loved us and made us co-inheritors in heaven. He held everything temporal in common with his disciples. We likewise are to make our brother an heir in temporal things with us here, bear and expect with him love and sorrow, good and evil, one with another. In this they will be recognized above all nations that they have one faith in Christ and are his true followers. Love is above all the symbol of devout and holy people.

John 17[:10]: Christ said: "(Father,) all mine are thine, and thine are mine." Thus it should be also in temporal goods and gifts with children of God.

John 12 and 13: Our precursor Christ held all things in common with his disciples. They had a common purse, and Judas was treasurer and carried whatever was given them.

Acts 2[:44–45]: When the Holy Spirit came he perfected the
community so that the three thousand and the five thousand [293]
at Jerusalem, indeed, "all who believed, were together and had all
things in common; and they sold their possessions and goods and
distributed them to all, as any had need."

Acts 4[:32, 35]: "Now the company of those who believed were
of one heart and soul, and no one said that any of the things which
he possessed was his own, but they had everything in common."
"There was not a needy person among them, for as many as were
possessors of lands or houses sold them, and brought the proceeds
of what was sold and laid it at the apostles' feet; and distribution
was made to each as any had need."

Acts 5[:1–5]: None of the others, however, were allowed to join
them. When Ananias and his wife Sapphira sold a piece of property,
he brought a portion of the money and gave it to the apostles but
kept back some of the proceeds. (No doubt they wanted to have
something in reserve if they were not able to remain with them; but
it is understood that later, when they had become disloyal, their
contribution was not returned to them.)† Both of them suffered sudden death because of their greed and the treachery of Belial.

Acts 2[:41–42]: "Those who received his [Peter's] word were
baptized, and there were added that day about three thousand souls.
And they devoted themselves to the apostles' teaching and fellowship, to the breaking of bread and the prayers." Just as it is necessary for us to hold to the teaching of the apostles in the breaking
of bread and in prayer, so it is also necessary to hold christian
community.

Acts 11 and 13: At Antioch they gathered as a church for a
whole year, and there were prophets and teachers there. If they then
gathered there as they did at Jerusalem, then they must also have
arranged their household as at Jerusalem. For those scattered because of the tribulation arising from Stephen's martyrdom came
there from Jerusalem and arranged things the same way at Antioch.

[294] 2 Corinthians 8[:3–5]: This was also done by the church at
Macedonia, who were praised by Paul himself saying: "For they
gave according to their means . . . and beyond their means, of their
own free will, begging us earnestly for the favor of taking part in

---

†According to Hutterite practice, if a person left the community after he
had become a full member, his former possessions were not returned to
him. If he decided to leave during the initial trial period, they were.

the relief of the saints—and this, not as we expected, but first they gave themselves to the Lord and to us by the will of God." Is this not a community such as at Jerusalem? No one can deny it.

1 [2] Thessalonians 3[:10–11]: The church at Thessalonica also lived in community, for Paul writes to them that those who led disorderly lives, who did not work and followed their own counsel, should eat their own bread. Therefore, they must have had common meals, for otherwise Paul could not have been able to write that they should eat their own food, if each person had previously eaten his own food.

1 Corinthians 10[:17]: We who are many are one bread, says Paul, that is, because we like grains of wheat exert our entire ability and stand in christian community.

Romans 12[:4ff.]; 1 Corinthians 12[:12ff.]; Ephesians 4[:16]; Colossians 3[:15]: We are one body and each is a member of the other. The apostles teach that we should therefore live accordingly. If you consider the image of the members of the body, then you can have no greater teaching for a christian community.

1 Corinthians 10[:24]; Philippians 2[:4]: Paul teaches: "Let no one seek his own good, but the good of his neighbor." If this is to be so, then we must always seek the equal and common good in the community.

1 Corinthians 13[:5]: If love does not insist on its own, then it certainly must seek the good of the community only.

Philippians 2[:5–9]: "Have this mind among yourselves, which you have in Christ Jesus, who though he was in the form of God, did not count [295] equality with God a thing to be grasped, but emptied himself, taking the form of a servant, being born in the likeness of men. And being found in human form he humbled himself . . . . Therefore God has highly exalted him . . . ." Through this he intends that we also, even though we may have been glorious and rich in the world, should not consider the taking away of these things to be deprivation. Rather we should empty ourselves and take on the form of a servant in the house of God. Though we were ourselves previously masters of that which we owned, now, however, we should be just like any other brother in Christ and humble ourselves. If we remain obedient until death, then God will exalt us. This is precisely why rich men are so unlikely to enter the kingdom of God, for they cannot bring themselves to do this.

2 Corinthians 8[:9]: "For you know the grace of our Lord Jesus Christ, that though he was rich, yet for your sake he became poor,

so that by his poverty you might become rich." In this he has given us an example that we should also gladly become poor for the sake of others and therefore love one another as he has loved us (Eph. 4). This is provided that we have put on Christ and renounced the old man.

1 John 1[:7]: "If we walk in the light, as he is in the light, we have fellowship with one another."

1 John 4[:21]: "And this commandment we have from him, that he who loves God should love his brother also."

We have sufficiently seen from this that Christ and the apostles diligently taught community. At all times they demonstrated christian community in every land and location or city, as much as was possible and according to the opportunity and to the extent it was possible to come together (1 Cor. 1[:2]). Thus we find that there was a church in the house of Prisca and Aquila (Rom. 16[:3–5]), and the church at Laodicea was in the house of Nympha (Col. 4[:15]). Archippus, the fellow soldier of Paul, also had the church dwelling in his house (Phil. 1). Paul writes that the brother Gaius at Corinth [296] was host to him and to the whole church when he wrote from there to Rome (Rom. 16[:23]).

He also admonished the Romans in that letter saying they should receive one another just as Christ had received them for the glory of God (Rom. 14). The apostle here intends that no person is to seek to have a separate residence or to keep and own one by himself only. Paul did not do this himself, but rather when he came to Rome as a prisoner and stayed two years in his own dwelling, he accommodated all who came to him. This was done so that the prophecy might be fulfilled where the prophet predicts that they will say: "Make room for me to dwell in" (Isa. 49[:20]; Heb. 10). Also so that it may be granted to us that we do not abandon our gathering as many people think. Rather that we may admonish one another and this the more so as we see that the day of judgment approaches.

Part 5

The Polish
Brethren

12   Letter to the Swiss Brethren at Strassburg

Editor's note

One of the more interesting descriptions of the beliefs and ordinances of the Polish Brethren (sometimes referred to as the Minor Church to distinguish them from the larger Reformed body in Poland) is found in the letter sent by Christopher Ostorodt to the Swiss Brethren at Strassburg in 1591. Ostorodt (d. 1611) was one of the German converts to the Socinian movement. He was born at Goslar in the Harz, the son of a Lutheran pastor. After securing a university education at Königsberg, he came into contact with Anti-trinitarians as a schoolmaster in Pomerania on the Polish border. After baptism in 1585 at the Socinian synod of Chmielnik, he soon became a leading pastor of an important church at Schmiegel in Greater Poland (near Poznań), and finally served as minister at Buskov by Danzig.

Ostorodt is primarily known in Polish Brethren history for his proselytizing trips to Germany and the Netherlands and for his literary activity. His letter to the Strassburg Anabaptists was an answer to questions they had sent in a communication, probably conveyed to him for reply by Andrew Wojdowski. Ostorodt devoted the first, and longer, part of the letter (here omitted) to a presentation of unitarian Christology. The Anabaptist recipients of the letter considered this to be unacceptable. They drafted an extensive critique of Ostorodt's answer that eventually found publication in the Netherlands in 1666.

This rebuff does not seem to have turned Ostorodt away completely from the Anabaptists because he used his influence among the Socinians to urge comparable positions on church questions. This led to some controversy within the Polish movement.

Ostorodt also wrote a pamphlet against the Hutterites which was answered by Andrew Ehrenpreis in 1654. Neither of the writings exists today.

The letter to Strassburg has been preserved in the state archive in Berne. This translation was made from its only publication by Theodore Wotschke in 1915.

Christopher Ostorodt   Letter to the Swiss Brethren
                                          at Strassburg (1591)

To the honorable and godfearing elders, servants [of the word], and
the entire church at Strassburg in Alsatia, known as the High-German
or Swiss Brethren, our dear friends and beloved brethren.

May the grace and peace of the one true God, namely the father,
and of the Lord Jesus Christ, his son, descended from the tribe of
Judah, born of the seed of David, be with you all. Amen.

Dear and gracious friends and brethren: We only received your
letter, dated May 28, on September 22 of this year [15]91. We were
most happy to receive it, for we otherwise have much tribulation and
are accustomed to mourn with the prophet David that the laws of the
Lord are not kept and the commandments of God are ignored
(Psalm 119). May the Lord Jesus grant his grace that not only you
and we but the whole earth might seek God and bow under the yoke
of the Lord Jesus, to the glory of the great, almighty God and to the
comforter of us all. Amen.

For the friendship and love toward us which we with gladness perceived in the words of your letter, we thank you very highly. We ask
God and his son that you might be recompensed with mercy for this
at the coming of the Lord. We also want you to understand that we
are inclined to serve you in every honest and christian way in the
love of the Lord Jesus. . . .

[150] That is then our simple confession of the one God, who is
the father of our Lord Jesus Christ, and of the same Lord Jesus, the
Messiah, and of the Holy Spirit, who is given by the father through
his son Jesus Christ to all those who are obedient to him, so that they
may be preserved until the day of salvation. In addition, although
you did not actually request it, we would like to add some brief information on some other points, such as baptism.

We immerse in water, for this is truly baptism, unlike what is practiced by the Antichrist who only sprinkles. He had to abandon immersion when he began to baptize children, lest he drown them. Also
because of the children, they abandoned the use of bread in the
Lord's supper and made little wafers out of it, so that they would
not choke, for in the papacy the [151] children were occasionally
given the idol to swallow.

Where there is no immersion, there is no true outward baptism.
The word baptism [*tauffen*] is old German and signified a dipping or
immersion [*teuffen, einduncken*]. On this point, inquire of your breth-

ren, the [Dutch] Mennonites, who call both of these *doopen* in their language. Also where there is no baptism or dipping in water, it is meaningless to baptize into the death, burial, and resurrection of the Lord Jesus (Rom. 6[:1–11]). It can also be seen in the scriptures that [baptism] occurred in this way. And the word *baptizare*, which in Greek is *baptizein*, is called in Latin *immergere*, or in German "dipping" or "plunging under." That is why Paul likened baptism to the Red Sea (1 Cor. 10[:17]), and Peter to the flood [1 Pet. 3:21].

This same baptism we practice publicly in waters or rivers (wherever it is possible) with confession of sins and of faith. And when strangers are present, which almost always happens, an admonition to the people is added.

Test this, and you will find it is the truth. Do not let ancient customs and traditions be your criterion, for that is antichristian, but rather look to the truth.

We observe the Lord's supper often, and if possible, every day, for we see that it was practiced in this way during apostolic times (Acts 2:42–46). We take bread and wine sitting at the table, not with the purpose as if we were to receive therein forgiveness for our sins or a seal and confirmation of our faith, but rather as stated by the Lord and by Paul, *ad commemorationem*, as a commemoration of the suffering and death of our Lord. We do not seek the body and blood of the Lord in the bread and wine, but bread and wine in the body and blood of the Lord, that is, in his church (1 Cor. 10:16). We do not consider the bread and the wine and the table of the Lord to be exactly like other bread and wine, but as the Lord's bread and wine and the Lord's table which are holy or blessed (1 Cor. 10:16). It is not proper for one who is unclean to sit and eat with the others, just as no uncircumcised person could eat of the pascal lamb. Indeed, not only the unbaptized but also the baptized who have again tainted themselves with sins must be excluded.

[152] The Lord's supper is observed with all devotion, admonition, prayer, and thanksgiving and exhortation so that each person may examine himself carefully to see whether he is really a member of Christ, lest he eat to his own damnation or to the Devil, as did Judas. The words *hoc est corpus meum* ("This is my body") we understand as in Exodus 12:27: "The lamb or the sacrifice is the pascal," that is the passover. This manner of speech is found often in the Old Testament, especially where a mystery is mentioned as in Ezechiel 5:5: "This is Jerusalem," etc. Such an obscure saying is clarified very simply by the question: "Why?" When they were eating

the Easter lamb and the children asked: "Why do you do that?" then the parents answered: "That is the passover," which is as if they said: "We do this because God spared our house as his angel went through Egypt and slew . . . in the night, when we came out," etc. Also with Ezechiel 5 [might be asked]: "Why do you divide (your) hair in this way?" The prophet answered: "This is Jerusalem," as if to say: "This I do in order to warn you that Jerusalem will be punished thus." So here in the same way.

People ask: "Why do you sit at the table, eat bread, and drink wine?" We answer: "This is the body of the Lord, who suffered death for us." This is as if we had answered: "Because our Lord Jesus Christ gave his body and blood for us, we do this as a commemoration and proclamation of his death as those having a certain hope (if we remain in his covenant which he sealed with his blood) that we will have fellowship in his body, that is in his church, and will drink with him in the kingdom of his father" (1 Cor. 10:16; Matt. 26:29).

We do not accept anyone into the congregation unless he previously has been baptized, has departed from evil and does good, does not live according to the flesh but according to the spirit, does not only love the brethren but also his enemies, is patient, suffers violence and injustice, and rejects war and bickering—indeed, not only rejects but also refuses to aid or abet such. In this the Mennonites, with whom you have united, err in no small measure. They do not themselves want to dress vainly, but yet make proud clothes for others, paint pictures, make muskets and similar things, which the world desires for the luxury and vanity of its way of life.*

If a brother or sister has a grievance against another brother or sister, they work it out together according to the teaching of Christ [Matt. 18:15–20]. If this is impossible, then they invite two or three more. If this does not settle it, then they take it before the church, not for the purpose of banning, [153] but rather for improvement and reconciliation. If, however, one party refuses to listen to the church, then he is placed in the ban.

If someone sins so that it causes public offense, then his [social] status is not considered but he is disciplined publicly and must do public penance. Or, if he is stubborn then he is placed in the ban

---

*The Dutch Mennonites enjoyed official toleration earlier than any of their fellow-believers. This led to prosperity and a higher standard of living, and thus to criticism by the more rigorous-minded. Several Dutch Mennonites became renowned artists.

and we do not eat or drink with him. This is not for his ruin but that
he might be ashamed, truly repent, and therefore be preserved.

We also have elders, that is teachers [*Lehrer*], superintendents
[*Aufseher*], exhorters [*Vermaner*], and also the deacons of the poor
[*Diener der Armen*], according to the holy scriptures. The exhortation occurs, insofar as possible, almost every day with public prayers,
thanksgiving, and singing, according to the teaching of Paul in the
vernacular, in Polish for the Poles and in German for the Germans
(1 Cor. 14:26).

Further, we abide in peace with everyone. Indeed, we would like
to hold communion with everyone who calls upon the name of the
Lord Jesus and is obedient to him, if he wishes to do so with us. For
we well know that all who fear the Lord, live in righteousness, and
call upon Lord Jesus will be saved. Why then should we not consider
them as our brothers, even if there are some points which they do
not yet understand?

However, those who wantonly resist the truth, even though they
may otherwise lead a decent life, we do not count among that number. We know well that a party spirit [*Sectenmachen*] is just as much
a work of the flesh as any other sin (Gal. 5[:2]). Therefore, we certainly want to tolerate others and not avoid them because of a different interpretation, as long as they are willing to be obedient to the
Lord Jesus and acknowledge us as brethren. It is just for this reason
that two of our brothers went to Moravia during Lent of this year
and approached, among other Anabaptists, your brethren in Austerlitz and Pausram on this point.† They presented our confession to
them but could not receive any answer to it.

[154] As regards our brotherhood, they wanted to consider the
matter and wanted to examine our church first. We did not react
negatively because we thought this right. Would to God that you and
they had been as careful before you turned to the Mennonites, among
whom there are much greater failings (that is, unless they now wish
to refrain from them), such as aiding pride, greed, usury, and a
curious confusion through much banning and separation. They have
also tasted of the spirit of the Antichrist, so that if a person disagrees
with their teachers he is placed in the ban.

This happened to several of our brethren who were with them for
a time. Yet their bishops were not able to resist them and stop their

---

†"Your brethren" is correct only in a general way, because the Hutterites
rejected attempts by the South German Anabaptists to bring about
union between them.

arguments (as is appropriate for true bishops) but proceeded to ban these devout and godly people. May the Lord grant them insight that they might understand what a great sin they have committed, forgetting what Paul said in Philippians 3:15–16. We do not write this out of envy or hatred or because we begrudge you your unity, God knows, but because we are heartsick that people who claim Christ are so separated and unreasonable. May the Lord have mercy upon them, upon you, and upon us, so that as far as possible, we may all become one people, saturated with the spirit of Jesus Christ, our Lord.

This we felt obliged to write in answer to your letter. Accept it in love and consider it well. Pray for us as well as yourselves. Greet your church from us diligently in the Lord. I, Christopher Ostorodt, servant of the church at Schmiegel, who wrote this letter, greet you in the name of the Lord. May the grace of the Lord Jesus be with you. Amen.

Written at Danzig, October 20, in the year of our Lord 1591. Your respected and beloved servants and brethren. [From] the brethren in Poland, Lithuania, Prussia, East Prussia, and Masovia, as well as Wolhynia, and Podolia, united in the name of him who was crucified and has risen from the dead, Jesus Christ our Lord.

13

Treatise on the Chief Points of the Christian Religion

Editor's note

A more ambitious product of Ostorodt's pen was his doctrinal volume *Treatise on the Chief Points of the Christian Religion*. This was first published in 1604; it was reprinted in 1612 and several times thereafter.

The order of presentation of topics and the material contained in the *Treatise* is very similar to that found in the famous Racovian Catechism of 1605. It is difficult to say what influence Ostorodt's book may have had on the catechism, written by three other Socinian leaders. What is known is that Ostorodt's treatise provided a popular summary of Socinian teaching. According to the standard history by E. M. Wilbur, "The work remained in print for more than two generations, and was long highly esteemed as the best manual of Socinian doctrine."

It differs from the catechism in its greater emphasis upon ethical issues, an emphasis thought to reflect Ostorodt's leaning toward Anabaptism. He included a long chapter on church discipline, which repeats in the main the same biblical citations and directions for practice used by Anabaptists. He also gave guidelines for christian standards of conduct in everyday matters such as eating, dress, and use of material resources.

In general, it could be observed that Ostorodt's position is not as rigorous as that of the Mennonites and the Hutterites. Avoidance, for example, is not held to be the duty of the family or of the servants of an erring member. The overriding commandment of charity must be kept foremost. Ostorodt's attitude is revealed well in the chapter on love which follows. His stress on christian tolerance reflects also the disappointment which the Polish Brethren felt in their lack of full acceptance even by those, such as the Anabaptists, with whom they otherwise had much similarity.

A copy of the 1612 edition in the University of Amsterdam Library was used as the basis for this translation.

Treatise on the Chief Points
of the Christian Religion
(1604)

Chapter Thirty-two
On Love: Wherein Is Also
Explained Who May Be
Considered a Brother in Christ

Up to this point we have examined and explained almost all of the commandments of Christ, insofar as we can remember, which are either little known at present and therefore controversial, or though known are held in low esteem. We have at the same time demonstrated that God has given us in the gospel a much more perfect piety and righteousness than, for example, under the law. Should we, however, have happened to forget anything in the previous part it will be made good in this chapter, for Christ's commandment on love embraces all others. And although previously we dealt extensively with it in the explanation of this commandment of Christ, we nevertheless deem it not only to be useful [246] but also necessary to treat of this love separately, thus concluding our discussion of several specific commandments of Christ with his universal and greatest commandment.

Very much, indeed, everything depends on its proper understanding, as no one who does not rightly understand this commandment can be obedient to it. If someone does not understand it and thus has no love, though he may understand everything, have all faith, give all he has to the poor, and finally deliver his body to be burned, he is nothing, says the apostle (1 Cor. 13:2–3). That is, all of his worship of God is in vain, does not please God, and therefore must be lost.

In order properly to understand this commandment, we shall point out the difference between the love which God commanded in the law through Moses and that in the gospel through Christ. This difference can be reduced and brought under two headings as in a *summa*, and can, for this reason, be considered to be two different things. For the difference consists either in those whom one should love or in how one should love.

Concerning the former, that is, whom one should love, we have previously shown that under the gospel one must love each and every enemy, which was not commanded under the law. Although it might well seem as if it were commanded to love the enemy under

the law [247] as well as under the gospel, we have clearly demonstrated that this is not true. In brief, as commanded by Moses, the
enemy, who was to be treated well in many ways and not to be
hated, was solely to be understood as another Israelite. That which
Christ commanded us, however, applies to all men without exceptions, so that our neighbor is not only our fellow believer but every
man regardless of nationality, class or religion. This can be clearly
seen from Christ's parable about the man who had fallen among
thieves and was left half dead, and who was ministered to by a
Samaritan (Luke 10).

Virtually none of our dear Christians today, many as there are,
understand this point in the least. We do not say this out of envy
or hatred, nor to despise them—far from it. That would indeed be
a most grievous sin if we, who are teaching others about love, ourselves sinned against love. To the contrary, we say this precisely
out of this very same love, so that mankind might for once awaken,
study this in all seriousness, and when they have recognized it, put
it into practice. Without such [deeds] no one will find mercy before
God, for without it faith is dead, and without faith—that is, living
faith—it is impossible to please God (Heb. 11:6).

Therefore, a Christian is required [248] to do good to every man,
whether he is friend or foe, whether he has done him good or evil,
whether he is his brother in faith or not, whether he has the right
belief or not. This is especially true if he is completely dependent
on their aid and is abandoned by those who ought rightly to help
him, just as the man who had fallen among robbers was abandoned
by his own countrymen and fellow-believers (Luke 10:31–32). Certainly one should not delay in aiding others. Without question it
pleases God much more when a person acts spontaneously in helping others. Indeed, it may be said of the Samaritan himself, who was
placed before us by Christ as an example, that he anticipated [the
help] of all others (Luke 10:33). In this story or parable it is not
stated that he knew this injured person had been deserted by those
who ought to have helped him. On the contrary, as soon as he saw
the injured man he was moved by mercy to take care of him.

One should pay due attention to this example because Christ
showed the scribes by means of his own statement that the Samaritan, although he was neither a Jew nor had the same religion as the
Jews—on the contrary (as Christ elsewhere said of the Samaritans)
he did not know what he worshipped, certainly a great error—
nonetheless was the Jew's neighbor. [249]. [He was] the neighbor

of the Jews who (as the same Christ said) worshipped what they knew (John 4:22). The Samaritan was his neighbor and that in an excellent and special way above the others. If he (who does not know what he worships is our neighbor and that in a special way above others) can therefore be such a person who shall be loved by us in a special way, how can those people now hate one another who *do* know whom they worship, namely God and his son Jesus Christ? We speak here about those (so that the matter may be clearly understood) who condemn others because of a particular understanding of the christian religion. That is, they do not recognize them as brethren in Christ but instead consider them to be godless people or at the least heretics. This error is the cause of all grief in Christendom and therefore there is hope neither for unity nor for restoration of the church of Christ until this prejudice has been completely eradicated from the hearts of men. This will occur when the poor misguided Christians understand the nature of faith in Jesus Christ, God's son.

We simply cannot believe that anyone who thinks that he himself believes in Christ could be so godless, or certainly so irrational, that he condemns him who believes in Christ and does not regard him as a brother [250] in Christ. Who can be so inexperienced in the christian religion that he does not know that God has through grace justified and therefore promised eternal life to each one who believes in Christ Jesus? Who would want to condemn such a man and not recognize him as his brother in Christ whom God has accepted as his child, inasmuch as it is evident that all who believe in Jesus Christ are the children of God (Gal. 3:26). Therefore it is appropriate for us to explain briefly the nature of faith in Christ. . . .

[252] It follows from this that each person who puts his trust in Christ and is obedient to him is a brother in Christ and shall therefore be considered a member of his church, although he differ from us in whatever points of religion he may. So that absolutely no doubt may remain and that the matter might be perfectly understood, we will not hesitate to make the effort to anticipate and meet those objections or refutations which might be raised against this.

Some one might say that now after we have set up two conditions for faith in Christ, namely trust and obedience, no one, according to our opinion could be regarded as a brother unless both parts—that is, not only obedience but also trust—are evident and manifest in him. This, however, is impossible because there are many who pretend to be obedient to God but [253] are not really so. Still less

could trust in God be observed by another person, because it is
located in the heart. The way therefore has not yet been demonstrated by which a brother in Christ can be recognized.

We answer this as follows: We gladly concede that it often happens that someone pretends to trust in Christ and to be obedient
to him, and yet is a hypocrite. However, it is not our opinion that
another person should not be regarded as a brother in Christ until
it is certain that he truly trusts in Christ and is obedient to him.
Rather, if someone publicly confesses this and thus by this deed
demonstrates it outwardly, no one can rightly suspect him of being
a hypocrite. This is what the apostles themselves did—they accepted
everyone without distinction who made this confession and had this
same outward appearance even though hypocrites were found among
them. We have clear examples of this in the case of Ananias and his
wife Sapphira and in Simon the magician (Acts 5[:1ff.], 8[:9ff.]).
Therefore, where there are no specific evidence and proofs of someone's unbelief or disobedience—as is the case with Papists, who are
idolators as will be shown later—one must conclude that each person who confesses with his mouth that he trusts in Christ and [254]
demonstrates his obedience to him outwardly is to be considered a
brother in Christ.

If someone were to say further that it does not necessarily follow
that if someone lives a devout life, even if this may be heartfelt and
honest, he therefore also trusts in Christ, inasmuch as someone may
do many good deeds and still revile Christ. For example, a pagan
may live according to reason (as may be seen with the philosophers)
and a Jew according to the law, yes, even a Muslim who keeps the
commandments of his Koran, and they may not even know Christ,
to say nothing of trusting in him. We say to this: The objection is
hardly worth an answer. If we did not know for a certainty that
many preachers consider this to be a very precious argument to
belittle good works and make great outcry about it, we would not
mention it, for it is really so childish that we are embarrassed on
their behalf.

It is certain that this rationalization of theirs does not serve to
weaken what we have just now concluded, inasmuch as we speak
of obedience to the commandments of Christ but they of certain
good works as if the two were the same. Since it is indeed possible
for a man to do many good works and yet not be obedient to Christ
(even though he may otherwise profess or pose as if he were obedient to Christ), how much less could those be considered obedient

to Christ [255] because of good works who do not even profess or pose to be obedient to Christ, indeed publicly deny this? What could be more gross and blasphemous than to compare the good works of the Muslims—who are not only full of superstition but also mingled with many wicked deeds and this according to Mohammed's own teaching—with the most holy and divine works which God has commanded us through Christ in the gospel?

It is truly not surprising that these same theologians see no difference between good works according to the law of Moses or to the gospel because they cannot even distinguish between the good works of the pagans or Muslims and those commanded in the gospel. Indeed, these people reveal publicly that they are completely ignorant of what a great and perfect holiness God demands from us in the gospel. They consider doing good works in accordance with Christ's teachings to be a very small matter which even a pagan can know and do on his own without special revelation. Therefore, it is false that a person can do good works, namely in the way Christ has commanded (for it is about this that we speak) and still not [256] trust in Christ.

To do the good works commanded by Christ is nothing other than to obey Christ's commandments (John 14:21). He who keeps Christ's commandments loves Christ, indeed, loves the Lord God himself, and that in a perfect way, as John says (1 John 2:5). Whoever keeps his word ("his word" should here be understood as Christ's commandment, as may clearly be seen from the preceding discussion), in him is the love of God perfected. Yes, whoever keeps his commandments knows Christ (1 John 2:3–4) and whoever knows Christ knows God. Therefore, it must necessarily follow that he believes in Christ who keeps his commandments, since no one can love or know Christ and God in a perfect way unless he believes in Christ.

Therefore, it is now clear and as evident as the sun shines at midday, that every person who is obedient to Christ also trusts in Christ. Since, however, trusting in Christ and being obedient to him is true faith in Christ (as shown above) then it must be concluded that all those who are obedient to Christ's commandment shall be considered members of Christ and thus our brethren in Christ.

This is the true love of Christ that one should bear with one another in differing understandings in religious matters, or not judge [257] or condemn one another because of different understandings

on certain points. The apostle clearly admonished us to do this in
the fourteenth chapter of Romans, which every person who holds
his salvation dear should diligently read and ponder. If this is done,
then all sects, heresies, and schisms will cease.

All those who love Christ, that is who keep his commandments,
will—regardless of their differences in several points—have love for
one another, consider each other brothers, praise God and Christ
together, and thus build up the house of the Lord together, that is
his church. But the hypocrites, the quarrelsome, and all those who
are fleshly minded will not be pleased by this, inasmuch as their
hypocrisy will become evident to everyone. May God grant his spirit
to all devout hearts that they might undertake this task with all
earnestness and zeal to the glory of his name. Amen.

Let this be enough said for now about whom one should love,
that is concerning the difference between the law and the gospel.
It is now time that we, according to our proposal, treat the other
difference between the law and gospel concerning love, which consists in the manner of loving.

It appears at first that the gospel does not command anything
more perfect [258] than Moses had done, inasmuch as the law says
expressly: "You shall love your neighbor as yourself" [Lev. 19:18].
In answer to this, first of all one should know that with Moses the
phrase "yourself" must not be understood literally but in a restrictive sense. For example, in the law it says "an eye for an eye," etc.
If, however, the commandment "love your neighbor as yourself"
were to be understood literally and not in a restricted sense, then
no one could demand an eye for his own from a neighbor. Anyone
who had struck out another's eye would not hope that his own would
be struck out in return but that he might be granted mercy.

In the gospel, however, this "love your neighbor as yourself"
must not be understood in a restrictive sense, but in a universal
sense and exactly as the phrase stands. Christ has forbidden us to
resist wickedness or to repay evil with evil; indeed, he commanded
us to overcome evil with good. This shows that there is indeed a
vast difference on this point between the law and the gospel.

In addition, one should know also that Christ wants something
else from us, namely, that we should love our neighbor even more
than we love ourselves, as we should gladly give our lives for one
another (John 15:13; 1 John 3:16). Thus, Christ's commandment
[259] about love is perfect, while the same commandment of Moses

was greatly lacking. Christ himself said: "Greater love has no man than this, that a man lay down his life for his friends" (John 15:13). This is Christ's own commandment, and that is, why he called it a new, that is, his commandment (John 13:34). Elsewhere from time to time in the New Testament it is called Christ's commandment in particular and justly so. He was not only the first to command and make it public, but he also fulfilled it in his own person and that as an example for us, which may be clearly seen from the passages which we referred to in the beginning.

Those who imitate Christ in this love and follow him, those and those alone are his disciples. For this reason he explicitly said: "By this all men will know that you are my disciples, if you have love for one another (as I loved you)" [John 13:35]. If this is true— and it must be true because he spoke it, in whose mouth there was no deceit (Isa. 53:9)—then the Lord certainly does not have many disciples today and there are therefore few Christians. This should be no cause for surprise, for such teaching has up to now been quite unknown. Instead of this other doctrines have been promoted which have to a large extent contributed to the suppression of the former. And yet all of us hope for eternal life, just as if we were true disciples of Christ.

[260] Inasmuch as love under the gospel is of such a nature that he who has it is ready to give his life for his brother, who can fail to see that this commandment of the evangelical or christian love includes all commandments dealing with the welfare and benefit of the brethren? It is simply impossible that he who has come to the point that he is ready and willing to give his life for his brethren would refuse to aid his needy brother. On the contrary, he would be concerned, even night and day, how he could further that person's welfare and good, and likewise he would serve everyone even in the least and the lowliest things.

Jesus Christ reminded us of this by his example, when he washed the feet of his disciples (John 13:5), which kind of task or service is very humble and about the most lowly of all. It should be noted here that we do not say that Christ did this so that we should actually wash one another's feet, although it may seem the case, first by the act itself and later by the words which Christ spoke at the time. Rather he meant to give us this as an example of true christian love and humility from which we should learn not to be ashamed or reject anything, be it as low or contemptible as it may be, as long as it helps the needs of our brother, [261] this very washing of feet not excluded.*

It is not sidestepping the truth to say that the word "footwashing" at the time of Christ and the apostles signified an everyday service, the most lowly which could be done for the needy. For beyond the words of Christ, this is clearly shown by the word of Paul when he dealt with the qualities and abilities of a widow who was to be enrolled, asking if she has "washed the feet of the saints" (1 Tim. 5:10). Others have noticed this before us. Christ, however, after having washed the feet of the apostles and exhorting them to do the same among themselves, added these words: "If you know these things, blessed are you if you do them" [John 13:17]. Who is so base as to think that if a person merely washes the feet of another he would thereby achieve his salvation? This is certain, that someone could wash the feet of the saints and still be lost. Therefore, it is evident that Christ meant by footwashing a perfect love which causes us gladly to serve all the needs of our brothers. It is this that makes us truly blessed and immortal, as John says: "We know that we have passed out of death into life, because we love the brethren" (1 John 3:14).

Wherever men are so minded that they humble themselves, hold others in higher esteem [262] than themselves, and therefore gladly serve them in the way we have described, there all wars, quarrels, strife and disharmony must cease, and peace, unity, and all good works will rule and flourish. There then would be no room for the daughters of self-love, such as envy, egotism, and ambition, from which grow greed, arrogance, and contempt of the neighbor. Let this be enough on christian love and the commandments of Christ, which are called morals or conduct.

We have now completed and treated both parts of the prophetic office of our Lord Jesus Christ and therefore the main part or summary of the whole christian religion, namely the promises and commandments of God revealed and given to us by Christ. Since no one can be saved without obeying these commandments, it is better to suffer much shame, scandal, misery, pain, and finally the most terrible death than to trespass against even one of them.†

---

*Several Anabaptist groups practiced the washing of feet as part of the observance of the Lord's supper, based on the passage John 13:1–17.

†Several concluding paragraphs are here omitted.

Part 6   The Collegiants

Editor's note

A representative of the little-known but influential circle of Dutch
Collegiants was Peter Cornelius Plockhoy (ca. 1620–1700). Two of the
Collegiants' chief qualities were their ecumenical spirit and their philan-
thropical zeal. Both of these were incorporated in the unusual career of
Plockhoy.

Plockhoy came from a Mennonite family in Zierik-zee in Zeeland and
was associated with the Collegiant movement in Amsterdam in the
mid-1600's. There were close connections commercially and culturally
between the Dutch and the English at this time, and it is not too surprising to find Plockhoy in England in 1658–60 as a would-be social
reformer. His tract, *The Way to the Peace and Settlement of These
Nations* (1659) included a plan to reform the established church by a
system of interdenominational assemblies. More important was the
scheme elaborated in his tract *A Way Propounded to Make the Poor in
These and Other Nations Happy* (1659), which went through three
editions.

The plan called for a series of self-supporting societies rather similar
in design to those which Charles Fourier (1772–1837) put forward
something less than two centuries later. Highly-placed Englishmen were
won by the detailed prospectus, which proposed societies in London,
Bristol, and Ireland. In fact, an Irish lord made available for this purpose
the town of Baelmullet, County Mayo, with surrounding lands, for a
period of ninety-nine years. The Restoration ended any possibility
of fulfillment.

Plockhoy's next proposal—a settlement on the Delaware River in New
Netherlands—was realized in 1663 but was soon destroyed by an English
raid during the Anglo-Dutch war of 1664. Plockhoy lived on as a
private citizen in the area, and appeared at the end of the century in
Germantown near Philadelphia as a public charge.

The following selection presents the invitation which Plockhoy circulated to interest potential members of his English societies. The text
(slightly revised) is taken from the copy of the first edition in the
British Library.

[*Peter Cornelius Plockhoy*]

An Invitation to the
Aforementioned Society or
Little Commonwealth:
Showing the Excellency of the
True Christian Love, and
the Folly of All Those Who
Consider Not to What End the
Lord of Heaven and Earth
Has Created Them

Matthew: 12:50: "Whoever does the will of my Father in heaven is my
brother, and sister, and mother."
London: Printed for G[iles] C[alvert] at the sign of the Black Spread
Eagle at the West end of Paul's Churchyard [1659]

An invitation to the aforementioned Society or little Commonwealth,
etc.

Though men are bound one to another upon several accounts
and knit together with very strait bonds, and that the likeness either
of manners, or of life and conversation, or of parentage and education, begets a mutual friendship between them, yet this is the most
perfect, and of all others the most blessed: When God by the dis-
pensation of his secret counsel joined some such together as do
agree with his divine will and with the rules of nature. And they
will not exchange their union or fellowship for all the riches in the
world.

But the more divine this state of friendship is, the more seldom
it is seen among us and the more is Satan (that enemy of mankind)
against it. He knows full well that he has not so much right or power
to meddle with this holy fire and the matter which maintains it, as
he has where either recreation or advantage only is looked after,
which kind of friendship he uses with very little trouble to dissolve.
But in this way of amity God only is the bond wherewith they are
tied together without being liable to be unloosed, and upon which
foundation being fixed, they resolve to withstand all assaults whatsoever.

If then there be any felicity in the life of man or any efficacious
remedy to prevent his future misery, I conceive nothing was ever
more solacing or reviving and coming nearer to the divine nature
than love, that is, true love which does so communicate itself in
and to that wherewith it reciprocates, that it seems to have exchanged
therewith, and made over thereto, whatsoever it did possess before.
So that among true friends there is such an agreement that no secret,

no joy, no profit, nor any cross or affliction is undivided, but whatever betides either of them is not otherwise than if it were the change
of one [24] alone, so that death itself can scarcely separate souls
so totally united. Certainly the heathens, who in all things pursued
that which they esteemed best, found nothing more excellent and
delightful than perfect friendship.

But how far does Christ excel all others in love, who by his doctrine and example has instituted a partnership or society of mutual
love by the denomination of brethren; abolishing among his disciples
all preeminence or domineering of one over another, requiring that
the gifts and means of subsistence in the world (for necessity and
delight) should be common; having called his people to a moderation and to a life suitable to pure nature, so that all Christendom
ought to be merely a certain great fraternity consisting of such as
(having denied the world and their own lusts) conspire together in
Christ, the sole head and spring of love, do well to one another and
for his sake distribute their goods to those that stand in need.

Oh, that we had this perfection and were answerable to the end
of our creation! Certainly there would not be such going to law,
such entrenching and encroaching of the bounds of land, such hiding
and close locking up of money, nor would there be such scraping
together of superfluous estates.

Oh total sum and highest pitch of good if any may be admitted
and that in due time to this divine favor! For even many decrepit,
aged persons do seldom attain to this, to be desirous to live after
such manner. Emperors, kings, princes, etc., having spent all their
years, all their strength of body and soul, have little or no time left
to them to serve a better master than the world. And therefore if
God joins some such together as endeavor after a life more regular
than their former, each of them being at a loss for a companion to
better and promote his resolution, one to whom he may communicate his secrets, a friendly reprover of his errors, a reclaimer of him
from the world's allurements, a comforter in adversity, a moderator
of joy in prosperity, and in all respects a sharer in that which God
has liberally given, and last of all one ready for all cases and conditions that may happen, I say and judge that these are the happiest
of all persons that ever were upon the earth. For as no more painful
or miserable thing can be thought of than that life which a man lives
according to the course of this world, so nothing is more acceptable
and lovely [25] in the universe than that harmony and concord
which has its origin from God and influence upon the man that is

joined with his fellow-man so agreeable to his mind. Which certainly can be found nowhere but there only where a firm love, agreement and concerned will in well doing, as also a liberal distribution and imparting of all created things is entertained.

It is evident that the most wise God would honor the sacred society of matrimony with the utmost perfection of this so great love, since they that are so joined together and built upon the right foundation have not only their goods, but also their joys and griefs common, and cannot be severed by any kind of reproaches or malicious endeavors of the envious.

The world has her delights in different degrees of dignities, states, titles, and offices, exalting themselves one above another. But Christ on the contrary wills that everyone shall perform his office as a member of one and the same body, in which no one exalts itself nor accounts itself worthier than [the] other. The eye is not puffed up because it sees; the foot is not grieved that it does not see. If any member of the body be blemished it is carefully covered by the other; if any be weak it is diligently provided for by the rest. Whereas on the contrary everyone in the world who by his office or title is differenced from others conceives he is quite another thing and, in himself, better than others; and [he] must be reputed as one that is set together and composed of some finer substance and designed to a sweeter life, yes, to a higher place in heaven than others.

Now if you only divest and strip the world of her riches, honors, and state, how naked and ruefully forlorn will she remain, and how very different will she be found from that she seems to be. And then it will be easy to believe that she is shored up by nothing else but worm-eaten props which, if they were once pulled away they would be fitted and made free for the imitation of Christ.

Do but see, oh man! what kind of things they are which do shut the door against true love and hinder communion or fellowship with Christ, that is, nugatory, frivolous things and trifles which only consist in a vain esteem and opinion, which some of the very heathen who saw a little farther than others did sometimes laugh at:

First, riches and estates which, as soon as our natures are satisfied, are altogether superfluous and very troublesome. The vanity [26] whereof—who does not see it? They are a burden to the rich, causing them to fill their houses with [a] variety of costly furniture, which in many years (or never) happen not to be useful to them. They are a trouble to get them, a perplexity to keep them, and a grief to part with them. Their houses are spacious and great, so that

there is either much void and empty room within, or else they put
themselves to a great deal of trouble and molestation in furnishing
and filling them.

Their clothes are so dainty and curious that they cannot sit down
anywhere with freedom, nor stand with ease, nor scarcely walk anywhere without fear of spoiling their apparel. And unless they have
some to behold their splendor, all is little to them; but if they have
spectators, they fear some will lurch and others filch away from
them. Their sleep is almost none. Oh, how great a misery and burden
it is to be laden with riches!

Secondly, honor and dignities which, if we measure according to
the design of nature and the rule of Christ may not otherwise be
distinguished than by several names or denominations of diverse
members of one and the same body. The name of the tongue, is that
any more worthy [a] name than the name of the finger? The name
of the eye, is that any more excellent than the name of the breast?
No, certainly that whereby the members are differenced does not
lift them up, as with us the name of lord and gentleman puffs up.
What else is it but a mere name? The vanity whereof, who sees it
not?

The very foundation of it is nothing else but the noise of the
tongue and the report of others, or the knee, or the hat, all fleeting
and variable things that are to be bought for a very small matter.
And yet we are oftentimes so foolish, that though such things commonly do not come from the heart, neither are they fruits of an
upright and sincere mind—no, when on the contrary our own mind
does suggest to us that there is I know not what kind of tacit deri-
sion in it, and does often signify nothing else but hatred and ill will
—yet we do delight in such trifles and give way to them so far that
we will rather hear a lie from a notorious parasite or flatterer, if it
be but on our side, than to hear the truth from an honest man if
it crosses our interest.

Do but now cast up your account, oh man! How dearly you have
ventured to buy the friendship of the world, which yet you have
never found to be your friend but feignedly and that for a spurt.
On the contrary, consider how little or almost nothing you have
bestowed to answer the love of God, who nevertheless would have
been the most assured, most faithful, and unchangeable friend.

[27] You have trimmed and decked your body, and in apparel
you have been passing sumptuous [so] that some silly creature might
gaze on you with admiration. In feasts you have been prodigal [so]

that your companions and associates might commend you. You have
distributed your gifts and presents [so] that you might seem liberal.
You have put forth your art and skill [so] that you may be called
and accounted learned. You have daubed your house with many
colors to cause them to stand still that pass by.

In the meantime your reward has been nothing else but a great
toil and the sudden uncomposed disagreeing and unreasonable judgment and censure of other men. Consider in the meanwhile whether
you have provoked God thereby or honored him. It is most certain
that you might have served God and have performed the office of
love to your neighbor at a far cheaper rate. For by how much pro-
fuse and lavish you have been in the service of the world, by so
much the more have you been parsimonious and sparing in the
service of God. For it is evident the world requires costly attendance
as to all her matters, being never solicitous of the heart (how it
stands with that) if you are but careful that nothing be wanting in
outward appearance, in dissembling and complemental deportments
or if there be but ceremony and external semblance and fine show
enough. So that by the very aspect it is plain that the slaves of the
world may be discerned from the true servants of God, inasmuch
as the first are movable, flexible, fickle, and variable, but the latter
have their eyes always fixed upon the mark which is set before them.

If we but once bring ourselves to the touch and travel through
the world with a free and pure mind, we shall be able to obtain so
much from ourselves as in christian simplicity, silence, and unencumberedness to exclude the wisdom, eloquence, and prudence of
the world, concluding (as in truth it is), that nothing is to be compared with our master Christ, and that none other knows anything
or can give any counsel that is savingly profitable but he. Nor shall
we repute them happy who have no other character or superscrip-
tion than the world's endowments, knowing that worldly knowledge
is not so great a thing as it is commonly esteemed, forasmuch as
under the title and disguise of [being] learned, the very shame of
being found ignorant does with many inventions and cheating sub-
terfuges endeavor [to keep] the hiding of itself from being discovered
to the eyes of the common people.

Shall we never be able to attain to that equal judgment in putting
a true value upon real virtue wheresoever it be found, as well in a
(beggar as in a)* [28] prince, and to leave off more to admire the

*The words "beggar as in a" are supplied from the second edition.

ornaments of a magistrate than the office he sustains, and the esteeming less of poverty than of superfluity, of the honor than of the state, of a good conscience less than of a popular or vain applause, of a piece of bread than of delicious dainties, of water than wine, of a green bank of turf than of a costly couch—shall we not be able to arrive at this, to esteem only one sentence of the holy scriptures more than the highest acuteness of all the world's philosophy? We shall be able to do it, if we did well weigh that the world's turn is but a short comedy, and that we are but actors who appear no more than once upon the stage. And if we did seriously consider that all things are described and represented to us in the world far otherwise than they are in themselves but especially when we have well pondered that honest and godly people after a very little while are to expect a participation and enjoyment of another kind of honor and dignity than any the world promises.

Shall we never be able to attain to this, to choose rather to lay up our estates in the hungry bellies of the poor than in a few bags, to lay the foundation of our praise upon the prayers of the poor, to make the cross of Christ our glory, and not to eschew the disfavor of man as the reward of our well doing: in a word, to put off all desire of fame and renown as also to refer all desire of revenge to the judgment of Christ. We shall be able to do all this if we do not forget that our God is the most faithful of debtors and the most sure of all securities, if also we never forget that his praise, which shall be given to us in the presence of men and angels, is the most glorious praise, and that his remunerations and recompenses are the most noble and everlasting.

To how happy an hour are we born, if we do enter upon this communion or fellowship, and from how many vexations will it release us! Whereof the heathens, having attained but a shadow, how magnanimously did they in their minds soar aloft above all kings and worldly glory: how did they despise all earthly affairs (as they that from above look down upon that which is below) and had pity of them, and so did indeed avoid the greatest miseries of man's life.

But since christian religion has come into the world it is a wonderful thing to consider what a light broke in together with it, that is, such a light that all they whose hearts were touched therewith, throwing all before them, betook themselves to it for refuge, as to a true and steadfast liberty [29] after a long and horrible captivity, easily forgetting their riches, state, rule, and possession, forsaking parents, wife, children, relations, and whatever before was most near and dear unto them, not being by any temptations of tyrants to be drawn from the sweetness of the christian life.

The same have appeared in the memory of our forefathers, when the bonds of Antichrist (it is strange to think how firm they were) were broken, when they who a little before were forced to creep upon the ground began to rise up. With what readiness that tyrannical worship of invocating so many deceased saints was rejected and the unconfined worship of God reentertained, and with what readiness that vain (though gainful) fancy of invocating Christ by so many intercessions came to nothing. So that it appears in all respects how much God has chalked out in nature itself the pure and true worship, as also the amicable and friendly conversation of man, and likewise how easily those things which are contrary to it perish and come to nothing, and how far our religion withdraws us from all theatrical or stage play, gestures and countenances, and all those troublesome ceremonies with which we torture ourselves in speaking, eating, saluting, walking, clothing, yes, and in all the actions of our life. But on the contrary how comfortable it makes us to the celestial hierarchy and natural policy. And yet in these petty and altogether childish things men are so hard to be convinced and drawn off from them, as if all their well-being depended thereon, and the beatitude or happiness of all mankind had all its foundation therein; and never give so much scope to reason and well-guided understanding, as either to acknowledge their vanity or, if it be known to them, rather to throw it off, than to retain and daily augment it with new and exotic baubles.

In truth, as often as we do strictly ponder to what end God the creator and ruler of all things has brought everyone of us into this great fabric of the world and yet for us to observe that the life of almost all men is either unprofitable, idle, wicked, or hurtful to mankind, we have reason to be afraid and jealous of ourselves, lest peradventure either by the corruption of the times or our education we have applied ourselves to some manner of life which is not suitable to the will of God and the end of our creation, being not able to give a just account of how we have lived to the glory of God and the advantage of mankind.

[30] Certainly to have eaten, to have drunk, to have slept, yes, to have read much, written much, seen, heard, and traveled much, and let this also be added, to have managed an estate, to have kept hounds, horses, and servants, to have had arts and learning in great esteem, to have trimmed up houses, to have often made banquets,

to have borne titles of honor, to have collected many books together —in a word, to have been employed and very busy to the uttermost in things which do not relate or belong to Christ, let them be what they will—certainly all that will never satisfy God, nor endure the touch or trial of the fire. But being consumed as a stubble it will leave man bare and naked, a malefactor and guilty in the presence of God for his lost time and neglect of friendship and union with God, together with the neglect of the endowments as well of body as spirit, so that there will be a horrible distance between them and those whose faith in God and love to man have been steadfast and firm.

Let us take heed, brethren, lest those among us who either in understanding, learning, riches, beauty or arts excel others, imagine that God is therefore more gracious and favorable to them than others, and that they have attained to the best life. For such men do grossly deceive themselves because the manner of God's judging is quite different from that of the world, his eyes are quite another kind of eyes, and his policy differs from the world's policy as much as heaven from earth, as one who chooses the unworthy and despised rejects and abhors that which the world does highly esteem.

If any think this our society or fellowship to be a new thing so that he cannot (as it was in the old time) so much as point out five pair of such friends, he has reason with me to lament that while men do curiously, and with anxiety of mind, search into the course of the stars and planets, the virtues† of plants and vegetables, yes, into the very bowels of the earth, yet they are so neglectful of their salvation that they do not in the least so much as seek and look after that life for which they would not need so much silver and gold, so many titles of honor, so many buildings, such clothes, so much furniture for their houses, so many messes and dishes at their meals, so many arms and ammunition or warlike provisions, so many judgments or decrees of law, so many medicines, nor so many books—all of which are causes of vast trouble. So that the men of the world themselves (if they were but wise) would avoid these occasions or (as they themselves confess) necessities of sinning.

[31] This society or fellowship has not always been so rare and so thinly sown, but was very rife in the primitive times until the enemies of the first innocence insinuated themselves into it. Whereby the life which men were bound to live as in obedience to the laws

---

†That is, qualities or efficacy.

of Christ began to be accounted such as a man may choose whether he would embrace or not, and take up a meritorius and supererogatory life (comprising such a sanctimony or holiness as was more than necessary to salvation and was only to be used by those who desired a greater reward in heaven than others). Which opinion gave a beginning to many orders of lazy and wanton beasts (I mean monks and the like) and of many thousand fables and cheats, which things, when men came to themselves, they did justly reject. And when they are grown wiser they will again totally cast off even those poor ones who now scrape and take together the riches of the world. As also those (seemingly) humble and lowly persons who now take up the high seats of the world and those pretended simple ones who now fill and disturb the whole world with their cunning and deceit.

But for us let us hold fast that which is in this life the best thing, that is, the universal love to God's creation. And if we be insufferable to the world and they be incorrigible or unbetterable, as to us, then let us reduce our friendship and society to a few in number, and maintain it in such places as are separate from other men, where we may with less impediment or hindrance love one another and mind the wonders of God, eating the bread we shall earn with our own hands, leaving nothing to the body but what its nakedness, hunger, thirst, and weariness calls for to help our necessity and health. Then it will appear how many things we may well be without, what things we may refrain, and what kind of matters we ought not to know, how many things we may avoid, in what things we may best quiet ourselves, and how far easier we may satisfy Christ in his little ones with a penny than the world with a pound.

For princes are not born on purpose to rear up stately palaces, the learned are not born for the writing of many unprofitable and (for the most part) frivolous books, the rich are not born to boast of their gold, silver and crystal vessels, the rest of the people are not born for so many various unprofitable handicrafts. In a word, mankind is not born for so many kinds of education, of being rich, and running into excess, but all these racks of the mind it has invested by itself, and now made a custom and habitual so that it has made the life [32] more grievous to itself every day, under so many painful and laborsome inventions.

Now I would that they that stand and admire the fine wits of our age and the sublime learning of our times did but consider with me whether those things which daily please our eyes with their novelty be indeed such for which we may justly rejoice, or whether on the contrary it were not much better, since they are the cause of so many griefs and troubles in man's life, that we were wished and advised by our learned men to put them away far from us.

For what greater fruit of wisdom or what greater glory of the new revived learning could there possibly be than by that to bring human matters to such a posture that we may attribute our well-being and felicity in this life to them under God, that by the wholesome instruction thereof, that which is superfluous, useless, and unnecessary might be thrown away, and that which is nugatory, trifling, and unprofitable might be cut off, and that we might be truly distinguished from the life of the barbarous and savage people, not by books, nor by titles of honor, nor by universities, but by such morality as christian philosophy does prescribe.

Let there come forth from the studies and libraries of our wise men into the light not a continuation or prosecution of old errors, or a heaping up of new to the old, but on the contrary a rule or direction for a new and reformed life in Christ, which may demonstrate that as professors of the best religion, we are also imitators of the best life. Then shall we return to their society or fellowship and be subject to their good laws and orders, and observe their rational customs.

In the meantime let them not take it ill that we do not make any great account of these sciences that are void of Christ, that we do not desire to know them, and if we have drunk in any such yet we desire to unlearn them, and with singleness of heart to become as children, who are altogether unacquainted with voluptuousness, ceremonies, riches, and foolish labor. Henceforward, we desire to live towards God in unencumberedness, void of caring for the multiplicity of superfluous things, exercising a delight in real equality, and for the rest acknowledge Christ only for our Lord and master. And in this school of his we hope that neither divine mysteries, nor secrets of nature, nor the contemplation of rare manners shall be wanting to us, since he [33] formerly has made it evident by the examples of his apostles and holy men how powerful he is in teaching. And then especially he displays his riches and opens his inexhaustible treasures when human wisdom ceased and the skill of the world melted away.

But that we now are so weak and that the strength of our religion is grown so faint with us that the majesty of the divine presence with the miraculous working is removed from us, whom shall we accuse for this but ourselves, who in the midst of the divine light have scarcely retained anymore than the bare name, being content if we may but be called Christians. As to the rest being altogether like to the world, so that it is no marvel that we who do not excel others in the pursuit of honest actions, as justice, mercy, and the propagation of the name of Christ, nor in the education of children, do not also in the least go beyond them in those gifts which were peculiar to upright and zealous Christians. And yet we ought in so clear a light of the gospel as we have, to be so far distinguished as to excel other men. So that if others do not commit adultery, we should not do so much as desire another man's wife; if they do not commit murder, we should not at all be angry with our brothers; if they love them that are like to them, we should love our enemies; if they do lend to those that have to give again, we should lend to those from whom we cannot hope to receive any thing again. For it becomes us who hope for the inheritance of an eternal life in all things to be beyond those that know only this present life. But if nevertheless we be found beneath these, or if we are found but like to them and no more, how much will their accusation press us down, and condemn us to the like, yes, to a more grievous punishment.

Let us look back to the former ages, and it will appear that the divine power was then most of all vigorous and eminent, when there was not such ostentation of fine wits, but that supreme knowledge and happiness then was placed in the cross of Christ. But now while matters go quite otherwise and the creatures of our brain do adumbrate or overshadow and obscure the works of God, we do things according to the will and pleasure of Satan, who, being the most subtle of all philosophers, logicians, and artists, is not afraid of us if we go his way; and by that occasion he insinuates himself more and more into us and glides in by means of such things which we most admire.

Do you not see, brethren, that by the goodness and longsuffering of God, it is in our hand and power, now we have tasted of the bitterness [34] of this world's pleasure, to rid ourselves of very many troubles, going on by a way that is not crooked but straight and smooth, tending to the true rest and highest pitch of all perfections by applying ourselves to this communion or society of which we have made mention, which suffers no pride, riot, excess, uncleanness, injustice, or any evils which have been portrayed in their native colors. From which society no man that professes the name of Christ and practices his doctrine is excluded, of what sect, party, or by name whatsoever he is called or known.

We desire, therefore, that all who love their own peace and welfare will consider of our order or institution, which is propounded for a general rule. For we judge it to be not only a true opposition to evil but also a means to rid the world of all unprofitable, and hurtful handicrafts, being the cause of sin and slavery. To which we hope that God, who is the husband of the widows and a father to the fatherless, will vouchsafe his blessing through Jesus Christ, that so the pure and uncorrupted worship (which consists more in well doing than in much speaking) may break forth to the glory of his holy name and the good of all mankind.

If any have a desire to speak with him who is instrumental in the promoting of so good a work; [they] may have knowledge of his residence by inquiring of the bookseller noted in the title page. Finis.

Part 7

The English Baptists

Editor's note

John Smyth or Smith (ca. 1565–1612) in his own person demonstrated
the gamut of Protestant church opinion in Puritan England. Educated in
theology at the University of Cambridge, he became a clergyman of
the Church of England at Lincoln. Although his talents seemed to
presage a brilliant career within Anglicanism, he left the established
church for reasons of conscience in 1602. A year later he was asked by
Puritan businessmen to become the preacher of the Brownist (Separatist)
congregation at Gainsborough. In 1608 he went into exile in Holland
with many of his congregation to escape the restrictions on nonconformist
religious practice.

In Amsterdam Smyth engaged in vigorous and sometimes bitter
religious polemics with other English refugee dissenters. By late 1608 he
had come to the conclusion that believer's baptism was necessary for a
true church. His congregation dissolved itself, and then reconstituted
itself once more on the basis of a new baptism conducted by Smyth, who
had first baptized himself (earning the tag "Se-baptist"—self-baptizer).
Later, dissatisfied with this baptism, he sought to unite his church with
the Waterlander Mennonite congregation in Amsterdam, and for this
purpose drew up articles of faith. A small number of his group under the
leadership of Thomas Helwys refused to repudiate the 1608 baptism,
broke with Smyth, and returned to England. There they organized what
is considered to be the first English General Baptist congregation near
London in 1611–12.

Smyth died in the Netherlands in 1612 before the Mennonites had
taken action to admit him, but his followers were enrolled three years
later. His name is included, however, in a list of pastors of the central
Amsterdam Mennonite congregation inscribed on a wall of the church
building.

The following document on the church was intended as a list of
principles and was therefore originally presented in outline form. It is
taken from the standard collection of Smyth's writings, edited by
W. T. Whitley.

[John Smyth]   Principles and Inferences
                                 Concerning the Visible
                                 Church (1607)

Matt. 22:29: "You are deceived, not knowing the scriptures."
1 Cor. 14:38: "If any one does not recognize this, he is not
recognized."
Job 19:4: "And even if it be true that I have erred, my error remains
with myself."
Job 19:19: "All my intimate friends abhor me, and those whom I
loved have turned against me."

[Preface]
The Author to the Reader

[250] Lo, hear, gentle reader, a short description of the New Testament which was once established by the blood of Christ, after (that)
the Old Testament by the blood of his cross was disannulled. Remember that there be always a difference put between the covenant
of grace and the manner of dispensing it, which is twofold: the form
of administering the covenant before the death of Christ, which is
called the Old Testament; and the form of administering the covenant since the death of Christ which is called the New Testament or
the kingdom of heaven. In this little treatise the ordinances of Christ
for the dispensing of the covenant since his death are described.

Read, consider, [and] compare the truth here expressed with the
frame, ministry, and government of the assemblies of the land, and
accordingly give sentence, judge righteous judgment, and let practice answerable to the truth follow thereupon. Fear not the face of
man, love not the world, be not deceived with the shapes of angels
of light, cast away all prejudice against the truth, remember that
anti-Christianism is a mystery of iniquity and that it began to work
early during the apostles' life, and so grew by little and little to this
strength and exaltation, from which it shall decline by degrees even
till the man of sin be destroyed, who the L[ord] shall consume with
the brightness of his coming, for God who condemns the whore of
Babylon is a strong Lord. Farewell.

Principles and Inferences
Concerning the Visible
Church

[251] A man may be a member of the visible church and no member
of the catholic church (John 17:12; Gen. 4:11–13; Heb. 12:17;

Fig. 4. A lay preacher and auditors of the English dissenters, by an unknown seventeenth-century engraver. Source: J. Taylor, *A Swarme of Sectaries, and Schismatiques* ([London], 1641), in the collection of the British Library. Reproduced by permission of the British Library.

2 Sam. 7:15). A man may be a member of the catholic church and no member of the visible church (1 Kings 14:13; Rev. 18:4; Rom. 11:4; 1 Kings 19:18). The catholic church is the company of the elect (John 17:20) and it is invisible (Col. 1:20).

The visible church is a visible communion of saints (Matt. 18:12; Acts 2:1, 41–42, 46 and 1:15 and 19:7; 1 Cor. 1:2; Phil. 1:1), all of which are to be accounted faithful and elect (Eph. 1:1, 4–5, 7, 11, 13–14) till they, by obstinacy in sin and apostasy, declare the contrary (1 John 2:19; 2 Tim. 4:10 and 1 [Tim.] 1:19–20; 2 Thess. 3:14–15; 2 Tim. 2:17, 18–21). It is one thing to be a saint, another thing to be of the visible communion of saints (1 Kings 14:13 compared with 2 Chron. 13:8–12). The communion of saints is either invisible or visible (Eph. 3:17; Matt. 18:10; Heb. 1:14; 1 Cor.

13:9–13). The invisible communion is with Christ (1 Cor. 15:28; Eph. 3:17); [with the] elect (1 Cor. 13:13). Invisible communion with Christ is by the spirit and faith (Eph. 3:17 and 4:4 and 2:22).

Invisible communion [is] with the elect men [or] angels (Heb. 1:14; 1 Cor. 13:13). Men elect are dead [or] living (Col. 1:20). Elect living are uncalled [or] called. Communion with the elect living is prayer proceeding from love (John 17:20) for them that are uncalled that [252] they may be called (Rom. 10:1), for them that are called that they may be confirmed (Col. 1:9–12). Communion with the elect angels is the help of their ministry (Matt. 18:10; Heb. 1:14; Gen. 28:12 and 32:1–2; Psalm 34:7), reverence of them (1 Cor. 11:10), and love unto them (1 Cor. 13:13).

A visible communion of saints is of two, three, or more saints joined together by covenant with God and themselves, freely to use all the holy things of God, according to the word, for their mutual edification and God's glory (Matt. 18:20; Deut. 29:12; Psalm 147:19 and 149:6–9; Rev. 1:6). This visible communion of saints is a visible church (Matt. 18:20; Acts 1:15 and 2:1, 41–42, 46). The visible church is the only religious society that God has ordained for men on earth (John 14:6; Matt. 18:20 and 7:13–14; 2 Chron. 13:8–12; Acts 4:12; Rev. 18:4; 2 Cor. 6:16–18). All religious societies except that of a visible church are unlawful: as abbeys, monasteries, nunneries, cathedrals, collegiates, parishes.

The visible church is God's ordinance and a means to worship God in (Eph. 4:6–6 [4–6]; Mark 13:34; 2 Chron. 13:10–11; Heb. 3:6 compared with Heb. 8:5 and 3:2–6). No religious communion [is] to be had but with members of a visible church (Matt. 18:17–20; 1 Cor. 5:12; Acts 4:11–12; 2 Cor. 6:16–18; Rev. 18:4). Whatsoever company or communion of men do worship God, being not of the communion of a visible church, sin (2 Chron. 13:9–10; Matt. 15:9; 1 Cor. 5:12–13).

The true visible church is the narrow way that leads to life which few find (John 14:6; Matt. 7:14). Other religious communions are the broad way that leads to destruction which many find (Matt. 7:13; Acts 4:12). God's word does absolutely describe unto us the only true shape of a true visible church (Mark 13:34; 1 Cor. 12:5; Heb. 8:5 and 3:2–6; Rev. 22:18–19; 2 Tim. 3:16–17; Rom. 14:23; Heb. 11:6). There is one only true shape or portraiture of a true visible church, for there is only one faith and truth in [253] every thing (John 14:6; Eph. 4:4–5; 1 Cor. 1:10–13; John 17:17).

Forms or shapes of visible churches or religious communions, to
worship God in or by, devised by men are intellectual idols or mental
idolatry (Ex. 20:4–5; Matt. 15:9; 2 Chron. 13:8–12; 1 Kings 12:33).
Visible churches or religious communions constituted according to
the forged devise of men are real idols, and to join to them and to
worship God in them is to join to idols or to worship God in or by
idols, by consequence from the former.

Visible churches or religious communions are either true or false
(John 14:6; Psalm 119:128; 2 Chron. 13:8–12; Eph. 4:4–6). True
visible churches are such as have the true essential causes and properties, which God's word ascribes to the true visible church, from the
definition. False churches are the contrary to the true, by proportion.

To a true visible church are requisite three things: (1) true matter;
(2) true form; (3) true properties.

The true matter of a true visible church are saints (Ex. 28:9–10,
15–21 compared with Rev. 21:14–21 and 1 Kings 5:17 compared
with 1 Pet. 2:5; Lev. 11 [in] toto, 13:43–44 compared with Rev.
18:2; 1 Pet. 2:9; Deut. 14:2; Rom. 1:7; 1 Cor. 1:2; Eph. 1:1; Phil.
1:1; 1 Pet. 1:2; Heb. 3:1). Saints are men separated from all known
sin, practicing the whole will of God known unto them (Col. 1:2 and
2:11–13; Rom. 1:7 and 6:2, 12–22), growing in grace and knowledge (2 Pet. 3:18), continuing to the end (1 John 2:19).

The true form of a true visible church is partly inward, partly outward. The inward part of the form consists in three things: (1) the
spirit; (2) faith; (3) love. The spirit is the soul animating the whole
body (Eph. 4:4; 1 Cor. 12:4, 7–10, 11–13; 1 Cor. 6:17). Faith unites
the members of the body to the head, Christ (Eph. 3:17 and 4:13–15
and 5:23–30; 1 Cor. 6:17). Love unites the members of the body to
each other (Eph. 2:20–21 and 4:3, 16; Col. 3:14–15).

[254] The outward part of the true form of the true visible church
is a vow, promise, oath or covenant between God and the saints: by
proportion from the inward form (see also Gen. 17:1–2 and 15:18;
Deut. 29:1, 8–13; 2 Chron. 29:10 and 34:30–32; Psalm 119:106;
Nehem. 9:38 and 10:29; 1 Cor. 12:25–26; Rom. 12:5, 15–16; Matt.
18:15–17). This covenant has two parts: (1) respecting God and the
faithful; (2) respecting the faithful mutually (Matt. 18:20). The first
part of the covenant respecting God is either from God to the faithful, or from the faithful to God (2 Cor. 6:16). From God to the
faithful (Matt. 22:32), the sum whereof is expressed (2 Cor. 6:16):
"I will be their God." To be God to the faithful is: (1) to give Christ;

(2) with Christ all things else (Isa. 9:6; 1 Tim. 4:8; 2 Pet. 1:3; Rom. 8:32; 1 Cor. 3:21–23). From the faithful to God (2 Cor. 6:16), the sum whereof is to be God's people, that is to obey all the commandments of God (Deut. 29:9). The second part of the covenant respecting the faithful mutually contains all the duties of love whatsoever (Lev. 19:17; Matt. 18:15–16; 1 Thess. 5:14; Matt. 22:39; 2 Thess. 3:14–15; Heb. 3:13 and 10:24–25).

The true properties of a true church visible are two: (1) communion in all the holy things of God; (2) the power of our Lord Jesus Christ (1 John 1:3; 1 Cor. 10:16 and 5: 4–5; Matt. 18:20; Isa. 55:3; Acts 13:34). The holy things of God are: (1) Christ; (2) benefits by Christ (Rom. 8:32).

The true church has title, possession, and use of Christ (Isa. 9:6; Song of Sol. 2:16; Matt. 18:20; 1 Cor. 3:21–23; Eph. 5:30).

The benefits which the true church has by Christ are the means of salvation and alms (1 Tim. 14[4]:8; 2 Pet. 1:3). The means of salvation are: the word, sacraments, prayers, censures, and the ordinances of Christ for the dispensing of them all (Rom. 3:2 and 4:11; Luke 19:46; Matt. 18:15–17; Acts 2:42; 1 Cor. 11:23–26; Matt. 28:19; Psalm 149:6–9). [255] Alms are the works of mercy yielded to the saints in distress (Acts 2:44–45 and 5:4; Matt. 25:34–40; Heb. 13:1–3; 1 Tim. 3:2 and 5:10).

The power of the L[ord] Jesus Christ given to the church has three parts: that is, power to (1) receive in (John 10:3; Acts 9:26–27 and 18:27 and 6:5); (2) preserve and keep within (1 John 2:19; 1 Pet. 1:5); [and] (3) to cast out (1 Cor. 5:13).

Power of Receiving

The true visible church has power to receive in: (1) members into communion (Acts 2:41 and 18:27 and 9:26–27); and (2) officers into office (Acts 6:5 and 14:23). The way or door whereby both members and officers enter in is Christ, that is the way taught by Christ in his word (John 14:6 and 10:3, 7–9 and 17:17; Mark 13:34–37). The way of receiving in of members is faith testified to by obedience (Acts 8:36–37; Matt. 3:6; Luke 7:29–30). Faith is the knowledge of the doctrine of salvation by Christ (1 Cor. 11:8; Gal. 3:2). Obedience is a godly, righteous, and sober life (Titus 2:11–12; Rom. 1:5).

Members thus received into communion are of two sorts: (1) prophets [and] (2) private persons (1 Cor. 14:24; 1 Sam. 19:20–23).

Prophets are men endued with gifts apt to utter matter fit to edification, exhortation, and consolation (1 Cor. 14:3; Acts 13:1; Rom.
12:6). These persons must first be appointed to this exercise by the
church (1 Cor. 14:40; Acts 13:1). The prophets' care must be to
prophesy according to the proportion of faith (Rom. 12:6; 1 Cor.
14:26). Let the prophets speak two or three and let the rest judge
(1 Cor. 14:29). If any thing be revealed to him that sits by let the
first hold his peace (1 Cor. 14:30, 40). All that have gifts may be admitted to prophecy (1 Cor. 14:31).

Private persons are: (1) men [and] (2) women.

Private men present at the exercise of prophecy may modestly
propound their doubts which are to be resolved [256] by the prophets
(Luke 2:46–47; 1 Sam. 19:20–23; 1 Cor. 14:30). Women are not
permitted to speak in the church in time of prophecy (1 Cor. 14:34;
1 Tim. 2:12; Rev. 2:20). If women doubt of anything delivered in
time of prophecy and are willing to learn, they must ask them that
can teach them in private, as their husbands at home if they be
faithful, or some other of the church (1 Cor. 14:35; 1 Tim. 2:12).

To this exercise of prophecy may be admitted unbelievers or they
that are without [the church] (1 Cor. 14:24; Acts 2:6–13). The exercise of prophecy, and the preaching of the word by them that are
sent, is that ordinary means God has appointed to convert men
(1 Cor. 14:24–25; Rom. 10:14–15). They are sent by God to preach
whom the church sends (Acts 13:2–4 and 8:14–15). If any man be
converted by other means it is not ordinary (Rom. 10:14–15; John
4:39–41; Acts 9:5–6). Therefore, they that are converted in false
churches are not converted by ordinary means (1 Kings 14:13 and
19:18; Rom. 11:13; Rev. 18:4).

The way of receiving officers into office is: (1) election; (2) approbation; (3) ordination: which must be performed with fasting and
prayer (Acts 6:5 and 14:23; 1 Tim. 3:10 and 5:22 and 4:14; Titus
1:5; Acts 13:3). The person to be admitted into office must first be a
member of that visible church whence he has his calling (Acts
1:21–22 and 6:3–5 and 18:27–28; 1 Cor. 1:22 and 3:6; 1 Tim.
3:2–3, 10). Election is by most voices of the members of the church
in full communion (Acts 6:5 and 14:23).

Query: Whether women, servants, and children admitted into full
communion yet under age may not give voice in elections, excom-
munications, and other public affairs of the church (1 Pet. 3:7; Eph.
4:4; 1 Tim. 5:9–10; Num. 30:5–16; 1 Cor. 14:34; Gen. 3:16; 1 Cor.
11:3–10; Gen. 18:19; Josh. 24–15).

Approbation is the examining and finding the officer [257] elect
to be according to the rules of his office (1 Tim. 3:10 and 5:9–10;
Acts 6:3). In approbation every member is bound to object what he
can, especially they that denied their voices (Acts 15:37–38; 1 Tim.
3:2–3, 10; Acts 6:3). Approbation must be after election, lest without cause the infirmities of the brethren be discovered, for there are
faults disabling men to offices which do not disable them to be members of the church (Ezek. 44:9–15; Acts 15:37–38; Matt. 18:21–22
compared with Prov. 10:12; 1 Pet. 4:8).

If the things objected bear weight against the officer elect, the
election is void and they must proceed to the choice of another
(1 Tim. 3:4–5 and 5:11; Acts 15:37–38; Ezek. 44:10; 2 Kings 23:9).
Defects or faults that cast men out of office are sufficient to hinder
men from entering into office: by proportion. If the thing objected be
frivolous the election is approved (1 Tim. 3:10) and they that dis-
sented are to consent to the rest, that so the whole church may agree
in one person (1 Cor. 1:10; Eph. 4:3 compared with Acts 1:26). If
the parties objecting still dissent without an approved reason, they
are to be reformed by censure (1 Cor. 11:17–18; Matt. 18:15–17).

Ordination is the dedication of the officer thus approved to his
office (Ex. 29:44 and 40:12–16; Num. 8:6–15; Heb. 5:4–5; Matt.
3:13–17; Acts 13:3–4; 1 Tim. 4:14; Heb. 6:2).

Ordination has three parts. The first is the power which the church
commits to the officer approved, to administer according to his office
(John 20:21–23; Matt. 18:15–20 compared with Ex. 29:1–38; Num.
8:10–11; Acts 6:3–5 and 14:23 and 20:28; 1 Tim. 4:14; 2 Tim.
1:6–14). The second is prayer made by the whole church for the
officer invested with this power that he may faithfully administer
(Acts 6:6 and 13:3 and 14:23; 1 Cor. 4:2). The third is a charge
given to the officer thus admitted to look unto his office in all the
parts thereof (Matt. 28:18–19; [258] 1 Tim. 5:21; 1 Pet. 5:1–2;
1 Tim. 6:13–14 compared with Deut. 1:16).

The ceremony used by the apostles in ordination is imposition of
hands, which ceremony first of all was used in the Old Testament
(Num. 8:10), then in the New [Testament], by Christ in praying for
children (Mark 10:16), by God the father in ordaining Christ to his
office of mediator (Luke 3:21–22), by Christ in ordaining the apostles
(Acts 2:3–4 and 1:4–8), by the apostles in giving the Holy Ghost
(Acts 8:15–17), in ordaining evangelists (2 Tim. 1:6), and in ordaining ordinary ministers (Acts 6:6 and 14:23), by the eldership or

church in ordaining officers (Acts 13:3; 1 Tim. 4:4), by the evangelists in ordaining officers (1 Tim. 5:22; Titus 1:5), and so may lawfully be retained and used in the church still (Heb. 6:12).

The use of imposition of hands is twofold. First to point out the officer in time of prayer made for him, as if it should be said: "This is the man" (by proportion from 1 Sam. 10:24; Matt. 3:17). Secondly to signify and to assure the officer to be ordained that the Lord by the church gives him power to administer (Acts 13:3–4 and 20:28; John 20:21).

Ordination and so imposition of hands appertains to the whole church as does election and approbation (Acts 13:3; Num. 8:9–10), yet for order's sake the fittest members lay on hands and perform all the other particulars of ordination for and in the name of the whole church (1 Cor. 14:40 compared with Num. 8:9–10 and Acts 13:3 and 1 Tim. 4:14, and by proportion from Lev. 4:15). The fittest persons are elders when the church has them (1 Tim. 4:14); when the church wants elders, men of best gifts appointed by the church (Num. 8:9–10). Thus after the apostasy of Antichrist arises a true ministry in the church (Rev. 15:4).

The officers of the true visible church thus admitted are then to administer faithfully (1 Tim. 3:10; 1 Cor. 4:2). The officers of the true visible church are all absolutely described in the word of God (Heb. 3:2–5 and 9:5; Rom. 12:7–8; Mark 13:34). These officers are of two sorts (1) bishops [and] (2) deacons (Phil. 1:1). [259] The bishops are also called elders or presbyters (Acts 20:17, 28; 1 Pet. 5:1). The bishops or elders jointly together are called the eldership or presbytery (1 Tim. 4:14 and 5:17 compared [omission in text]).* The eldership consists of three sorts of persons or officers: that is, the pastor, teacher, governors (1 Tim. 4:14 and 5:17). All the elders or bishops must be apt to teach (1 Tim. 3:2; Titus 1:9). The pastor is a bishop excelling in the word of wisdom or exhortation (Rom. 12:8; 1 Cor. 12:8); he is called the angel of the church (Rev. 2 and 3). The teacher is a bishop excelling in the word of knowledge or doctrine (Rom. 12:7; 1 Cor. 12:8). The governor is a bishop excelling in the quality of wise government (1 Tim. 5:17; Rom. 12:8). The pastor and teacher also have power to administer the sacraments (Matt. 28:19; Eph. 4:12; 2 Cor. 11:23). All the bishops deal by office in the government of the church (1 Tim. 5:17) and are conversant about the soul and spiritual part (John 18:36; 2 Cor. 10:3).

*Here, as in several places following, there is a gap in the text.

The deacons are officers occupied about the works of mercy respecting the body or outward man (Acts 6:2). The deacons are: (1) men; or (2) women deacons or widows (Acts 6:2; Rom. 16:1). Men deacons collect and distribute with simplicity the church's treasury, according to the church's necessities and the saints' occasions (Rom. 12:8; 2 Cor. 8:2–8; 1 Cor. 16:2–3).

The church's treasury is silver, gold, or money worth, freely given by the members of the visible church for the common good (Lev. 27 [*in*] *toto*; 2 Kings, 12:4–16; Luke 21:4; Acts 4:34–35; 2 Cor. 8:2–8 and 9:7). The church's treasury is holy (Matt. 27:6; Luke 21:4). Query [omission]. None of those that are without [the church] may cast of their goods into the treasury, lest the treasury be polluted (2 Cor. 8:4; Josh. 6:17–19). Query [omission]. Nothing that is gotten by fraud, violence, or any wicked means, may be cast into the church's treasury (Deut. 23:18; Micah 1:7; Isa. 66:3).

[260] The use of the church's treasury is peculiar to the saints, and it consists in provision for holy things or holy persons (Deut. 14:2–3, 21; Ex. 30:12–16). Query [omission]. Holy things: as bread and wine for the Lord's supper, places and instruments serviceable to holy uses (Ex. 25:2–8; Matt. 27:7 to the contrary). Holy persons: as the maintenance of church offices and the poor brethren, either of that particular visible church or of any other true church (1 Cor. 26[16]:2–3; 2 Cor. 8:7; 1 Cor. 9:6–14; 1 Tim. 5:17–18).

In the necessity of the church if they that are without bestow anything upon the saints they may receive and use it with thanksgiving (1 Cor. 10:25–26). If it be manifested by evidence that the goods of them that are without offered to the saints be the treasures of wickedness, the saints are not to receive and use them, to avoid offense (1 Cor. 10:28–29).

Women deacons or widows are [at least] of sixty years of age, qualified according to the apostles' rules (1 Tim. 5:9), relieving the bodily infirmities of the saints with cheerfulness (Rom. 12:8 and 16:1).

Power of Preserving

Hitherto of the church's power of receiving in: now follows the church's power of preserving and keeping within.

The power of preserving within is manifested by the heedful use of all the holy things of God by the whole church jointly, and by every member particularly (Mark 13:33–37; Heb. 10:24; 1 Thess.

5:14; Matt. 18:15–17; Acts 6:1). The pastor's chief endeavor must
be to make the church zealous, holy, and obedient (Rom. 12:8;
1 Cor. 12:8; Rev. 3:19 by proportion). The teacher's chief care must
be to preserve the church from ignorance and error (1 Cor. 12:8;
Rom. 12:7; 1 Cor. 3:10–12 compared with Titus 1:9).

The chief office of the governors consists in preserving peace and
order in the church (1 Cor. 14:40; Rom. 12:8; 1 Tim. 5:17). The
deacons' chief care must be that none of the saints want bodily
necessaries, and that due provision [261] be made for holy things
and persons (Rom. 12:8; John 13:29) and that with simplicity (John
12:6). The widows' chief office is to visit and relieve the widow,
fatherless, sick, lame, blind, impotent, women with child, and dis-
eased members of the church (1 Tim. 5:9; Rom. 12:8; Matt.
25:35–40). The care of the eldership must be to order, direct, and
moderate the public actions of the church (1 Cor. 14:40; 1 Tim.
5:17). The prophets' chief care must be to resolve doubts, difficulties,
and dark places, and to give true expositions, translations, and
reconciliations of scripture (1 Cor. 14:26–30; Luke 2:46–47). The
office of the pastor and teacher in the exercise of prophecy is to
moderate and determine all matters out of the word (1 Cor. 14:32;
1 Sam. 19:20).

The care of the whole church jointly must be to keep her power
given her by Christ, and not to suffer any open known sin, or any
tyranny or usurpation over them (Matt. 18:15–17; Mark 13:37; Col.
4:17; 3 John 9–10; Rev. 2:2; Gal. 1:8–9). The chief care of every
member must be to watch over his brother (Mark 13:37; Heb. 10:24),
in bearing one another's burden (Gal. 6:2; 1 Cor. 10:24, 28–29),
admonishing the unruly, comforting the feeble-minded (1 Thess.
5:14), nourishing the excommunicate (2 Thess. 3:15), restoring them
that are fallen (Gal. 6:1).

Here, special care must be had of admonition (Matt. 18:15–17).
Admonition must be administered with prayer and in love (1 Tim.
4:5; Gal. 6:1; Lev. 19:17; 1 Tim. 1:5; Rom. 13:8). Prayer is needful
that it may please God to give his blessing to the admonition administered (Matt. 7:7–8; James 1:5 and 4:2–3). Love must be manifested to the offender that he may be the better won (Eph. 4:2; Col.
3:14; Lev. 19:17; 1 Pet. 4:8).

Admonition is either private or public (Matt. 18:15–17). Private
admonition is either solitary or before witnesses (ibid.). [262] Private
admonition is performed by one particular brother offended to another brother offending, and that in secret (Matt. 18:15). The ad-

monisher must not tell the fault of the offender to another, but himself must admonish the offender (Psalm 15:3; 1 Pet. 4:8; Prov. 25:9). If the offender repent upon admonition, the fault must be covered (Prov. 10:12); if not, the admonisher must proceed to the second degree of admonition, that is to admonish the offender before witnesses (Matt. 18:16).

The fittest witnesses must be chosen (1 Kings 21:10–13; Matt. 26:59–61 and 28:12–15); the fittest witnesses for the most part are the elders, who for their wisdom and authority can best sway the delinquent. If the offender repent upon admonition before witnesses the fault must yet be covered also (Prov. 10:12; 1 Pet. 4:8; James 5:20). If the offender admonished before witnesses deny the fact, then protestation or an oath of God must end the matter (Ex. 22:11). Though the admonisher know the fact to be so, and the offender deny the fact before witnesses, yet the admonisher is not to forsake the offender's communion (John 3:31 and 13:26), notwithstanding he must still seek to bring him to repentance (Lev. 19:17). If the offender acknowledge the fact and repent not, the admonisher and witnesses must bring the matter to the church (Matt. 18:17).

In bringing the matter to the church, if the elders be not already interested in the cause, it is meet to use the advice and help of the eldership who are fittest to deal in all public business (1 Cor. 14:33, 40; 1 Tim. 5:17). The matter being before the church, the offender is to be dealt with by all possible means, that he may come to repentance, as by admonition, by threat, by intreaty, by prayer for him, etc. (Gal. 6:1; 2 Cor. 2:6). If the offender repent upon the church's admonition, he is still to be continued and accounted a brother (2 Cor. 2:6; Matt. 18:17). Thus the church and all the members thereof shall be [263] preserved and kept pure within, and their communion shall be holy (Lev. 19:17; 1 Tim. 5:22; 1 Cor. 6:20 and 5:6), and so shall increase with the increasing of God (1 Cor. 11:17; 2 Pet. 3:18).

All the degrees of admonition must be administered upon the offender before the church have any communion with him (Matt. 18:15–17; 1 Cor. 11:17; 1 Tim. 5:22; Lev. 19:17; Matt. 22:39). If a man see his brother sin and admonish him not, but suffer his sin unreproved, he is defiled therewith (Lev. 19:17; Matt. 18:15 and 22:39; 1 Tim. 5:22). In solitary admonition, if the admonisher stay in the first degree of admonition, the offender not repenting, he is defiled with the sin. In admonition before witnesses, if the admonishers cease and stay in the second degree of admonition, the offender not repenting, they are defiled with the sin. In admonition before the church, if the church bear with the party offending and bring him not to repent, but leave him in sin and impenitence and yet hold him in communion, then the whole church is defiled. And so that is verified, a little leaven leavens the whole lump (1 Cor. 5:6 and 11:17; Matt. 13:33). If a sin be publicly known in a church, or if more sins be openly known and suffered, the whole church is defiled and leavened (ibid.). No communion can be had with, nor no joining can be to, a church thus leavened without manifest consenting to sin (ibid.).

Therefore, if the church will not reform open known corruptions, after due proceedings separation must be made from it till reformation come. Therefore separation may be made from true churches for incorrigible corruptions, and to separate from a defiled church that is incorrigible is not to forsake the communion of holy things, but the pollution and profanation of holy things.

Thus much for the second part of the church's power of preserving and keeping within.

Power of Casting Out

The church's power of casting out follows, which is twofold. [264] First, of officers out of office (Acts 14:23 compared with Col. 4:17; Rev. 2:2; Gal. 1:8–9). Second, of members out of communion (Matt. 18:17; 1 Cor. 5:4–5; 2 Thess. 3:6–14; 1 Tim. 1:20).

The cause[s] of casting officers out of office are apostasy or disability (Ezek. 44:10; Num. 8:23–26). Apostasy is when the officers shall fall to open idolatry, atheism, heresy, or other sins equipollent† of the first or second table (Ezek. 44:10 and by proportion drawn from 2 Kings 23:9; 1 Tim. 3:2; Lev. 22:1–5 and 21:16–24; Ezra 2:61–62). The officer upon repentance after apostasy or sin equipollent thereto may be retained as a member of the church, but not as an officer (Ezek. 44:13–14; Matt. 26:69–75 compared with John 21:15–18; Acts 13:38). Query [omission].

Disability is either of age, or sickness, or maiming, etc. Disability of age is when the officer can no longer by reason of old age discharge the works of his office. Then he may retain his dignity and ought to be honored of all (Num. 8:23–26; Philemon 9). Disability by sickness as frenzy, madness, melancholy, or by maiming, as loss of the tongue, in the pastor or teacher, etc., or by any other infirmity

†Equivalent.

disabling him to the actions of his office (Lev. 21:16–24 compared
with 1 Tim. 3:2; Titus 1:6–9). Query: Whether an officer may refuse
an office imposed upon him by a lawful calling (Ex. 4:14; Jer. 1:6–7,
17). Query: Whether the church may suffer her officers to be translated from herself to other churches upon any ground (Acts 20:28;
1 Pet. 5:2; Acts 13:4). Yes, though it be granted that she have members so fit for offices as her officers are in present; yes, though the
life of the officer be endangered (Acts 9:25; Matt. 10:23; 1 Kings
18:4).

The cause of casting members out of communion is only one: that
is, sin obstinately stood in without repentance and confession after
due conviction (Matt. 18:17; Job 31:33; Prov. 28:13). Due conviction is the discovery of the sin by manifest evidence (Job 19:4 and
32:12–13 and 39[34]:37). Manifest evidence is either of the fact or
sinfulness [265] of the fact. The fact is evident either by confession
of the party that committed the fact, or by sufficient witnesses (Matt.
26:65; Deut. 19:15; John 5:31). Query: Whether the testimony of
them that are without [the church] is sufficient or not. The sinfulness
of the fact is evident either by direct scripture, or by necessary consequence from the scripture (Matt. 22:31–32 and 4:4).

Due conviction is perceived two ways: first, by the delinquent's
shiftings, cavils, excursions, tergiversations, etc. (1 Tim. 1:6; Titus
3:11); secondly, by the conscience of them that have the power to
censure the fact (Psalm 36:1; Prov. 27:19; Titus 3:10; 1 Cor. 2:15
and 12:10). Obstinacy in sin is the refusing of confessing and forsaking the crime (Prov. 28:13; Matt. 18:17; Josh. 7:19). If the
matter be not evident, but doubtful and controversial, communion
still must be preserved peaceably, notwithstanding diversity of judgment, until the truth be discovered (Phil. 3:15–16; 1 Cor. 13:49–
79[?]).

Persons that differ in judgment are either strong or weak (Rom.
15:1). The strong must not maintain controversies with the weak nor
despise them, but bear their infirmity and burden (Rom. 15:1 and
14:1–3; Gal. 6:2; 1 Cor. 13:5–7 and 9:22 and 10:23–24). The weak
must not censure or judge the strong as delinquents, but meekly
desire instruction and satisfaction (Rom. 14:3; Matt. 7:1–3). Thus
must men walk in diversity of opinion during which time all men
must carefully search out the truth and labor for information (1 Cor.
1:20; 2 Pet. 3:18; Phil. 3:15; James 1:5).

The power given the church for casting out obstinate convicted
offenders is the power of excommunication (2 Cor. 10:3–5 and

1[Cor.]5:4–5; 1 Tim. 1:20; Gal. 5:12; 2 Thess. 3:6–14; Matt. 18:17). Query: Whether delivering to Satan be not or contain some bodily punishment inflicted upon the offender: see Acts 5:5–10; 1 Cor. 12:10. Excommunication is the depriving of the offender of the visible communion of saints, and the benefit of all [266] the holy things of God given to the church (1 Cor. 5:4–5, 11–13; 2 Thess. 3:6–14; Matt. 18:17). Query: Whether separating, withdrawing, turning away from false teachers and wicked livers be the same with excommunication (2 Thess. 3:6; 1 Tim. 6:5 and 2:3–5; Matt. 18:17; 1 Cor. 5:4–5). Excommunication duly administered is ratified and confirmed in heaven (Matt. 18:18; John 20:23). Therefore, the party excommunicate is in the hands of Satan, and out of the Lord's protection and blessing, being deprived of all the public means of salvation (Matt. 18:17; 1 Cor. 5:5; Isa. 4[24]:5–6).

In excommunication consider two things: first, the decreeing of it, which must be done by the whole church (1 Cor. 5:4), wherein the church must proceed as in approving her officers. Secondly, the pronouncing of excommunication which must be performed by the fittest person deputed thereto by the church (1 Cor. 14:40). The end of excommunication is not the destruction of the offender, but the mortification of his sin, and the salvation of his soul (1 Cor. 5:5; 2 Thess. 3:14–15; 1 Tim. 1:20). The party excommunicate is not to be counted as an enemy, but to be admonished as a brother (2 Thess. 3:15). Query [omission].

The members of the church are to avoid all religious and civil communion with him that is excommunicate (Matt. 18:17; 1 Cor. 5:11), except that subjects, servants, children, parents, wife or husband, etc., that are bound to him may perform civil and natural offices to him (1 Cor. 7:5, 12–13 and by proportion). The party excommunicate upon repentance is to be admitted again into the communion of the visible church (2 Cor. 2:6–8), yet so as that the church always have an especial eye to him, as being a suspicious person that durst despise the church (Matt. 18:17; Ezek. 44:10; 2 Pet. 2:22; Heb. 10:26 by proportion). Query: Whether an officer excommunicate, upon repentance may be admitted into office; and whether must he have new vocation by election, approbation, ordination: yes or no?

[267] The visible church walking in this holy order has in it the presence and protection of Christ (Isa. 4[24]:5–6; Matt. 28:20 and 18:20). To this visible church must all sorts of persons resort that desire to be saved (Acts 4:12; Matt. 7:13–14; John 14:6).

True visible churches are of two sorts: first, pure where no open known sin is suffered (Rev. 2:7–13 and 3:8–11); second, corrupt, wherein some one or more open known sin is tolerated (Rev. 3:1–6; 1 Cor. 11:17, 21–22). True visible churches are so far forth good as they agree to the pattern of the word (Heb. 8:5; Rev. chaps 2 and 3; 1 Cor. 11:2, 17–22). Every true visible church has title to [the] whole Christ and all the holy things of God (Isa. 9:6–7; Song of Sol. 2:16; Eph. 1:22–23). Every true visible church is of equal power with all other visible churches (Rev. chaps 2 and 3; 1 Cor. 5) and has power to reform all abuses within itself (1 Cor. 11:2, 17), which power is spiritual as is Christ's kingdom, not worldly, bodily, nor carnal (John 18:36; 2 Cor. 10:3–5).

The erecting of visible churches appertains to princes and private persons. Princes must erect them in their dominions and command all their subjects to enter into them, being first prepared and fitted thereto (2 Chron. 29 and 24 and 17).‡ Private persons separating from all sin and joining together to obey Christ their king, priest, and prophet, as they are bound, are a true visible church, and have a charter given them of Christ thereto, being but two or three (Matt. 18:20; Acts 14:19–20; Heb. 11:38) and further power than to reform themselves they have none.

Every man is bound in conscience to be a member of some visible church established into this true order (Matt. 7:13; Rev. 18:4), because every man is bound to obey Christ in his kingdom and spiritual regiment and no other (Luke 19:14–27) and the true visible church is Christ's kingdom and house (Mark 13:34 with Luke 19:14–27; Acts 1:3; Heb. 12:28 and 3:6). Therefore, they that are not members of this visible [268] church are no subjects of Christ's kingdom (Luke 19:27; 1 Cor. 5:12). This true visible church is called Christ (1 Cor. 12:12).

Thus much concerning the true church. The false church or the church of Antichrist follows to be considered.

Whatsoever thing is contrary to this order of the visible church is antichristian by notation of the word compared with it (1 Cor. 12:12). Whosoever takes upon him to erect new forms or shapes of visible churches and to appoint new officers, laws, ministry, worship, or communion in the church is Antichrist (1 John 4:3; 2 Thess. 2:4; Rev. 13:16, 17). Whosoever yields or submits to any other constitu-

‡Baptists were noted for their staunch advocacy of separation of church and state. This statement probably represents a remnant of Smyth's former Anglicanism.

tion, laws, officers, ministry, or worship than that of Christ's appoint-
ment is the subject or servant of Antichrist, by necessary consequence
from the former (Rom. 6:16). A man cannot be both the servant of
Christ and of Antichrist (Matt. 6:24).

The author entreats the gentle reader not to cavil or wrangle at
the contents of this present treatise, nor to traduce or calumniate his
person in secret, but by writing to discover the errors thereof, which
he desires may be manifested to him, remembering that therein he
shall perform a charitable work: for he that converts a sinner from
going astray out of his way shall save a soul from death, and shall
hide a multitude of sins (James 5:20).

16

An Appeal to the Parliament,
Concerning the Poor, That
There May Not Be a Beggar
in England

Editor's note

Seventeenth-century England was a period of great upheaval, not only
politically but also economically and socially. English historians have
described the lot of the agricultural and industrial workers as generally
poor. A standing observation of contemporaries was the numbers of
workingmen reduced to beggary. The Poor Laws passed in Elizabethan
times seem to have been badly administered or neglected.

One of the proposals to Parliament to rectify this social evil was
contained in *An Appeal to the Parliament* (1660). Not content with
pointing out the problem, the author outlined a plan which in his
estimation would provide a nationwide solution. Later commentators
have found the suggestion of a labor-exchange to be the most practical
part of the program.

Strangely, two different religious bodies claim the author of the tract,
identified only by the initials "T. L." According to Quaker bibliographers
and historians, this stands for Thomas Lawson (1630–91), a former
Anglican priest, later a school teacher and botanist while a member of
the Society of Friends. Lawson was considered a leading herbalist of his
times and authored eight volumes of doctrinal discussion.

It is more likely that the author was Thomas Lambe (d. 1686), a
leading Baptist pastor and philanthropist. For a time a member of a
Separatist (Congregationalist) church, he became a Baptist in 1653 but
eventually returned to the Church of England. That he was more
probably the author of the tract is indicated by the remarkable zeal he is
known to have exerted in aiding the poor, both from his private means
and by appeals to others. He secured the liberation from prison of
several hundred debtors. Throngs of petitioners surrounded him at all
hours, we are told, seeking his aid. He refused to take vacations so that he
could continue his care and hired an agent to assist him when he
became infirm.

The catalog of the Angus Library, Regent's Park College, Oxford,
attributes their copy of the tract to Lambe, although there is no
contemporary notation of authorship, nor is there on any of the three
copies in the Library of the Society of Friends, London.

T. L.

An Appeal to the Parliament,
Concerning the Poor, That
There May Not Be a Beggar in
England (1660)

In the midst of many and great undertakings, let not a settlement for the poor be forgotten, but revive, ad[d], and execute all wholesome laws, and encourage all good means, to supply poor people with labor and relief, and so prevent the ill breeding, wicked life, and bad end that many thousands have fallen into through idleness. To this end, give order that the ensuing platform may be fully executed. Although this thing be warrantable, yet if there be not an absolute necessity laid on them (whom it does concern) to execute their office, this work may fail and come to little or nothing, notwithstanding the means may be sufficient; but if carried on as it ought, the cure is certain: No beggar in Israel [Deut. 15:4].

The Platform or Way How Poor
People May Be Supplied with
Labor, and Relief

Every parish, according to the various places and employments, and as their poor are increased, agree with some able man, or men, that rightly understand their work, that may undertake and by the parish be assisted:

I. To take notice how many old [people], impotent, and young children be in the parish, and supply them by collection; and also help such whose labor is not sufficient to yield them maintenance. But if any in the parish want employment that are able to work, set them to work according to the wholesome laws of the nation.

II. To take the most orderly way for the manner of doing, according to the variety of places, and kinds of work. If there be twenty persons in a country village that want employment, then the parish [is to] agree with some clothier, stuff- or stockingmaker to furnish them with so much work as they can do: so in great towns, and places of clothing, one clothier take ten, another twenty, being brought in by authority. For though there may be work enough, yet the idle will not come for it. To have work and want government [direction)], is as if they wanted work. Some parishes have means enough, and yet the poor want work, food, and government.

So in great cities, where is much trading on silk, wool, hair, winding, weaving, button-making, etc., every parish or division agree with some tradesman, or men, to provide for ten or twenty as aforesaid, and so may rise to hundreds or thousands by the same rule. So in parishes where the poor are much increased and have no trade,

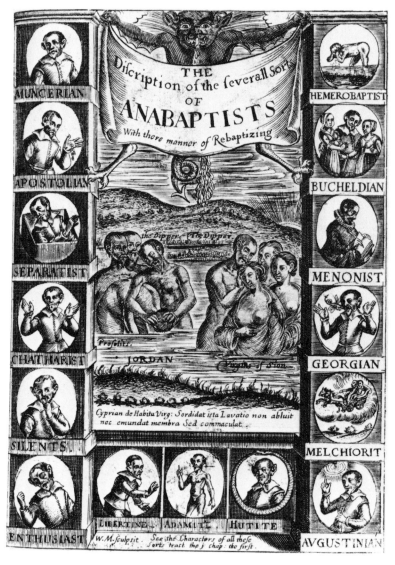

Fig. 5. A caricature of different
Anabaptist groupings, by an
unknown seventeenth-century
engraver. Source: D. Featley, *The
Dippers Dipt. Or, the Anabaptists
Duck'd and Plunged* . . . (London,
1645), frontispiece, in the collec-
tion of the British Library.
Reproduced by permission of the
British Library.

179 An Appeal to the Parliament,
Concerning the Poor, That There
May Not Be a Beggar in England

or where some great trade is wholly decayed, there some other [trade] is to be sought for with discretion. In parishes where [there] are no poor, their account is soon given, and they [are then] fit to help others. Some near London said they had not a beggar dwelling in their parish, and yet have had thirty travelling beggars in one week.

III. To settle a poor man's office: First, where handcraftsmen and laborers that want work, and such as want workmen, may inquire. Secondly, where boys that would or are fit to go apprentice, may inquire of masters, and such as want servants in city or country, or whom they have spoken to, may inquire. Thirdly, where maids that would and are fit to go apprentices, or covenant servants, or some that want such, may inquire. (But none to be put to service until they be first taught to spin, knit, sew, learn some trade, or way of livelihood; who else are neither fit for service nor can in after [3] times do any thing for themselves.) Fourthly, where all poor people that are in distress or in danger of perishing, may make their conditions known, that means may be used to supply their wants.

IV. That all persons whatsoever may have free access and acceptance without molestation to give in true information concerning any neglect of the poor to any in authority, justice of the peace, or any in power, as there may be cause; and that every one that neglects his duty, restore to the poor so much as they have done them wrong, and that distress be made if they refuse to pay presently.

V. That all judges of assizes and sessions lay open the sad condition of the poor in their charge, and what the law provides, and take account of what is done; and receive all true information concerning any neglect of the poor, and see the penalty justly executed: The law is made for the lawless and disobedient.

VI. That no poor people be denied their former liberty, nor strict course taken against them, until some good means be used to supply their wants.

Much might be added concerning the means how there may be work enough; how to order things to the best advantage in cities, towns, and villages; how to take a list, or the just numbers in great cities, out-streets and alleys, tenants, in-tenants and inmates, where may be many perish, many idle hard to be found, and settled in order; how to encounter with the great charge this may amount to. But honest labor and good government may save the rich from charge and the poor from hunger. And to speak to particulars may be more seasonable when this work is come into practice, and more suitable to the divers places, persons and various kinds of trading.

If any object [to] the trouble: To have such multitudes of beggars in this fruitful kingdom, is not that trouble? To hear them cry and not give, is not that trouble? To hear their cry, and give, is trouble also, not knowing whether it does good or harm. But if every parish keep to their own, the condition of the poor may be known.

I have considered of cities, towns, and villages, but no place have I found where this platform may not be [4] suitable, with little or no alteration. Although it be short, it concludes enough to effect the work, and with little trouble or charge in comparison of some proposals concerning the poor. And being faithfully executed, there may not be a beggar in England, which is the desire and hope of one that has no intention of evil to any, but wishes the good of all, who, having been many years exercised among the poor, and much desired their good, and through long experience have seen the ground of their misery, the easiness of the remedy, and the benefit.

Postscript

This work of charity does not concern Parliament men and the officers of the poor only, but all other[s] in authority to exercise their power in their respective places for the general good. And all not in authority also; rich men to encourage it every way, being best able; and the middle sort do their endeavor, lest they [be] like small iron creepers in a chimney, who bear the burden and heat of the fire until they be wasted to cinders; and the poor to avoid idleness, which is oftentimes the cause of beggary. And hearken to the counsel of the wise man, Ecclesiastes 40: "My son, lead not a beggar's life, for better it is to die than to beg" (verse 28). "The life of him that depends on another man's table, is not to be accounted a life" (verse 29). "Begging is sweet in the mouth of the shameless, but in their belly there burns a fire" (verse 30).

That this platform, or some other, may be put in practice when the days lengthen is likely, because of the necessity, and cannot safely with good conscience be wholly omitted. But that all join in the execution—there lies the stress. Many good things have been begun, but men being selfish, careless, and unconstant, the work has failed. I have in some measure unloaded my conscience in this thing, and laid it before others that all might be clear from the cry of the poor. But he that stops his ears at the cry of the poor, he also shall cry and not be heard.
T. L.

London: Printed for Robert Wilson, at the Black Spread Eagle and Windmill, in Martins Le Grand, 1660.

17

The Records of a Church of Christ

Editor's note

The early Baptist congregations were known for the seriousness with which they took the matter of church discipline. One of their (many) objections to the Church of England was the policy of inclusiveness or comprehension that was intended to bring all Englishmen into the fold of the church. This could be carried out only by emphasizing conformity to the observances and sacraments of the national church, with consequent neglect of the day-to-day life of many of the parishioners.

For the Baptists the church covenant not only extended to agreement on matters of doctrine and church order, but also to quite specific issues of conduct and daily occupation.

English Baptists of this early day had a rule that a member not present for worship of a Sunday should be visited by church officers during the following week to learn the reason for the absence. If it was not considered satisfactory, he would be admonished by the congregation. The scope of congregational interest was not limited to attendance. John Christmas of the Fenstanton Baptists was taken to task for being unkind to his wife, but was forgiven upon a change in his former conduct and his expression of regret. A young member of the London Particular Baptist congregation led by William Kiffin was excommunicated in 1666 because he falsely represented himself as a man of property in order to marry a young woman member of the congregation of higher social class.

The manner of proceeding and the spirit of such church discipline can be gleaned from the records of early English Baptist congregations. One that can stand for others is from Broadmead, in Bristol, compiled by one of its members, Edward Terrill. The church book is at present in the Angus Library, Regent's Park College, Oxford. The source of the following excerpts is the edition by Nathaniel Haycroft in 1865.

But to a brief narration and history of God's leading this church of Christ. So that, by reason of this Act for Banishment, we were fain to move from house to house; and one Lord's day, of the 11th month Jan[uary], Anno 1664, a meeting being at Brother Terrill's, then living in Corn Street, the mayor's sergeants came up and dissolved the meeting [and] carried away one Mr. Zephaniah Smith and three or four Londoners before the mayor. The minister, Mr. Smith, was sent to Newgate Prison, and, he being a stranger in a manner here, then the next week they released him, upon his telling them he was to be gone out of town, and they charging him to depart in a few days.

Upon the 7th of the 12th month [February], Anno 1664, at the close of a day of [57] prayer, upon the consideration of several persons in the congregation not walking orderly, some remiss in their duty of assembling with the church by reason of these troubles, the church appointed a monthly meeting of the brethren only, to consider persons or things amiss in the congregation; and so appointed the first sixth day of the week, or Friday, that should happen in any month; and afterward it was altered to the first second day [Monday] in the month.

Anno 1665—in the 4th month [June], 1665, the church ordered that Brother Terrill should ingross all the members' names in parchment, and that they should be called over always at breaking bread, to see who do omit their duty.

Upon the 4th of the 6th month [August], 1665, it was resolved and ordered that once a month for the future there should be constantly a select meeting of the members only, to stay after others were departed from the public exercise (which might be that Lord's day fortnight after we break bread); to this end, that there might be an opportunity for the pastor, and for any other brother, to minister a word proper to church members for information, or exhortation to their duty, or reproof, etc., that we might more often see the whole church together.

Upon [the] 3rd of the 9th month [November], 1665, it was determined (after dealing, and several months' waiting), that these six members, namely, John Evans, John Hicks, and John Harris that went to New England, with Sister More, Sister Stoakes, and Martha Moggs, be declared no members, and to be looked upon as persons not to have full communion with us; some for neglecting their duty of assembling through fear, some for evils in their conversation, three of them.

In the ninth month, 1665, there came a troop of horse to this city as reported on purpose to suppress the meetings; and they were very abusive to those meetings they found. . . .

[64] Upon the 22nd day of the 10th month [December], 1667, Sister Sandy was proposed, and afterwards spoken with, and joined to the congregation.

Upon the 2nd of the 12th month [February], 1667, S[ister] Marsh was proposed, spoken with the 23rd day, and afterwards added to the church.

In this 12th month, 1667, Brother Brag and Sister Moore, after divers times dealing with them from the church, and long patient waiting their reforming their conversation and place in the church, they were both ejected, by declaring them no members of this congregation.

Anno 1668: upon the 15th of the 12th month [February] 1668, aged Mr. Teather was propounded to the church, spoken with the 2nd of [the] first month following, and afterwards baptized in the River Froome, though above eighty years of age, and joined member to this church.

Br[other] Robert Bodenham upon the 21st day of the first month [March] 1668, was proposed, and afterwards spoken with, and baptized, and joined a member to this said congregation.

Anno 1669: S[ister] Martha Griffen, in the 3rd month [May], Anno 1669, proposed to join with the congregation, and thereabout spoken with, and gave a good account for us to hope there was a true work of God on her soul; but she was not then received. For there was little done this year, by reason our pastor, Mr. Ewins, declined very fast. But our public meetings were supplied by other ministers during his weakness, which at last was so great that he kept his house and chamber near five months. . . .

[68] In this year, 1670, our pastor being deceased, the church did not break bread (until we had another pastor), yet kept up our monthly day of prayer, as we used to do before breaking of bread. And the church, though they had no pastor, yet they did, notwithstanding, deal with members that walked irregular in their conversations; and they cast out some from among them, and received in others to be members with them. Thus, having ruling elders, by them

they carried on and managed the church power, and kept up all their meetings duly, only forbore breaking of bread, that holy ordinance, till they had a pastor, whose proper work it is to administer the same.

One person cast out was Philip Sciphard; who then being a member was, after divers times dealing with (according to the rule of our Lord) for his scandalous walking in excess of drinking, though he several times covered, evaded, and justified himself for want of due proof. At last his sin that he lived in found him out: for it happened that two brethren saw him overcome in drink, and therefore at a church meeting, he being present, his evils were laid before him, and by the eldest ruling elder, Brother Ellis, at his house. The said Philip Sciphard was cast out of the congregation, in the fifth month [July], Anno Domini 1670.

Part 8   The Society of Friends

Editor's note

The document known as the Balby Advices is the first church discipline to emerge from the Quaker movement. It was intended for meetings in the North, which were more fully settled than those in the South. It thus represents a second stage of organization and order following the dramatic and charismatic early ingatherings. Quaker leaders felt a desire for some clear guidance to deal with matters of misconduct or need which had arisen or could arise.

A meeting was held in Balby, Yorkshire, in November, 1656, to compile such advice. Representative elders from meetings in Yorkshire, Lincoln, Derby, and Nottingham drafted and sent out the epistle. It is signed by Richard Farnsworth (d. 1666), William Dewsbury (d. 1688), and other Friends. It may well have been originally written by Dewsbury.

"Disorderly walking," marriages, and care for the poor were practical matters requiring attention by Quaker meetings. "To suggest wise lines of action in respect to these matters, and to exhort Friends in their various relations of life to walk worthily of their calling, was all that seemed of urgent necessity to the framers of this document" (W. C. Braithwaite). Several commentators have emphasized that the advices were written in a spirit of mutual exhortation, and were not to be considered as a binding or legal code. The postscript underlines this point: "These things we do not lay upon you as a rule or form to walk by, but that all with the measure of light which is pure and holy may be guided."

Other Quaker advices soon followed, many reflecting the language and spirit of the Balby counsels. The compilations later evolved into a comprehensive system of "Queries" which were to be read annually in the meetings and answered by every member. The questions entered into every aspect of the life of the Quaker, from spiritual attainment and family relations to everyday conduct. It cannot be denied that in time they took on a legalistic bent but this was antithetical to the intentions of the first framers of the advices.

These Advices are taken from the valuable compilation of documents by A. R. Barclay, *Letters, etc., of Early Friends.* An improved, critical edition is anticipated in a forthcoming issue of the *Journal of the Friends' Historical Society.*

William Dewsbury and Others The Balby Advices (1656)

The elders and brethren send unto the brethren in the North these necessary things following: To which, if you, in the light wait, to be kept in obedience, you will do well. Fare you well.

1. That the particular meetings, by all the children of the light, be duly kept and observed, where they are already settled, every first-day of the week, except they be moved to other places. And that general meetings be kept in order and sweet in the life of God, on some other day of the week than on the first-day, unless there be a moving to the contrary that so in the light and life, the meetings be kept to the praise of God.

2. That care be taken that as any are brought into the truth, meetings be in such places among them, as may be for the most convenience for all without respect of persons, and that hands be laid on none suddenly, lest the truth suffer.

3. That if any person draw back from meetings, and walk disorderly, some go to speak to such as draw back to exhort and admonish such with a tender, meek spirit, whom they find negligent or disorderly. And if any, after admonition, do persist in the thing not good, let them again be admonished and reproved before two or three witnesses, that by the mouth of two or three witnesses, everything may be established. And if still they persevere in them, then let the thing be declared to the church: and when the church has reproved them for their disorderly walking, and admonished them in the tender and meek spirit, and they do not reform, then let their names and the causes, and such as can justly testify the truth therein, and their answers, be sent in writing to some whom the Lord has raised up in the power of his spirit to be fathers, his children to gather in the light—that the thing may be known to the body and with the consent of the whole body, the thing may be determined in the light.

4. That as any are moved of the Lord to speak the word of the Lord at such meetings that it be done in faithfulness, without adding or diminishing. And if at such meetings any thing at any time be otherwise spoken by any out of the light, whereby the seed of God comes to be burdened, let the person or persons in whom the seed of God is burdened speak in the light (as of the Lord they are moved) in meekness and godly fear, to him; but let it be done in private between them two, or before two or three witnesses, and not in the public meetings, except there be a special moving so to do.

188

5. That collections be timely made for the poor (that are so indeed) as they are moved, according to order—for relief of prisoners and other necessary uses, as need shall require. And all monies so collected, an account thereof to be taken; from which every need may be supplied as made known by the overseers in every meeting, that no private ends may be answered but all brought to the light, that the gospel be not slandered.

6. That care be taken for the families and goods of such as are called forth into the ministry or [who] are imprisoned for the truth's sake, that no creatures be lost for want of caretakers.

7. That as any are moved to take a brother or sister in marriage (marriage being honorable in all, and the bed undefiled) let it be made known to the children of the light, especially to those of the meeting of which the parties are members, that all in the light may witness it to be of God. And let them be joined together in the Lord and in his fear, in the presence of many witnesses, according to the example of the holy men of God in the scriptures of truth recorded (which were written for our example and learning) that no scandal may rest upon the truth, nor anything be done in secret, but all things brought to the light that truth may triumph over deceit. And that they who are joined together in the Lord may not by man be put asunder, whom God has joined together. That there may be a record in writing, witnessing of the day, place, and year, of such things, kept within that meeting of which the one or both are members, under which writing the witnesses present may subscribe their names (or so many of them as be convenient) for the stopping of the mouths of the gainsayers and for the manifesting the truth to all who are without.

8. That a record be kept in every meeting of the births of the children of such who are members of that meeting, and of the burials of the dead (who die in the Lord) as they depart out of the body; which be done after the manner of the holy men of God, recorded in the scriptures of truth, and not after the customs of the heathen who know not God.

9. That husbands and wives dwell together according to knowledge, as being heirs together of the grace of life. That children obey their parents in the Lord and that parents provoke not their children to wrath, but bring them up in the nurture and fear of the Lord, walking before them as good examples, in gravity and godliness, providing things honest in the sight of God and man.

10. That servants be obedient to them that are masters in the flesh in things that are good, in singleness of heart as unto Christ, not with eye-service as men-pleasers, but as the servants of Christ; doing the will of God from the heart, with good-will doing service as to the Lord and not to men; knowing whatsoever good thing any man do, the same shall he receive of the Lord, whether bond or free. And that masters give to their servants that which is just and equal, forbearing threatening, knowing that their master is also in heaven, neither is there respect of persons with him.

11. That care be taken that none who are servants depart from their masters, but as they both do see in the light; nor any master to put away his servant but by the consent of the servant. And if any master or servant in their wills do otherwise, it is to be judged with Friends in the light.

12. That the necessities of the poor, widows, and fatherless may be truly supplied. And that such as are able to work, and do not, may be admonished; and if, after admonition, they refuse to work, then let them not eat. And that the children of such as are in necessity, be put to honest employment, that none be idle in the Lord's vineyard.

13. That care be taken that as any are called before the outward powers of the nation that in the light obedience to the Lord be given.

14. That if any be called to serve the commonwealth in any public service which is for the public wealth and good, that with cheerfulness it be undertaken and in faithfulness discharged unto God, that therein patterns and examples in the thing that is righteous, they may be, to those that are without.

15. That all Friends that have callings and trades do labor in the thing that is good in faithfulness and uprightness, and keep to their yes and no in all their communications. And that all who are indebted to the world, endeavor to discharge the same, that nothing they may owe to any man but [to] love one another.

16. That no one speak evil of another, neither judge one against another, but rather judge this that none put a stumbling-block or occasion to fall in his brother's way.

17. That none be busy bodies in others' matters, but each one to bear another's burden and so fulfill the law of Christ. That they be sincere and without offence, and that all things which are honest be done without murmurings and disputings. That they may be blameless and harmless, the sons of God without rebuke, in the midst of

a crooked and perverse nation, among whom they may shine as light in the world.

18. That christian moderation be used towards all men; they who obey not the word may be won [by] those that in the word dwell, to guide in an holy life and godly conversation.

19. That the elders made by the Holy Ghost feed the flock of God, taking the oversight thereof willingly, not by constraint, but of a willing mind, neither as lords over God's heritage but as examples for the flock of Christ.

20. That the younger submit themselves to the elder—yes, all be subject one to another and be clothed with humility, for God resists the proud but gives grace to the humble.

Given forth at a General Meeting of Friends in the Truth at Balby in Yorkshire, in the ninth month 1656.

From the spirit of truth to the children of light, to walk in the light, that all in the order be kept in obedience to God; that he may be glorified who is worthy over all, blessed for ever. Amen!

Dearly beloved Friends, these things we do not lay upon you as a rule or form to walk by, but that all, with a measure of the light which is pure and holy may be guided, and so in the light walking and abiding these things may be fulfilled in the Spirit, not in the letter; for the letter kills but the spirit gives life.

Richard Farnsworth, William Dewsbury, etc.

Editor's note

Historians agree that George Fox played the central role in shaping the course of the Quaker movement. To be sure, there were Quaker-like currents before he became active, and there were also contemporaries with greater gifts as preachers and biblical exegetes. But it was Fox who wove together the divergent strands into the sturdy and plain Quaker fabric.

An important tool for this task was his prolific correspondence directed to individuals, particular meetings and, increasingly, the entire movement. Many of these letters have been collected in the published works of Fox. Others are preserved in manuscript. Fox had little formal schooling, and his original letters are often crude and ungrammatical. This caused them to be extensively worked over by later editors sensitive to public respectability. Yet the native vigor and drive of their writer manifest themselves despite the editing.

For the purposes of this collection, three letters by Fox from the early years of Quakerism have been selected. The first (1656) encouraged all Friends to persist in caring for needy members. During both the Commonwealth and Restoration periods the Society of Friends bore the brunt of churchly and government measures to control or eliminate nonconformity. The peculiar practices of Quakers, including the rejection of oaths, the refusal to doff hats to social superiors ("hat-honor"), the use of "thou" to all, matched with stout directness and persistence, caused them great suffering, steadily endured

The second letter went out in 1658 as a typical expression of Fox' pastoral concern. The hardships and struggles of their existence were not to be allowed to hamper mutual care and concern. There is contemporary evidence that the support of Quakers for each other was widely noticed by outsiders and proved effective in attracting new members.

In late 1662 or early 1663 Fox wrote a general letter to Friends appealing for support of those traveling abroad. It was the fifth such collection. Fox mentions specific needs which required immediate attention, involving Quakers in Hungary, the Near East, and the American colonies.

George Fox

Epistles to Friends and
Brethren (1656–62)

**To Friends, to Take Care of
Such Who Suffer for Owning the
Truth (1656)**

Friends, in the wisdom and power of God dwell, by which all things
must be ordered to his glory, in which you may do all things to his
glory; and that with the wisdom of God you may order and preserve
the creation, and everything that is good. And if any servants be
convinced and turned from their places for truth's sake, Friends [are]
to be tender to them, that they be not lost, but that they may be
preserved. And if any soldiers be put out of the army for truth's
sake, that they may be nourished and cherished. Or any children be
turned from their parents, or believing wives from their unbelieving
husbands, that they may be admonished to walk wisely towards them.

And that all prisoners that have but little of their own, there may
be care taken for them, and for the lame and sick. And that if any
Friends be oppressed any manner of way, others may take care to
help them. And that all may be as one family, building up one
another, and helping one another. And if any desire meetings any
way for truth's service, Friends not to look out, but to dwell in the
life and power of God, and therein to answer it.

And all Friends everywhere, in the power, and life, and seed of
God, keep your meetings that over all the top-stone may be laid, and
you all in the wisdom and patience may be preserved, and as a sweet
savor may be kept to God and in the hearts of all people. And every
one be obedient to the life and power of the Lord God, and that will
keep you from being as a wilderness, but be faithful and still, till the
winds cease and the storm be over.

G. F.

**To Friends and Brethren
Everywhere (1658)**

Friends and brethren everywhere, dwell in that which makes for
peace and love, for blessed are the peacemakers, for theirs is the
kingdom, that stands in righteousness, joy, and peace in the Holy
Ghost and in power. Therefore seek the peace, in which is the welfare and good of everyone. And take heed of strife and contention,
for that eats out the good, and does not edify, nor make for peace,
for it is love that edifies the body. Therefore keep in the seed, and

know that which was before enmity was, in which there is both peace and life.

And all be careful to watch over one another for one another's good. And be patient and keep low and down in the power of the Lord God, that there you may come to enjoy the kingdom of peace and sit down with Abraham, Isaac, and Jacob in the same. For blessed are you that lie down in the power of the Lord and rise up in it, and in faith remain. Through which power you come to be preserved and united to the God of life and truth.

And take heed of any words or carriage that do not tend to edification and building up in the love and life. Therefore, you that have tasted of the power of God, and of his good word, and of his light, wait for wisdom and in it walk, that you may be preserved in unity, in the light and life, and in fellowship with God, and one with another. That to the Lord God you may be a good savor, and to him a blessing in your generation, strengthening one another in the faith, in the grace, [and] in the word, by which all things were made and created.

And keeping the word of patience, herein you will see the Lord keeping you from all temptations which come to try them that dwell upon the earth. By which word of God you may all be preserved in the sweet and holy life, in which there is unity in the word which was before enmity, which word does fulfill the words. Therefore in that live that you may all feel life abundantly through the light and power that comes from the word, which was in the beginning, through which immortal word you immortal souls may be brought up to the immortal God, where is joy, peace, and comfort.

So, above all things live in that which stops strife, contentions, and janglings, and live in that by which you come to serve one another in love, even in the love of God, which thinks no evil, nor envies not, neither is it easily provoked. Therefore, live in that which is not easily provoked and thinks no evil, which fulfills the law, which is love out of a pure heart. And let not prejudice boil in any of your hearts, but let it be cast out by the power of God, in which is the unity, and the everlasting kingdom, that you may all witness your being made heirs of the same kingdom of peace, and to be inheritors of it, sitting down in the same, knowing your own portion, and increasing in the [123] heavenly riches. And this is above all strife, that is below, and the man of it, which is born of the Egyptian woman, which genders to bondage.*

*Genesis 16.

Therefore know the seed, the second man, the heir of promise over all set, and the blessing and presence of the Lord, which was before strife was. Therefore know the seed of life, and peace to reign in you all, which possesses the kingdom, where there is no end.

The grace of our Lord Jesus Christ be with you all, to teach, season, and establish you, which brings your salvation.

G. F.

An Appeal for Money (late 1662)

Dear Friends:

In the everlasting seed of God, by which all things was made and created, in which all may feel every one's condition as their own. And now as the Lord God of Heaven and earth, who by his mighty power and hands is spreading his truth over all the earth, to the exalting [of] his kingdom and his name. And this island being as a family of prophets and training up by the virture of the God of life to go forth into other barren nations and wildernesses beyond the seas, where some are cast into prison, by the hard hea[r]ted dark powers of the earth. As two lie in prison about Hungary, going towards the Turk's camp to declare the message of truth to him, and two women have long lain in Malta and are lately come forth, who have left a sweet savor behind them and given a good report to truth, whom the Lord has brought back safe.

And also a ship that Friends of necessity was fain to hire in the beginning of last winter was a twelve month to carry the king's letter in behalf of our poor friends that lay in prison in New England, about forty then lying in prison. And some of them had been banished on pain of death and were returned back again after banishment and being in prison the general court of Boston drew near, who had murdered four of our dear friends before. And knowing their bloody minds we were necessitated to hire a ship on purpose, the hire of which came to 140 £, who ventured their lives (going so near winter) for their lives, and that brought the truth over them all, through which Friends have their liberty and it has not been so bad since.

And besides Friends are under great sufferings that way where truth is but young. And George Wilson is lately dead in irons in a prison in Virginia, and though some are bad, yet truth prospers and spreads and has a good report, even among the very heathen. And

Friends are daily going over, and there is 240 £ and upwards paid out, more than what has been received.†

And therefore it is thought fit that a general manifestation of your loves might be manifested by way of a collection in every county and sent up to Gerrard Roberts, Amor Stoddartt, John Bolton, or Thomas Coveny. And you may show this at every Men's Meeting that is appointed [99] for such services, and also to every particular meeting in every county. And consider the thing with care and speed, and send up the thing together and not by pieces with speed, as everyone as he is moved freely of the Lord God. For outward things is the least love, for many Friends are moved of the Lord to pass beyond the sea who have not much of the outward, and this is only for such. For they that have of their own, they can spend it no way better than in the service of the Lord.

So this is the intent that nothing may be lacking, then all is well and all is preserved low, as a family in the order of the everlasting life, which was with the father before the world began.

G. F.

And whereas there have been several collections formerly concerning this service, all being disbursed upon the same account before mentioned, as by o[u]r accounts may appear to any who desire to see them: so our desire is that you mind the thing, it being of so public concernment to the general good of spreading the truth, and the supply of Friends who are moved thereunto.

This is from London where Friends had a meeting where was many of the ministers of the everlasting truth and gospel of God.

Francis Howgill	Thomas Briggs
Samuel Fisher	Thomas Thurston
George Whitehead	Adam Gouldney
Joseph Fuce	Josiah Coale
John Moone	Joseph Coale

---

†The Friends secured a royal decree on September 9, 1661, ordering the magistrates in New England to stop hanging Quakers. The special ship hired to take this order to America arrived in October or early November, traveling during an unseasonable time for Atlantic crossings. Wilson wrote a diary, which has been preserved, describing his harsh captivity. He died as a result of his imprisonment.

20   **To All the Magistrates in
                                London**

Editor's note

Along with the crusade of George Fox for religious revival went his
strongly phrased appeals to the authorities for social and economic
justice. Never one to mince words, Fox condemned in ringing phrases
the carelessness and inactivity of those responsible for the public
welfare.

A representative sample of his social criticism is the brief tract
addressed to the London magistrates (1657). It was not inappropriate
during the Commonwealth to appeal to the religious conscience of
magistrates, for they claimed a christian basis for their rule. Strictures
from the Old and New Testaments had more than passing importance
for Puritans.

Later writers on socialism noted the importance of the Quaker cries
of conscience. The treatment by Eduard Bernstein, German Marxist
revisionist, is among the more thorough. It cannot be said that these
appeals had immediate results, but most students of the subject credit
the Friends with helping to develop greater sensitivity in England
on social issues.

It is not difficult to understand the Quaker concern for social
justice. Although there was an important bourgeois element, many came
from the laboring class. Propertied Friends experienced at first hand
the terrible conditions facing the poor when their goods were seized
by court action, or when they refused on principle to pay the cost of
imprisonment and therefore suffered the lot of the penniless.

Moreover, the basic Quaker theological position which saw "that of
God" in every man was bound to have humanitarian implications. A
Calvinist with a certain understanding of predestination could more
easily judge poverty to be the rightful penalty of divine wrath upon
the unfaithful. Later Puritan thought developed a direct relationship
between prosperity and salvation, penury and damnation, to the
satisfaction of the christian middle classes. Early Quakers would have
none of this, although later Quietist Quakerism displayed rather similar
attitudes, but always tempered by reform impulses.

The tract is taken from the collected works of Fox.

George Fox   To All the Magistrates in
                      London, etc. (1657)

Friends, that are called Christians, and christian magistrates: are you not worse than the Jews that took tithes and had store houses whereof all the strangers, and widows, and fatherless were satisfied, and there was not to be a beggar in Israel? [Deut. 15:4]. And your blind men, widows, and fatherless children, crying up and down, laying in every corner of your streets, crying up and down half a dozen together, up and down your streets crying for bread, poor and lame—is not this a shame to your Christianity?

How dwells the love of God in you? How clothe you your own flesh? How feed you the hungry? Are you not come here under the reproof of James [1:27]? How are you in the pure religion, to visit the sick, the fatherless, and the widows, when both blind, and sick, and halt, and lame lie up and down, cry up and down almost every corner of the city, and men and women are so decked with gold and silver in their delicate state that they cannot tell how to go.

Surely, surely, you know not that you are all of one mold and blood that dwell upon the face of the earth. Would not a little out of your abundance and superfluity maintain these poor children, halt, lame, and blind, or set them at work that can work, and they that cannot, find a place of relief for them; would not that be a grace to you? Is not that a disgrace to you, for them to lie up and down in corners of your streets, and highways, and steeple-house* doors! Does not this show that you want the wisdom of God to order the creation? And is not this a grief, think you? And do you not believe it is so, to all the tender and sober people? Is this true christian religion to see so much preaching, praying, sermons, lectures, and to see so many blind and lame, poor men and women and children up and down the streets, and at the steeple-house doors—is not this an ill savor among you, and in you, and the high profession you profess?

Deal your bread to the hungry, honor the Lord God with your substance; hide not yourself from your own flesh; give to him that asks of you, or would borrow of you; lend, hoping for nothing again. "He that turns his ear from hearing the cry of the poor, the Lord will not regard. He that despises the poor, despises his maker" [Prov. 14:21, 31]. So see, this is the [106] word of the Lord God to you all, and a charge to you all in the presence of the Lord God. See all the

---

*The early Quaker term for church buildings.

poor, the blind, [the] lame, the widows, the fatherless, that cry up and down your streets for bread, for maintenance at your steeple-house doors, and highways, and corners of streets and alleys, that these be taken up and provided for. And they that can work, that they may be set to it, and they that cannot, that they may be looked to, that there may be a good savor in your streets, that the Lord may come with a blessing upon you, and give you an increase double another way.

Then you show the fruits of true religion, and the works of charity, and the fruits of love, and the fruits of the spirit; but now the fruits of the flesh which have superfluity, which say: "I have enough; I have superfluity; I have gold; I have money and goods in store; I have fine apparel, and jewels, and rings, and dainty diet, dressing my self in glasses, and buying glasses and pictures, and spices," and con-sider not the poor which is ready to be starved, crying in the streets. And you are so proud that you cannot tell how to go up and down the streets in your laced shoes, and clothes, and hats. How are many with their hair powdered like bags of meal? How are many in their jewels, and rings, and gold, and costly attire, which the apostle speaks against and checks such for [James 2:2–3]. They regard not their own flesh, they regard not their creator that regard not their fellow creature that he created—who created the one as well as the other, and causes the sun to shine upon the just and the unjust—but destroy the creatures upon their lusts when others are in want of the crea-tures, slackening their hand, and not giving to the poor.

God loves a cheerful giver, for God gives cheerfully and freely and liberally. "He that gives to the poor, lends to the Lord, for the Lord restores him double again" [Prov. 19:17]. But people's hearts are hardened, and they mind not to disgrace the truth; and the custom of the cries of the blind, the lame, the widows, and the fatherless have taken away the sense of compassion. Therefore, let there be a store-house where all may be relieved, and let none want, that all may have enough. The Lord can take away from you as much in a week that would (it may be) serve thousands of the poor, and cross you by sea and by land for your hardheartedness; which otherwise you would see as a blessing and feel as a blessing both within and without, in store, in field, by sea and land.

As you come into the wisdom of God, and stand in it, and are preservers of the creation, then God will bless you, and what you take in hand will prosper. A preserver of the creation visits the sick and the fatherless, and causes not the blind to wander. Cannot God bring the proudest of you all down, and make you as poor as them that wander in the streets, because you do not do good in your life time? Therefore, come to work, and do the work of the Lord while you have poor, you great ones; and come to the feeling of these things, you magistrates, that none of these may lie up and down your streets, while it is in your power to do good.

From a lover of mercy and compassion to all that see the wounded, and feeble, lame, and blind, and helpless. So in tenderness these things consider; for there is so much destroyed in your superfluity and vanity that would maintain the weak, lame, and blind, that is spent on your lusts. Oh, be a good savor, and do that which may be a good savor to the Lord God and in the hearts of all people in your generations!

From a lover of truth and a friend of all your souls,

G. F.

Editor's note

Striking evidence of the Quaker belief in mutual aid is found in their readiness to suffer on behalf of their fellows. This is noted repeatedly in the histories of early Quakerism. When Quakers approached Oliver Cromwell with the request to be allowed to substitute themselves for some of their number whose health had been broken by long confinement and ill-treatment, they were refused. However, the Lord Protector remarked at the time to his entourage that they would scarcely do the same for him if the situation were reversed.

Perhaps the most appealing example of this readiness came out during the period of rule by Richard Cromwell. In April, 1659, Quakers presented a memorial to the Parliament giving details of the sufferings of Friends at that time and the recent past. Later the same month 164 Friends gathered in the chambers of Parliament offering their bodies in substitution for fellow-believers held in English jails.

The Quaker initiative did not immediately meet with success, because the legislators replied that they were not willing to take cognizance of a situation which would reflect scandal on magistrates and ministers. The petitioners were ordered to disperse to their homes. There is some evidence that the consciences of some members of the Parliament were reached by the evidence submitted and by the stance of those offering themselves as replacements.

In later periods of persecution of Quakers, the persistence of their representatives in calling attention to judicial and administrative abuses was often rewarded by the release of their brethren. Certain leading Quakers become skilled at this form of lobbying. They were also successful in negotiating the release of non-Quaker dissenters as well.

The declaration is taken from Joseph Besse's *Collection of Sufferings of the People Called Quakers* (1753). The comment by George Fox is from his *Journal* (1659).

Henry Abbott and 163
Other Quakers

A Declaration to
Parliament (1659)

Friends, who are called a Parliament of these nations:

We, in love to our brethren that lie in prisons, and houses of correction, and dungeons, and many in fetters and irons, and [who] have been cruelly beat by the cruel jailors, and many have been persecuted to death, and have died in prison, and many lie sick and weak in prison, and on straw. So we in love to our brethren do offer up our bodies and selves to you, for to put us as lambs into the same dungeons and houses of correction, and their straw, and nasty holes and prisons, and do stand ready [as] a sacrifice for to go into their places in love to our brethren, that they may go forth, and that they may not die in prison, as many of the brethren are dead already.

For we are willing to lay down our lives for our brethren, and to take their sufferings upon us that you would inflict upon them. And if our brethren suffer, we cannot but feel it. And Christ says, it is he that suffers and was not visited [Matt. 25:43]. This is our love towards God and Christ and our brethren, that we owe to them and our enemies, who are lovers of all your souls and your eternal good.

And if you will receive our bodies, which we freely tender to you for our friends that are now in prison for speaking the truth in several places, for not paying tithes, for meeting together in the fear of God, for not swearing, for wearing their hats, for being accounted as vagrants, for visiting friends, and for things of like nature, according to a paper entitled *A Declaration to the Parliament, etc.*, delivered the 6th day of the second month called April, 1659 [v] to the then speaker of the said house: We whose names are hereunto subscribed (being a sufficient number to answer for the present sufferers) are waiting in Westminster Hall for an answer from you to us, to answer our tenders, and to manifest our love to our friends, and to stop the wrath and judgment from coming from our enemies.

Henry Abbott [and 163 other Quakers]

[The title and sub-title of the declaration referred to were: *A Declaration of the Present Sufferings of Above 140 Persons of the People of God (Who Are Now in Prison) Called Quakers* (London, 1659).]

To the Parliament of the Commonwealth of England, being a declaration of the names, places, and sufferings of such as are now in prison for speaking the truth in several places—for not paying

tithes—for meeting together in the fear of God—for not swearing—
for wearing their hats—for being accounted as vagrants—for visiting
Friends and things of the like nature—in all about 144. Besides,
imprisoned and persecuted till death, twenty-one. Alsc a brief narrative of their sufferings within the last six years or thereabouts, of
about 1,960 persons already returned; being but part of many more,
whose names and sufferings are not yet returned; all of which it is
desired may be read and considered of by this Parliament, that right
may be done.

[A contemporary journal *Mercurius Politicus* noted the Quaker initiative:]

Friday, April 15:
   This day, and the following, a great number of a sort of people
called Quakers, come up to London from several parts, assembled
themselves in Westminster Hall, with intent to represent somewhat
to the House touching the men of their way.
Saturday, April 16:
   A paper (written on the outside thereof, with these words, namely:
"For the Speaker of the Commons assembled in Parliament. These
are for him to read to the House of Commons") was this day read.
And upon the reading thereof, the same (among other things) referred to another paper, entitled, *A Declaration to the Parliament,
etc., Delivered the Sixth Day of the Second Month Called April,
1659, to the then Speaker of the said House.* The said papers were
presented by certain persons commonly called Quakers; and some
of them being called in by order of the House, received the answer
following at the bar, that is: That this House has read their paper,
and does declare their dislike of the scandals thereby cast upon
magistracy and ministry; and does therefore order that they do forth-
with resort to their respective habitations, and there apply themselves
to their callings, and submit themselves to the laws of the nation, and
the magistracy they live under.

[On May 10, 1659, a committee of the succeeding Parliament was
appointed "to consider of the imprisonment of such persons who
continue committed for conscience sake, and how and in what manner they are and continue committed, together with the whole cause
thereof, and how they may be discharged, and to repeat the same
to the Parliament" (*Journals of the House of Commons*).]

The Comment of George Fox

Now it was a time of great sufferings; and many Friends being in prisons, many other Friends were moved to go to the Parliament, to offer up themselves to lie in the same dungeons, where their friends lay, that they that were in prison might go out, and not perish in the stinking jails. This we did in love to God and our brethren, that they might not die in prison; and in love to those that cast them in, that they might not bring innocent blood upon their own heads; which we knew would cry to the Lord, and bring his wrath, vengeance, and plagues upon them. But little favor could we find from those professing Parliaments; instead thereof they would rage, and sometimes threaten those Friends that thus attended them, that they would whip them, and send them home.

Then commonly soon after the Lord would turn them [members of Parliament] out, and sent them home; who had not a heart to do good in the day of their power. But they went not off without being forewarned, for I was moved to write to them, in their several turns, as I did to the Long Parliament, unto whom I declared, before they were broken up, that "thick darkness was coming over them all, even a day of darkness that should be felt."

And because the Parliament that now sat was made up mostly of high professors, who, pretending to be more religious than others, were indeed greater persecutors of them that were truly religious, I was moved to send them the following lines, as a reproof of their hypocrisy:

"Oh friends, do not cloak and cover yourselves; there is a God that knows your hearts, and that will uncover you. He sees your way. 'Woe be to him that covers, but not with my Spirit,' says the Lord. Do you act contrary to the law, and then put it from you? Mercy and true judgment you neglect. Look, what was spoken against such: my Savior spoke against such: "I was sick, and you visited me not; I was hungry, and you fed me not; I was a stranger, and you did not take me in; I was in prison, and you visited me not.' But they said: 'When did we see thee in prison, and did not come to thee?' 'Inasmuch as you did it not unto one of the least of these, you did it not to me' [Matt. 25:41–45].

"Friends, you imprison them that are in the life and power of truth, and yet [you] profess to be the ministers of Christ. But if Christ had sent you, you would bring out of prison, and bondage, and receive strangers. You have lived in pleasure on the earth, and

[have] been wanton; you have nourished your hearts, as in a day of slaughter; you have condemned, and killed the just, and he does not resist you."

G. F.

22

Some Reasons Why the People Called Quakers Ought to Enjoy Their Meetings Peaceably

Editor's note

An excellent example of early Quaker literature is the broadside written by Thomas Atkins and published in London in 1660. It reflects the situation at the start of the Restoration period when Quaker meetings were illegal. The king's proclamation forbade gatherings of seditious bodies and conspirators, and nonconformist religious bodies were held to fall under these categories. The uprising by left-wing Puritans known as the Fifth Monarchy added to this suspicion. The king himself was not at first opposed to the Quakers and released some 700 of them imprisoned during the Commonwealth. However, local authorities and army officers were alarmed by the Quaker insistence upon holding regular meetings and their refusal to swear oaths of allegiance.

Notable in the Atkins broadside is the argument that the Quakers should be allowed to meet because of their contribution to society. The care for their own poor and assistance given to others are put forth as reasons that an enlightened government would do well to tolerate them.

Quakers maintained that they were no threat to the crown because of their pacifist convictions. This position was put forth by Fox when he was arrested near Lancaster in the first days of the reign of Charles II. He was allowed to proceed to London for his trial on his own recognition. At the trial he pointed out that if he were the dangerous traitor claimed in the writ he would hardly have been allowed to come to London on his own, but rather would have been gathered on the way by "a troop or two of horse."

The tract provides clear insight into the self-understanding of the Quakers in relation to the state and also to their attitude toward those in need in society. The author, Thomas Atkins, was an obscure person who did not play a large role in the affairs of the Society. The broadside is contained in the collection of the Library of the Society of Friends, London.

Thomas Atkins Some Reasons Why the People
Called Quakers Ought to
Enjoy Their Meetings Peaceably. Published for the information of those, who are not
acquainted with their way, and
to prevent mistakes concerning
them (1660)

Knowing the purity of the above-named people's principles, together
with the integrity of their lives, I drew forth this testimony concerning them, though they lie at the present under restraint, yet inno-
cently. Many of them, who are real friends to this nation, lie in
prison: some upon straw, and some upon the bare ground (or
boards) to bear witness and to testify that they have right to meet.

I. Because for the liberty to meet in the exercises of their tender
consciences they have the word of God for it, seconded by the word
of a king (yes, of King Charles the Second): therefore they have a
right to meet.

II. Though the king's proclamation does forbid unlawful and
seditious meetings, yet seeing the Quakers made no ill use of their
opportunities in meeting together (neither was the proclamation
occasioned through any miscarriage in them): therefore they ought
to meet.

III. Because the ground or cause of the law is the bottom or
foundation whereon it takes hold (or it is the subject matter against
which the law is placed): therefore, as those persons whose principles and practices afford no ground nor bottom for any such law,
there the law [be]comes void concerning them. But the ground or
cause of the coming forth of that proclamation, that is "Because
that some made so ill an use of their liberty as to take those times
as opportunities to plot against the peace of their neighbors" (whom
they ought to love as themselves). But from all such practices, plots,
or conspiracies, as to go about or to compass any hurt either to the
king or to any of his subjects, the people called Quakers are wholly
free from both in thought, word, and deed; so the cause of the
proclamation touches them not; therefore they ought to meet.

IV. Because they are the greatest friends to magistracy that may
or can be, for their whole aim, end, and drift of all their preaching
and living is to discountenance sin and vice and to encourage virtue,

that is goodness, meekness, mercy, and truth together with love, long-suffering, and patience exercised toward all men in the true fear of the living God, this is that [which] they seek and in good measure find. So this being that which the magistrate is to defend, both the magistrates' work and theirs agree. Thus they cleave close to the magistrate in substance, and that is more than others, who cleave to him by flattery or for self[ish] ends: therefore ought these people to meet.

V. Because in their meetings they desire and seek no other thing nor liberty for themselves than they are willing all men should have and enjoy: therefore they have right to meet.

VI. Because in their meetings they seek the good of all men: therefore they ought to meet.

VII. Because in their meetings they do meet in the spirit of truth: therefore they have right to meet.

VIII. Because that when they meet they seek to bring others out of their wicked ways into the obedience of the truth: therefore of right they ought to meet.

IX. Because that in their meetings they make no plots against any man's person or estate: therefore they have right to meet.

X. Because that in their meeting together they do nothing against the true peace of this nation, but seek to bring all men into the peace of God which passes understanding: therefore they ought to meet.

XI. Because in their meetings they edify one another in love, calling and warning all men to repent from the wickedness of their ways and with speed to turn to the Lord before it is too late: therefore they ought to meet.

XII. Because in their meetings they take care for the poor that there may not be a beggar among them: therefore they ought to meet.

XIII. Because that in their meetings they take care to pay the rent of the poor widows, who are not of ability to pay it themselves: therefore they ought to meet.

XIV. Because in their meetings they provide for such fatherless children that are among them who are in want, and do pay for the nursing of some and the schooling of others, etc.: therefore they ought to meet.

XV. Because that in their meetings they take order and provide for such poor people as are among them who are out of work, by setting their families to work when work is scarce and by giving them better wages than shop-keepers will: therefore they have right to meet.

Fig. 6. The Quakers Meeting, by Egbert van Heemskerk (1610–1680). Source: Engraving by Marcel Lauron in the collection of the Friends' Historical Library, London.

XVI. Because that in their meetings they appoint fit persons to look to such as are sick among them, who administer suitable supplies to such, according to their necessities: therefore they have right to meet.

XVII. Because that in their meetings they take care to provide for such young traders who want stock, by lending them certain sums of money (according to their capacity who are to use it) for a time freely: therefore they ought to meet.

XVIII. Because that in their meetings their compassion is extended to the poor who come from beyond the seas with letters or request to this nation, by a free contributing to their necessities: therefore they have right to meet.

XIX. Because they disown all such among them who walk disorderly, not becoming the gospel of Christ: therefore they have right to meet.

XX. Because they use no violence to any man: therefore they ought to meet.

Here follow certain scriptures which show that the people of the Lord formerly assembled together, and that, notwithstanding they were forbidden by those who were in power not to speak at all in the name of Christ, yet they chose rather to obey God than man as you may read in Acts 4, verse 18: "So they called them (that is Peter and John) and charged them not to speak or teach at all in the name of Jesus."

Verse 19: "But Peter and John answered them: 'Whether it is right in the sight of God to listen to you rather than to God, you must judge.' " See also Acts 5:28.

See Hebrews 10:24: "And let us consider how to stir up one another to love and good works." (Verse 25) "not neglecting to meet together, as is the habit of some, but encouraging one another, and all the more as you see the Day drawing near." (Verse 26) "For if we sin deliberately after receiving the knowledge of truth, there no longer remains a sacrifice for sins."

Which is to show that it is a wilful sinning, if such should not (after they have received the truth) assemble themselves together according to Paul's exhortation. Read also [Hebrews 10] verse 27. See also Acts 12:12. Acts 28:30–31: "And he [Paul] lived there two whole years at his own expense, and welcomed all who came to him, preaching the kingdom of God and teaching about the Lord Jesus Christ quite openly and unhindered."

Whereby it does appear that Paul under the Roman governors, being heathens, had more liberty to meet than the people called Quakers have here in England, being already deprived of it by such who call themselves Christians.

Written by one who has had good experience of them [the Quakers], having these many years watchfully observed them.

Thomas Atkins

London: Printed for Robert Wilson at the sign of the Black Spread Eagle and Windmill, in Martins le Grand, 1660.

Appendix

Ordinance of the Common Chest at Wittenberg

Editor's note

In his important tract *Address to the Christian Nobility of the German Nation* (1520) Martin Luther called for the abolition of begging as an urgently needed reform. For Luther, this included doing away with the mendicant monks as well as with common beggars. Every town should provide for its own poor, taking care to distinguish between those who were actually in need and those who were unwilling to work.

The first effort to put this appeal into practice was in his home town of Wittenberg, but it took place during Luther's protective custody in the Wartburg Castle. The man who inspired the reform was his somewhat older colleague and later critic, Andreas Bodenstein of Carlstadt (ca. 1480–1541). He had first taken a cautious position toward change in traditional church practices, but by late 1521 Carlstadt concluded that drastic reform was needed. Against the specific ruling of the authorities, he celebrated the first Protestant Eucharist in Wittenberg; following a sermon which he preached in ordinary dress rather than in the customary vestments, he administered both bread and wine to the communicants.

Soon after this, he wrote a passionate treatise against the use of images in churches, which, together with his other reform measures, has earned him the label "puritan" among historians. The full title of the tract was *On the Putting Away of Pictures and that There Should Be No Beggars Among Christians.* The second half of the title emphasizes a conviction which was to appear time and again among radical Protestant groups. Christians should care for their own in a spirit of fraternal love. "It is a sure sign that a city is but weakly christian when you see beggars about the streets."

Under Carlstadt's leadership, the Wittenberg town council issued in January 1522 a sweeping ordinance to mandate evangelical changes in the town, also embodying many of Luther's desired reforms. Among other provisions, the ordinance forbade begging by medicant orders, and directed the institution of a common chest for relief of the poor and for loans to needy artisans. The general ordinance was supplemented by a specific ordinance detailing how the chest was to be supplied and the funds distributed. The second ordinance is here published in translation. It is important as the first ordinance dealing with the poor to be influenced by Protestantism. The original document was first published in Herman Barge, *Andreas Bodenstein von Karlstadt* (1905).

[*Andreas Bodenstein of Carlstadt*]

Ordinance of the Common Chest, for maintaining the household and other needy persons, established here at Wittenberg. How it is to be done, etc. (1521–22)

First, a chest kept locked with three separate keys is to be placed in the parish [560] church in a place where it can be seen, where the money which has been collected or otherwise received through begging, is to be deposited.

Second, the other collection plate [*Taffel*], which heretofore has been passed in the parish church solely for the benefit of the hospital, from now on is to be used for all infirm and needy persons in the congregation, but in such a way that the poor in the hospital (according to the good judgment of the stewards of the common purse) may not be overlooked.

Third, this same collection plate may be passed weekly in the parish church, whenever the people are gathered for worship, notwithstanding the fact that up to now this particular collection was permitted along with others only at weddings.

Fourth, it is necessary that such men be made stewards of the common purse who are well acquainted with the town and with the poor as to their property, character, status, origin, and integrity, and who are capable of discerning those willing to work from the idle ones, judging conditions and making decisions. They [must be men who] judge not from love or hate but solely on the basis of need, lest the idle be preferred to the diligent, the dishonest and licentious to those who are burdened with many children and who wish to earn their own living honorably to the best of their abilities.

Therefore it has been deemed good that henceforth the lord mayor [should charge] four honest, prosperous, and faithful citizens, who are to be elected from the four quarters of the town, to inquire from the town councillors and others among their neighbors of the grievances and needs of the poor, infirm, and needy people, so that they may give them their aid, salvation, and comfort from the common purse according to their best judgment.

Fifth, those from the four quarters who are thus installed by the three councillors are to have the two keys and the lord mayor is to have one. They are to give full account of their deposits and expenditures to the new [mayor] as well as to the three councillors and

217

to the pastor, in order to avoid any suspicion. At the same time there is to be consultation and discussion of this new good work as it is being received and beneficially distributed. Whenever it is deemed necessary by the council of three and the pastor to appoint different stewards, this shall also be in their power.

Sixth, the council is to see to it that the Jacobite brethren, the mendicant monks, and other vagabonds are not admitted but solely our own people who earn their living among us by their labor and other honest means. By the same token, the mendicant monks, who cajole legacies from our simpleminded folk, and who generally bother the people with their begging, may be reduced and subdued with a good conscience, for thanks be to God, there are enough priests among us.

Seventh, those men from the four quarters are to be required to call on the mayor on behalf of these matters every Sunday after the sermon. There they are to decide in a suitable place who during the following week is to be given an advance or an outright gift for the love of God from the common money. Further [they are] to visit the poor householders personally [561] to inquire diligently into their need and deprivation, not to wait until they are penniless and in extreme poverty. For there are many these days who are ashamed to beg and yet are in need of alms.

Eighth, if it is possible to receive donations from good christian people given through His grace—if we have enough faith, it will be done—that it might be possible to buy a supply of grain. Thus the stewards are to purchase it when the price is reasonable and store it in the hospital, so that the poor may be aided in times of high prices. [It should be given] to those who have some means for money, to the sick and infirm who cannot pay for the love of God. This is always to be based on the insight of the stewards and each person's capability is to be estimated.

The same principle should be applied to firewood in the summer, so that the poor may be saved from frost in the winter.

At times of death also, the poor are to be given care and attention at a special place apart from other people, as this and all other things are to be done in accordance with and under the supervision of the stewards, etc.

The same applies to the shiftless people. Everything is to be in honor of God and the saints, and for christian love which each is to bear toward the other, etc.

Notes

Notes

Abbreviations

ARG	*Archiv für Reformationsgeschichte* (1903–)
Bilder	*Bilder und Führergestalten aus dem Täufertum 1–3,* W. Wiswedel (Kassel, 1928–52)
BQ	*The Baptist Quarterly* [London], New Series (1922–)
BRN	*Bibliotheca Reformatoria Neerlandica*, eds. S. Cramer and F. Pijper (The Hague, 1903–14)
CH	*Church History* (1932–)
Chronik	*Die älteste Chronik der Hutterischen Brüder*, ed. A. J. F. Zieglschmid (Philadelphia, 1943)
DNB	*Dictionary of National Biography*, eds. L. Stephen and S. Lee (London, 1885–)
Doctrinals	*Gospel Truths Demonstrated in a Collection of Doctrinal Books [of] George Fox 1–3* (London, 1706)
Epistles	*A Collection of Many Select and Christian Epistles, Letters and Testimonies. Written [by] George Fox* (London, 1698)
JFHS	*Journal of the Friends' Historical Society* (1903–)
Journal	*The Journal of George Fox 1–2*, ed. N. Penney (Cambridge, 1911)
Linke Flügel	*Der linke Flügel der Reformation*, ed. H. Fast (Bremen, 1962)
ME	*The Mennonite Encyclopedia*, eds. H. S. Bender and C. Krahn (Scottdale, Pa., 1955–59)
MQR	*The Mennonite Quarterly Review* (1927–)
Quakerism 1	*The Beginnings of Quakerism*, rev. ed., W. C. Braithwaite (Cambridge, 1955)
Quakerism 2	*The Second Period of Quakerism*, rev. ed., W. C. Braithwaite (Cambridge, 1961)
QGT	*Quellen zur Geschichte der (Wieder) Täufer* (Leipzig/ Gütersloh, 1930–), a sub-series of the *Quellen und Forschungen zur Reformationsgeschichte*

QGT, 1   *Württemberg*, ed. G. Bossert (1930)

QGT, 2   *Bayern I*, ed. K. Schornbaum (1934)

QGT, 3   *Glaubenszeugnisse oberdeutscher Taufgesinnter I*, ed.
L. Miller (1938)

QGT, 4   *Baden und Pfalz*, ed. M. Krebs (1951)

QGT, 5   *Bayern II*, ed. K. Schornbaum (1951)

QGT, 6   *Hans Denck, Schriften I–III*, eds. G. Baring and W. Fell-
mann (1955–60)

QGT, 7   *Elsass I*, eds. M. Krebs and H. G. Rott (1959)

QGT, 8   *Elsass II*, eds. M. Krebs and H. G. Rott (1960)

QGT, 9   *Balthasar Hubmaier, Schriften*, eds. G. Westin and T.
Bergsten (1962)

QGT, 10   *Bibliographie des Täufertums*, ed. H. J. Hillerbrand
(1962)

QGT, 11   *Öesterreich I*, ed. G. Mecenseffy (1964)

QGT, 12   *Glaubenszeugnisse oberdeutscher Taufgesinnter II*, eds. R.
Friedmann and others (1967)

QGT, 13   *Öesterreich II*, ed. G. Mecenseffy (1972)

QGT (Schweiz) *Quellen zur Geschichte der Täufer in der Schweiz I*, eds.
L. von Muralt and W. Schmid (Zürich, 1952)

QGT (Hessen) *Wiedertäuferakten 1527–1626*, eds. G. Franz and others
(Marburg, 1951)

SAW   *Spiritual and Anabaptist Writers*, eds. G. H. Williams and
A. M. Mergal (Philadelphia, 1957)

Schriften   *Die Schriften Bernhard Rothmanns*, ed. R. Stupperich
(Münster, 1970)

Studies   *Hutterite Studies: Essays by Robert Friedmann*, ed. H. S.
Bender (Goshen, Ind., 1961)

Writings   *The Complete Writings of Menno Simons*, ed. J. C.
Wenger (Scottdale, Pa., 1955)

ZKG   *Zeitschrift für Kirchengeschichte* (1877–)

Introduction

1. W. A. Visser 't Hooft, *The Pressure of Our Common Calling*
(London, 1959), p. 28.

2. For a recent discussion, see John H. Yoder, "A People in the
World: Theological Interpretation," in *The Concept of the Believers'
Church*, ed. James Leo Garrett, Jr. (Scottdale, Pa., 1969), pp. 250–83.

3. The motto appeared on all of Hubmaier's known publications; see
QGT, 9.

4. George H. Williams, *The Radical Reformation* (Philadelphia,
1962); Franklin H. Littell, *The Origins of Sectarian Protestantism* (New
York, 1964), formerly published as *The Anabaptist View of the Church*
(1952, rev. ed. 1958); Max Weber, *Die protestantische Ethik I*, ed.
J. Winckelmann (Munich, 1969), published in his collected works
(1920). There is a discussion of terminology in Donald F. Durnbaugh,
The Believers' Church (New York, 1968), pp. 3–33. The terms are used
interchangeably here.

5. A convenient summary of the shift in international scholarly assessment is available in Littell, *Origins*, pp. 138–61. See also: H. S. Bender, "The Historiography of the Anabaptists," *MQR* 31 (1957): 88–104; Bernhard Lohse, "Die Stellung der 'Schwärmer' und Täufer in der Reformationsgeschichte," *ARG* 60 (1969): 5–26; Antonio Rotondò, "I movimenti ereticali nell'Europa del Cinquecento," *Rivista Storica Italiana* 78 (1966): 103–39; Jean Séguy, "Problèmes historiques et sociologiques actuels de l'anabaptisme," *Archives de Sociologie des Religions* 7 (1959): 105–15; Gunnar Westin, "Döparrörelsen som forskningsobjekt. Ett reformationshistoriskt problem," *Kyrkohistorisk Årsskrift* 52 (1952): 52–92.

6. "Reply to Gellius Faber," in *Writings*, pp. 739–44.

7. Dirk Philips, "The Church of God," in *Enchiridion*, ed. Abram B. Kolb (Elkhart, Ind., 1910), reprinted in *SAW*, pp. 228–60. A systematic presentation of Philips's thought is found in William E. Keeney, *The Development of Dutch Anabaptist Thought and Practice from 1539–1564* (Nieuwkoop, 1968). See also J. ten Doornkaat Koolman, *Dirk Philips: Vriend en Medewerker van Menno Simons, 1504–1568* (Haarlem, 1964).

8. William Penn, "Preface," *Journal*, 1:xxix–xxx. A modern historian lists "the sharing of material and spiritual goods" among the practical consequences of the early Quakers' "living in the Light": Frederick B. Tolles, *Quakers and the Atlantic Culture* (New York, 1960), pp. 1–2.

9. *Luther's Works*, ed. Helmut T. Lehmann (Philadelphia and St. Louis, 1955–), vol. 53, *Liturgy and Hymns*, ed. Ulrich S. Leupold (Philadelphia, 1965), pp. 53ff. The quotation from Riedemann is found in "Die erste Rechenschaft," *QGT*, 12: 14.

10. Quoted in John Horsch, "The Faith of the Swiss Brethren," *MQR* 5 (1931): 140. See also J. W. Fretz and H. S. Bender, "Mutual Aid," *ME*, 3:796ff.

11. Christian Meyer, "Wiedertäufer in Schwaben," *ZKG* 17 (1897):252.

12. *Journal*, 1: 185, 470; in the revised *Journal of George Fox*, ed. John Nickalls (Cambridge, 1952), pp. 169, 373. The account reports that sometimes several hundred non-Quakers would come for aid, "for all the country knew we met about the poor."

13. *Schriften*, p. 244.

14. "Schriften von Jacob Hutter," *QGT*, 3:184.

15. The pioneer investigation by Ernst Correll, *Das schweizerische Täufermennonitentum: Ein soziologischer Bericht* (Tübingen, 1925), has been supplemented by Paul Peachey, *Die soziale Herkunft der Schweizer Täufer in der Reformationszeit* (Karlsruhe, 1954), Claus-Peter Clasen, *Die Wiedertäufer im Herzogtum Württemberg und in benachbarten Herrschaften* (Stuttgart, 1965) and other studies.

16. H. S. Bender, ed., "The Discipline Adopted by the Strasburg Conference of 1568," *MQR* 1 (1927): 64; "An die Gemeinde Gottes zu Horb: Brief Michael Sattlers 1527," *Mennonitische Geschictsblätter* 14 (1957): 31.

17. Wolfgang Schäufele, *Das missionarische Bewusstsein und Wirken der Täufer* (Neukirchen, 1966), p. 172; Franklin H. Littell, "The Anabaptist Theology of Missions," *MQR* 21 (1947):5–17.

18. C. E. Whiting, *Studies in English Puritanism from the Restoration to the Revolution, 1660–1688* (London, 1931), pp. 217–18.

19. *QGT*, 5:34. This is discussed in *Bilder*, 2: 91. See also *QGT*, 5: 129.

20. *Quakerism 2*, pp. 554–97.

21. *QGT*, 6/2:82; Bernhard Lohse, "Hans Denck und der 'linke Flügel' der Reformation," in *Humanitas-Christianitas: Festschrift Walther von Loewenich* (Witten, 1968), pp. 74–83. See William Klassen, *The Forgiving Community* (Philadelphia, 1966).

22. Christopher Ostorodt, *Unterrichtung von den vornemsten Hauptpunckten der Christlichen Religion . . .* (Racovia, 1612), pp. 195–96; *QGT*, 5:66. See also *QGT (Hessen)*, pp. 254–55, 439–40; *QGT*, 7:209–12, 290; *QGT*, 8:28. Dirk Philips's writings on the ban are found in *BRN*, 10:249–65, 657–66. Zwingli's criticism of Anabaptist discipline is discussed in *Bilder*, 3:11–12.

23. *QGT (Schweiz)*, 1:17; in English translation in *SAW*, p. 79. The link between discipline and communion is described in Correll, *Täufermennonitentum*, p. 52. Littell, *Origins*, p. 36, and Williams, *Radical Reformation*, pp. 449–50, portray Reformed disciplinary measures. See also Franklin H. Littell, "New Light on Butzer's Significance," *MQR* 36 (1962):256–74.

24. Williams, *Radical Reformation*, pp. 485ff., speaks of Anabaptism become "Anabanism." See also Frank C. Peters, "The Ban in the Writings of Menno Simons," *MQR* 29 (1955):16–33, and A. L. E. Verheyden, *Anabaptism in Flanders, 1530–1650* (Scottdale, Pa., 1961), pp. 9–12. A more general discussion is John T. McNeill, *A History of the Cure of Souls* (London, 1952), pp. 270–86.

25. Published in Robert Barclay, *The Inner Life of the Religious Societies of the Commonwealth* (London, 1876), pp. vii–xiii of the appendix to Chap. 6 following p. 117.

26. Penn, "Preface," *Journal*, 1: xliii. A recent statement on the issue is Yoder, "A People in the World," p. 266. Dietrich Bonhoeffer wrote in *Life Together*, trans. J. W. Doberstein (New York, 1954), p. 107: "Nothing can be more cruel than the tenderness that consigns another to his sin. Nothing can be more compassionate than the severe rebuke that calls a brother back from the path of sin."

27. H. S. Bender, "The Anabaptist Vision," *CH* 13 (1944): 3–24, and *MQR* 18 (1944): 67–88; Ethelbert Stauffer, "Märtyrertheologie und Täuferbewegung," *ZKG* 52 (1933): 545–98—in English translation, "The Anabaptist Theology of Martyrdom," *MQR* 19 (1945): 179–214. The story of the Quaker substitutes is found in document 21.

28. Champlin Burrage, *The Early English Dissenters* (Cambridge, 1912), 2:177.

29. Hugh Barbour, "The Meeting: The Nurturing Ground of Quakerism," in *The Three M's of Quakerism: Meeting, Message, Mission* (Richmond, Ind., 1971), pp. 8–9.

30. Abram R. Barclay, ed., *Letters, etc., of Early Friends* (London, 1841), p. 305.

31. W. L. Lumpkin, *Baptist Confessions of Faith* (Philadelphia, 1959), p. 121. A concise Mennonite view of the church is presented by J. Lawrence Burkholder, "Die Gemeinde der Gläubigen," in *Die*

Mennoniten, ed. Hans-Jürgen Goertz, vol. 8 of *Die Kirchen der Welt* (Stuttgart, 1971), pp. 53–69.

32. Christian Neff and Robert Friedmann, "Community of Goods," *ME*, 1: 658–60; Peter J. Klassen, *The Economics of Anabaptism, 1525–1560* (The Hague, 1964); Correll, *Täufermennonitentum*, pp. 15ff. A recent defense of Melanchthon's position is Robert Stupperich, "Melanchthon und die Täufer," *Kerygma und Dogma* 3 (1957): 150–70.

33. *QGT*, 9: 178; a similar statement by Hubmaier is *QGT (Schweiz)*, 1: 148. The cumulative evidence in the sources makes this conclusion inescapable despite many contemporary claims by opponents to the contrary. An incomplete list is *QGT*, 1: 683, 915; *QGT*, 2: 36, 44, 93–95, 130, 139, 187, 219, 225, 238, 240, 334, 335, 339; *QGT*, 4: 193; *QGT*, 5: 11, 34, 127, 140, 153, 169; *QGT*, 7: 63, 66, 185; *QGT*, 11: 42, 44; *QGT (Hessen)*, pp. 1: 64–69, 174–75; *QGT (Schweiz)*, 1: 49–50, 215–17. Comments in opposition to this in Elsa Bernhofer-Pippert, *Täuferische Denkweisen und Lebensformen im Spiegel oberdeutscher Täuferverhöre* (Münster, 1967) have been effectively refuted by Klassen, *Economics of Anabaptism*, pp. 29ff.

34. *QGT*, 2: 49.

35. Quoted in *Bilder*, 2: 81; *QGT*, 5: 169.

36. *QGT (Hessen)*, p. 435. See Theodor Sippell, ed., "The Confession of the Swiss Brethren in Hesse, 1578," *MQR* 23 (1949): 22–34.

37. Barclay, *Inner Life*, p. xiii following p. 117.

38. [Thomas Piggott], "The Life and Death of John Smith (Smyth)," in Barclay, *Inner Life*, p. xiv following p. 117.

39. *QGT*, 3:222 and Rudolf Wolkan, *Die Hutterer* (Vienna, 1918), p. 154. There is an English translation in *SAW*, pp. 274–84.

40. Ernst Troeltsch, *The Social Teaching of the Christian Churches* (New York, 1931), 1: 332 (originally published in 1912).

41. This is discussed in Robert Friedmann, ed., "An Epistle Concerning Communal Life: A Hutterite Manifesto of 1650 and Its Modern Paraphrase," *MQR* 34 (1960): 252, and elsewhere. The image was first used in the *Didache* (Teaching of the Twelve Apostles) of the early second century and by Martin Luther in a sermon on the sacraments (1519): Lydia Müller, *Der Kommunismus der mährischen Wiedertäufer* (Leipzig, 1927), p. 66. See also *QGT*, 6/2: 82. A comparison of Hutterite and Mennonite views is Donald Sommer, "Peter Ridemann and Menno Simons on Economics," *MQR* 28 (1959): 205–23.

42. Robert Friedmann, ed., "A Notable Hutterite Document: Concerning True Surrender and Christian Community of Goods," *MQR* 31 (1957): 58–59, slightly revised. Of Friedmann's many essays on this topic, see especially, "The Christian Communism of the Hutterite Brethren," *ARG* 46 (1955): 196–209.

43. *Journal*, 2:76.

44. *Writings*, p. 200; see also p. 538.

45. Leland Harder and Marvin Harder, *Plockhoy from Zurik-zee* (Newton, Kans., 1952), pp. 24–47.

46. The latest discussion is by Anthony R. Epp, "Voltaire and the Anabaptists," *MQR* 45 (1971): 145–51. For Voltaire's interest in the

Quakers, see Edith Philips, *The Good Quaker in French Legend* (Philadelphia, 1932).

47. Some general treatments are: Cornelius J. Dyck, "Anabaptism and the Social Order," in *The Impact of the Church Upon Its Culture, Essays in Divinity*, ed. Jerald C. Brauer (Chicago, 1968), 2: 207–29; J. Winfield Fretz, "Mutual Aid Among the Mennonites," *MQR* 13 (1939): 28–58, 187–209; W. J. Kühler, "Dutch Mennonite Relief Work in the Seventeenth and Eighteenth Centuries," *MQR* 17 (1943): 87–94.

48. A typical incident was the dialogue between Martin Bucer and Anabaptist leaders in Hesse: *QGT (Hessen)*, pp. 223–24. See also Correll, *Täufermennonitentum*, pp. 46–48 and *Bilder*, 3: 55, 82. Some discussions of Quaker efforts are: E. D. Bebb, *Nonconformity and Social and Economic Life, 1660–1800* (London, 1935); Dietrich von Dobbeler, *Sozial Politik der Nächstenliebe* (Goslar, 1912); Paul Held, *Quäker im Dienst am Nächsten* (Basel, ca. 1956); Walter Koch, *Die Stellung des Quäkertums zur sozialen Frage* (Munich, 1921).

49. Littell, *Origins*, pp. 109–37; Schäufele, *Bewusstsein*. Another volume in this series will be devoted to this topic.

50. *Journal*, 1: 316 (rev. ed., p. 263).

51. Fritz Blanke, "The First Anabaptist Congregation: Zollikon, 1525," *MQR* 27 (1953): 17–33. The documentary record is available in *QGT (Schweiz)*, I.

52. *Chronik*, pp. 157–58.

53. The latest discussion is Barrie R. White, "Baptist Beginnings and the Kiffin Manuscript," *Baptist History and Heritage* 2, no. 1 (1967) 27–37.

54. Frederick B. Tolles, "1652 in History: Changing Perspectives on the Founding of Quakerism," *Bulletin of the Friends' Historical Association* 41, no. 1 (1952): 12–27, and his "Introduction," in *Quakerism 2*, pp. xxv–xxxvi.

The Anabaptists

Document 1. Source: *QGT*, 2: 47–49, 66. Most of the documents on pages 25–111 involve Spittelmaier; many were first published in Alexander Nicoladoni, *Johannes Bünderlin von Linz und die oberösterreichischen Täufergemeinden in den Jahren 1525–1531* (Berlin, 1893), pp. 223ff. Materials for Spittelmaier's biography are found in *Chronik*, pp. 52ff.; Herbert C. Klassen, "Ambrosius Spittelmayr: His Life and Teachings," *MQR* 32 (1958): 251–71; and Wilhelm Wiswedel, "Ambrosius Spittelmayr, der bibelfeste Täuferlehrer," *Bilder*, 2: 8–17. See also Herbert C. Klassen, "Spittelmayr (Spittelmaier), Ambrosius," *ME*, 4: 599–601, and Nicoladoni, *Bünderlin*, pp. 51–60.

Document 2. Source: *QGT*, 9: 338–46. There is one publication in English translation: John H. Yoder, trans., "On Fraternal Admonition," *Concern No. 14* ([Scottdale, Pa.], 1967), pp. 33–43. Two other English translations exist in manuscript: H. C. Vedder, Library of the Colgate Rochester Divinity School, Rochester, N.Y., and G. D. Davidson, William Jewell College Library, Liberty, Missouri (*SAW*, pp. 287–88). For other Hubmaier statements on discipline, see *QGT*, 9: 316–17, 366–

78. The treatise is published in modernized German in *Linke Flügel*, pp. 45–58. The most thorough examination of Hubmaier's life, but not a complete biography, is Torsten Bergsten, *Balthasar Hubmaier: Seine Stellung zu Reformation und Täufertum, 1521–1528* (Kassel, 1961). Other important studies are: Franz Lau, "Luther und Balthasar Hubmaier," in *Humanitas-Christianitas: Festschrift Walther von Loewenich* (Witten, 1968), pp. 63–73; Johann Loserth, "Hubmaier, Balthasar," *ME*, 2: 826–34; Wilhelm Mau, *Balthasar Hubmaier* (Berlin/Leipzig, 1912); Carl Sachsse, *D. Balthasar Hubmaier als Theologe* (Berlin, 1914); R. Wilhelm Schulze, "Neuere Forschungen über Balthasar Hubmaier von Waldshut," *Alemannisches Jahrbuch* (1957), pp. 224–72; Wilhelm Wiswedel, *Balthasar Hubmaier, der Vorkämpfer für Glaubens- und Gewissensfreiheit* (Kassel, 1939); John H. Yoder, "Balthasar Hubmaier and the Beginnings of Swiss Anabaptism," *MQR* 33 (1959): 5–17; and Jarold K. Zeman, *The Anabaptists and the Czech Brethren in Moravia, 1526–1628* (The Hague, 1969), pp. 122–76.

Document 3. Source: *QGT*, 3: 136–43. There is a partial English translation in Klassen, *Economics of Anabaptism*, pp. 128–33. See also Nicoladoni, *Bünderlin*, pp. 300–301, excerpt. For his activity in Austria see *QGT*, 11: 64ff. His death is described in the *Chronik*, pp. 65–66 and in T. J. van Braght, *A Martyrology of the Churches of Christ, commonly called Baptists, During the Era of the Reformation*, ed. E. B. Underhill (London, 1850–53), 1: 102–3. There is a brief biography by Christian Neff, *ME*, 1: 404–5; see also Nicoladoni, *Bünderlin*, pp. 29–32.

Document 4. Source: *Linke Flügel*, pp. 130–37. The document is translated by William Klassen, "A Church Order for Members of Christ's Body, Arranged in Seven Articles by Leopold Scharnschlager," *MQR* 38 (1964): 354–56, 386 and, partially, in Klassen, *Economics of Anabaptism*, pp. 120–22. Information on Scharnschlager is found in Heinold Fast, "Pilgram Marbeck und das oberdeutsche Täufertum: Ein neuer Handschriftenfund," *ARG* 47 (1956): 212–42; Gerhard Hein, "Leopold Scharnschlager (†1563), Swiss Anabaptist Elder and Hymn Writer," *MQR* 17 (1943): 47–52; Gerhard Hein and William Klassen, "Scharnschlager, Leupold," *ME*, 4: 443–46; and J. ten Doornkaat Koolmann, "Leupold Scharnschlager und die verborgene Täufergemeinde in Graubünden," *Zwingliana* 4 (1926): 329–37.

The Münsterites

Document 5. Source: *Schriften*, pp. 239–48, 255–56. A basic collection on the history of the Münsterite revolution has been reprinted: C. A. Cornelius, ed., *Berichte der Augenzeugen über das Münsterische Wiedertäuferreich* (Münster, 1965), first published in 1853. There is a wealth of literature, both older and recent, in German on Münster. A few of the recent contributions are: Gerhard Brendler, *Das Täuferreich zu Münster, 1534/35* (Berlin, 1966), a Marxist interpretation; Cornelius Krahn, "Die niederländischen Täufer und Münster," *Mennonitische Geschichtsblätter* 24 (1967): 30–46; Karl-Heinz Kirchhoff, "Die Täufer im Münsterland: Verbreitung und Verfolgung des Täufertums im Stift Münster, 1533-1550," *Westfälische Zeitschrift* 113 (1963): 1–109, one of his many published articles on the subject; and Otthein Rammstedt, *Sekte und Soziale Bewegung: Soziologische Analyse*

der Täufer in Münster, 1534–35 (Cologne/Opladen, 1966). Among
the treatments in English on Münster and Rothmann may be mentioned:
Norman Cohn, *The Pursuit of the Millenium*, rev. ed. (London, 1970),
pp. 252–80; John Horsch, "The Rise and Fall of the Anabaptists of
Münster," *MQR* 9 (1935): 92–103, 129–43; A. F. Mellink, "The
Mutual Relations between the Münster Anabaptists and the Netherlands,"
ARG 50 (1959): 16–32; Christian Neff, Ernst Crous, and William
Klassen, "Rothmann, Bernhard," *ME*, 4: 367–70; Jack W. Porter,
"Bernhard Rothmann (1495–1535): Royal Orator of the Münsterite
Anabaptist Kingdom," Ph.D. dissertation, University of Wisconsin,
1964; James Stayer, "The Münsterite Rationalization of Bernhard
Rothmann," *Journal of the History of Ideas* 28 (1967): 179–92; and
Frank J. Wray, "The 'Vermanung' of 1542 and Rothmann's 'Bekent-
nisse.'" *ARG* 47 (1956): 243–51. The Hutterian Brethren attempted
to distance themselves from this "cruel abomination set up and
contrived by the Devil" (*Chronik*, pp. 144–45).

The Mennonites

Document 6. Source: *The Complete Writings of Menno Simons, c.
1496–1561*, ed. John Christian Wenger. Copyright 1956 by Mennonite
Publishing House, Scottdale, Pa., 15683. Used by permission.
Pp. 1030–35, slightly revised. It was taken from [G. L.] von Reiswitz
and [F.] Wadzeck, *Beiträge zur Kenntnis der Mennonitengemeinden in
Europa und Amerika* (Berlin/Breslau, 1821–29), 1: 22ff. There is a
full listing of Menno's writings: Irvin B. Horst, ed. *A Bibliography of
Menno Simons* (Nieuwkoop, 1962). This epistle is noted on p. 123,
no. 104. The only critical edition of Menno's publications is *Dat Funda-
ment des Christelycken Leers*, ed. H. W. Meihuizen (The Hague, 1967).
However, a complete critical edition is planned in the series *Documenta
Anabaptistica Neerlandica*. The basic collection is *Opera omnia
theologica, of alle de godtgeleerde Wercken van Menno Symons*
(Amsterdam, 1681). For information on Menno and the Dutch
Mennonites, see Ernst Behrends, *Der Ketzerbischof: Leben und Ringen
des Reformators Menno Simons, 1561* (Basel, 1966); H. S. Bender
and John Horsch, *Menno Simon's Life and Writings* (Scottdale, Pa.,
1936); J. A. Brandsma, *Menno Simons von Witmarsum: Vorkämpfer
der Täuferbewegung in den Niederlanden* (Kassel, 1962); Keeney,
Dutch Anabaptist Thought; Cornelius Krahn, *Dutch Anabaptism:
Origin, Spread, Life and Thought, 1450–1600* (The Hague, 1968);
W. Kühler, *Geschiedenis der Nederlandsche Doopsgezinden*, 1–3
(Haarlem, 1932–50); Franklin H. Littell, *A Tribute to Menno Simons*
(Scottdale, Pa., 1961); H. W. Meihuizen, *Menno Simons* (Haarlem,
1961); Karel Vos, *Menno Simons, 1496–1561* (Leiden, 1914); and N.
van der Zijpp, *Geschiedenis der Doopsgezinden in Nederland*
(Arnhem, 1952).

Document 7. Source: *The Complete Writings of Menno Simons, c.
1496–1561*, ed. John Christian Wenger. Copyright 1956 by Mennonite
Publishing House, Scottdale, Pa., 15683. Used by permission. Pp.
558–60, slightly revised by comparison with the *Opera omnia theologica*,
pp. 504–6. Horst, p. 96, no. 50. The quotation from Menno repudiating
community of women is from p. 660. The question of community of
goods is discussed by Keeney, *Dutch Anabaptist Thought*, pp. 135–36

and by Krahn, *Dutch Anabaptism*, pp. 141–43. Hutterite attitudes toward the Mennonites are found in Robert Friedmann, ed., "An Epistle Concerning Communal Life," *MQR* 34 (1960): 249–74, with the quotation about Menno on p. 267, and in L. Neubaur, "Mährische Brüder in Elbing," *ZKG* 33 (1912): 447–55.

Document 8. Source: *The Complete Writings of Menno Simons, c. 1496–1561,* ed. John Christian Wenger. Copyright 1956 by Mennonite Publishing House, Scottdale, Pa., 15683. Used by permission. Pp. 739–42, slightly revised by comparison with the *Opera omnia theologica,* pp. 298–300. See the discussion in Cornelius Krahn, *Menno Simons (1496–1561): Ein Beitrag zur Geschichte und Theologie der Taufgesinnten* (Karlsruhe, 1936), pp. 113–29. There is a recent dissertation on Menno: Christoph Bornhäuser, "Leben und Lehre Menno Simons," Ph.D. dissertation, University of Heidelberg, 1969; see also the article by Bornhäuser, "Die Gemeinde als Versammlung der Gottesfürchtigen bei Menno Simons," *Mennonitische Geschichtsblätter* 27 (1970): 19–36.

The Hutterian Brethren

Document 9. Source: *Chronik*, pp. 430–40. The quotation on their origins is found on p. 87. Modern studies of the European history include: Hans Fischer, *Jakob Hutter: Leben, Frömmigkeit, Briefe* (Newton, Kans., 1956); *Studies;* Klassen, *Economics of Anabaptism*; Hermann Schempp, *Gemeinschaftssiedlungen auf religiöser und weltanschaulicher Grundlage* (Tübingen, 1969); Williams, *Radical Reformation*; and Zeman, *Anabaptists and Czech Brethren*, with a valuable bibliography. An article which links the *Chronik* to the medieval tradition of monastic annals is Josef Szövérffy, "Die Hutterischen Brüder und die Vergangenheit," *Zeitschrift für deutsche Philologie* 82 (1963): 338–62. Older works which are still valuable are: John Horsch, *The Hutterian Brethren, 1528–1931* (Goshen, Ind., 1931); Johann Loserth, "Der Communismus der mährischen Wiedertäufer," *Archiv für österreichische Geschichte* 81 (1894): 135–322; Frantisek Hruby, *Die Wiedertäufer in Mähren* (Leipzig, 1935); Lydia Müller, *Der Kommunismus der mährischen Wiedertäufer* (Leipzig, 1927); and Rudolf Wolkan, *Die Hutterer* (Vienna, 1918), reprinted 1965.

Document 10. Source: Taken from the book *Account of Our Religion, Doctrine and Faith*, by Peter Rideman. Used by permission. Copyright 1970 by the Plough Publishing House of The Woodcrest Service Committee, Inc., Rifton, New York. Pp. 42–43, 85–91, slightly revised. The best summary of Riedemann's contribution is Robert Friedmann, "Peter Riedemann: Early Anabaptist Leader," *MQR* 44 (1970): 5–44, an expansion of his biographical sketch in *ME*, 4: 326–28. See also Franz Heimann, "The Hutterite Doctrines of Church and Common Life: A Study of Peter Reidemann's Confession of Faith of 1540," *MQR* 26 (1952): 22–47, 142–60, a translation by Robert and Betty Friedmann of the dissertation for the University of Vienna, 1927; Dieter Hillerbrand, "Am Rande der Reformation: Ein Wiedertäufer in Nürnberg," *Zeitschrift für bayerische Landesgeschichte* 30 (1967): 333–36; Robert Holland, *The Hermeneutics of Peter Riedemann, 1506–1566* (Basel, 1970), critical; William Klassen, *Covenant and Communion* (Grand Rapids, Mich., 1968); Lydia Müller, *Kommunismus,* especially chap. 1; Donald Sommer, "Peter Rideman and Menno

Simons on Economics," *MQR* 28 (1954): 205–23; and Wilhelm
Wiswedel, "Peter Riedemann, ein Gefangener Jesu Christi," *Bilder*,
1: 169–94.

Document 11. Source: *Chronik*, pp. 285–96. The history of the
several forms of the *Five Articles* was told by Robert Friedmann, "Eine
dogmatische Hauptschrift der hutterischen Täufergemeinschaften in
Mähren," *ARG* 28 (1931); 80–111, 207–40; 29 (1932): 1–17. It was
printed in *QGT*, 12: 59–317. The third chapter of the expanded version
is available in English translation in Robert Friedmann, ed., and
Kathleen Hasenberg, trans., "A Notable Hutterite Document: Concerning True Surrender and Christian Community of Goods," *MQR*
31 (1957): 22–61. See also George H. Williams, "Popularized German
Mysticism as a Factor in the Rise of Anabaptist Communism," in
Glaube—Geist—Geschichte: Festschrift für Ernst Benz (Leiden, 1967),
pp. 290–312.

The Polish Brethren

Document 12. Source: Theodor Wotschke, "Ein dogmatisches
Sendschreiben des Unitariers Ostorodt," *ARG* 12 (1915): 137–54.
Information on Ostorodt and Socinian contacts with Anabaptists of
several kinds is found in: *Chronik*, pp. 440–58; Otto Fock, *Der
Socinianismus nach seiner Stellung in der Gesamtentwicklung des
christlichen Geistes* (Kiel, 1847), 1: 190–92; Robert Friedmann, "The
Encounter of Anabaptists and Mennonites with Anti-Trinitarianism,"
MQR 22 (1948): 139–62; Robert Friedmann, "Ostorodt, Christoph,"
ME 4: 92–93; Stanislas Kot, *Socinianism in Poland: The Social and
Political Ideas of the Polish Antitrinitarians in the Sixteenth and
Seventeenth Centuries*, trans., E. M. Wilbur (Boston, 1957); W. J.
Kühler, *Het Socinianisme in Nederland* (Leiden, 1912), pp. 53–57,
106–11; J. C. van Slee, *De Geschiedenis van het Socinianisme in de
Nederlanden* (Haarlem, 1914); Earl M. Wilbur, *A History of
Unitarianism* (Cambridge, 1946–52), 1: 397ff., especially 417; Williams,
Radical Reformation, pp. 685–707.

Document 13. Source: Christoph Ostorodt, *Unterrichtung von den
vornemsten Hauptpunckten der christlichen Religion, in welcher
begriffen ist fast die ganze Confession oder Bekentnis der Gemeinen in
Königreich Polen . . .* (Racovia, 1612), pp. 245–50, 252–62. A list of
Ostorodt's writings is found in Christopher Sand, *Bibliotheca anti-
trinitariorum* (Freistadt [Amsterdam], 1684), reprinted Warsaw, 1968,
Biblioteka Pisarzy Reformacyjnych 6, pp. 90–92. See further: Delio
Cantimori, *Italienische Häretiker der Spätrenaissance*, trans. Werner
Kaegi (Basel, 1949), pp. 391–405; Edward Kupsch, "Der Polnische
Unitarismus (Fratres Polones): Anfang und Entwicklung des polnischen
Unitarismus 1535–1600," *Jahrbücher für Geschichte Osteuropas*, 5
(1957): 401–40; Françoise Le Moal, "Les dimensions du Socinianisme,"
Revue d'Histoire moderne et contemporaine 15 (1968): 557–96; Günter
Mühlpfordt, "Deutsche und polnische Arianer: Eine frühaufklärerische
Gemeinschaft der radikalen Reformation," in *Deutsch-slawische
Wechselseitigkeit in sieben Jahrhunderten: E. Winter zum 60. Geburtstag
dargebracht* (Berlin, 1956), pp. 74–98; Theodor Wotschke, *Geschichte
der Reformation in Polen* (Leipzig, 1911), pp. 219–26; Paul Wrzecionko,

"Die Theologie des Rakower Katechismus," *Kirche im Osten* 6
(1963): 73–116; and Paul Wrzecionko, "Humanismus und
Aufklärung im Denken der polnischen Brüder," *Kirche im Osten*
9 (1966): 83–100. The quotation is found in E. M. Wilbur, *History*,
1: 417.

The Collegiants

Document 14. Source: Peter Cornelius [Plockhoy] van Zurik-zee,
An Invitation to the aforementioned Society or Little Common-wealth
(London, [1659]), bound with his tract, *A Way Propounded to Make
the Poor in These and Other Nations Happy by Bringing Together a
Fit, Suitable, and Well-Qualified People into One Hous[e]hold-
government, or Little Common-wealth* (London, 1659). The text is
revised and compared with other editions. Both of these tracts have
been published by modern authors: in English by Harder and Harder,
Plockhoy, pp. 134–73 along with other Plockhoy materials; in French,
by Jean Séguy, *Utopie Coopérative et Oecuménisme: Pieter Cornelisz
Plockhoy van Zurik-Zee, 1620–1700* (Paris, 1968), pp. 179–203. These
basic monographs may be supplemented by W. H. G. Armytage,
Heavens Below: Utopian Experiments in England, 1560–1960 (London,
1961), pp. 9, 29; and Irvin B. Horst, "Pieter Cornelisz Plockhoy: An
Apostle of the Collegiants," *MQR* 23 (1949): 161–85. The details
on the Irish lord, a Captain Shane, are provided in the third edition
of the *Invitation* (1660), in the Harvard University Library. The best
studies, although dated, of the Collegiant movement are: W. J. van
Douwen, *Socinianer en Doopsgezinden* (Leiden, 1898); G. B. Hylkema,
*Reformateurs: Geschiedkundige Studien over de Godsdienstige
Bewegingen* . . . (Haarlem, 1900–1902), 2 vols.; Kühler, *Socinianisme*,
pp. 144–52, 184–92; and especially, J. C. van Slee, *De Rijnsburger
Collegianten* (Haarlem, 1895).

The English Baptists

Document 15. Source: John Smyth, "Principles and Inferences
Concerning the Visible Church," in *The Works of John Smyth, Fellow
of Christ's College, 1594–9*, ed. W. T. Whitley (Cambridge, 1915),
1: 249–68. A new edition of Smyth's writings is planned for the series
Domumenta Anabaptistica Neerlandica. Discussions of Smyth and the
early Baptists are found in: Johannes Bakker, *John Smyth: De Stichter
van het Baptisme* (Wageningen, [1964]); Walter H. Burgess, *John
Smyth the Se-Baptist* (London, 1911); Burrage, *Early English Dissenters*;
Henry W. Clark, *History Of English Nonconformity* (London, 1911–13),
1: 182ff.; B. Evans, *The Early English Baptists* (London, 1862–64);
William Haller, *The Rise of Puritanism* (New York, 1957), originally
published in 1938; Robert G. Torbet, *A History of the Baptists*, rev.
ed. (Valley Forge, Pa., 1963), pp. 33–57; A. C. Underwood, *A History
of the English Baptists* (London, 1947); W. T. Whitley, *A History of
British Baptists* (London, 1923), pp. 17–58; and N. van der Zijpp,
"Smyth (Smith), John," *ME*, 4: 554–55.

Document 16. Source. T. L., *An Appeal to the Parliament Concerning
the Poor, That There May Not Be a Beggar in England* (London,

1660). It was published in *BQ* 1 (1922): 128–31, with a commentary entitled "Lambe's Tract," pp. 131–34, and a biography of Lamb, pp. 134–35. Basic information on Lamb is found in Richard Lucas, *A Sermon Preacht at the Funeral of Mr. Thomas Lamb, July 23, 1686* (London, 1686) and Richard Spurrier, ed., *Memorials of the Baptist Church Worshipping in Eld Lane Chapel, Colchester* (Colchester, 1889), based on a manuscript by Joshua Thomas, pp. 7–9. See also Thomas Crosby, *The History of the English Baptists from the Reformation to the Beginning of the Reign of King George I* (London, 1738–40), 3: 55ff. and Alexander Gordon, "Lambe or Lamb, Thomas," *DNB*, 32 (1892): 3–5. Biographical information on Lawson is in C. Fell-Smith, "Lawson, Thomas (1630-1691)," *DNB*, 32 (1892): 297–98 and *Quakerism 1–2, passim*. The earliest Quaker attribution of the *Appeal* to Lawson is [John Whiting], *A Catalogue of Friends Books, Written by Many of the People, Called Quakers* (London, 1708), p. 90.

Document 17. Source: Edward Terrill, comp., *The Records of a Church of Christ Meeting in Broadmead, Bristol, A.D. 1640 to A.D. 1688*, ed. Nathaniel Haycroft (London, 1865), pp. 56–57, 64, 68. Also published in Edward B. Underhill, ed., *The Records of a Church of Christ Meeting at Broadmead, Bristol, 1640–1687* (London, 1847) and in a forthcoming edition, Roger Hayden, ed., *The Records of the Church of Christ in Bristol: 1640–1687*. Information on the church and its pastors is found in Roger Hayden, "Broadmead, Bristol in the Seventeenth Century," *BQ* 23 (1970): 348–59. A comparable record is Robert Steed, comp., "Baptist Church Discipline, 1689–1699," ed. H. Wheeler Robinson, *BQ* 1 (1922–23): 112–28, 179–85. See also T. Dowley, "Baptists and Discipline in the 17th Century," *BQ* 24 (1971): 157–66. The examples of Baptist discipline noted in the introduction are taken from C. E. Whiting, *Studies*, p. 96.

The Society of Friends

Document 18. Source: Abram R. Barclay, ed., *Letters, etc., of Early Friends* (London, 1841), pp. 277–82. The section (part 2) on "Documents Illustrative of the Early Discipline and Testimonies of the Society," pp. 275–354, has other examples. An outline of the Advices is provided by Braithwaite in *Quakerism 1*, pp. 310–14, with an assessment of its importance in the development of Quaker organization. The quotation by Braithwaite is found on p. 314. The Balby Advices have often been noted in histories of the Friends. See, among others, Arnold Lloyd, *Quaker Social History, 1669–1738* (London, 1948), p. 33, and John Sykes, *The Quakers: A New Look at Their Place in Society* (Philadelphia, 1959), pp. 54–55.

Document 19. Source: *Epistles*, pp. 94, 122–23 for the letters of 1656 and 1658; the appeal for funds was published by Kenneth L. Carroll, "George Fox's 1662 Appeal for Money," *JFHS* 51 (1966): 96–106. The article describes the background of the appeal and gives information on those mentioned in the letter and on those signing it. The two Friends in the Hungarian prison were John Philley and William Moore, who visited the Hutterite settlements on their trip. Moore reported in a letter of 1663 to Amsterdam that they "were pretty kindly entertained by some of them" and "had pretty good service among

them" in preaching. The record of their adventures was published in
Joseph Besse, comp., *A Collection of the Sufferings of the People
Called Quakers* (London, 1753), 2:420ff.; reprinted in William and
Thomas Evans, eds., *The Friends Library* (Philadelphia, 1840), 4:
469–79. A recent description is Edward Goerke, "Quakers in Hungary,
1662," *Friends Journal* 2 (1956): 771.

Document 20. Source: *Doctrinals*, pp. 105–6. Similar warnings are
found on pp. 29–31, 73–76, and 127–30. Some references to Quaker
social concerns can be found in: Eduard Bernstein, *Sozialismus und
Demokratie in der grossen englischen Revolution* (Stuttgart, 1922); Isabel
Grubb, *Quakerism and Industry before 1800* (London, [1930]);
Margaret James, *Social Problems and Policy During the Puritan
Revolution, 1640–1660* (London, 1930); Auguste Jorn, *Quakers as
Pioneers in Social Work*, trans. Thomas K. Brown (New York, 1931),
originally published 1912; Wilhelm Schenk, *The Concern for Social
Justice in the Puritan Revolution* (London, 1948); and Richard B.
Schlatter, *Social Ideas of Religious Leaders, 1660–1668* (London,
1940).

Document 21. Source: Besse, *Sufferings*, 1:iv–vi. It is also published
in Barclay, *Letters*, 63–66, where additional information is given. The
description from the *Mercurius Politicus* was found in "Quakers and
Parliament," *Bulletin of Friends' Historical Society* 5, no. 1 (April 1913):
32. Fox's comments are located in the *Journal*, 1: 439–40 (rev. ed.,
349). See also Maria Webb, *The Fells of Swarthmoor Hall and Their
Friends*, 2nd ed. (Philadelphia, 1896), pp. 158–63.

Document 22. Source: Thomas Atkins, *Some Reasons Why the
People Called Quakers Ought to Enjoy Their Meetings Peaceably*
(London, 1660), broadside. The Fifth Monarchy uprising is described in
Champlin Burrage, *The Fifth Monarchy Insurrection* (London, 1910),
reprinted from the *English Historical Review* 25 (1910): 722–47, and
Louise Fargo Brown, *Political Activities of the Baptists and Fifth
Monarchy Men During the Interregnum* (London, 1912), reprinted as
Burt Franklin Research and Source Works Series no. 97 (New York,
1964.)

Appendix

Source: Hermann Barge, *Andreas Bodenstein von Karlstadt* (Liepzig,
1905), 2: 559–61. The best recent study of Carlstadt's life and
importance is Gordon Rupp, *Patterns of Reformation* (Philadelphia,
1969), pp. 47–153. Helpful information on the Protestant poor
ordinances is found in *Luther's Works*, ed. Helmut T. Lehmann
(Philadelphia and St. Louis, 1955–), vol. 45, ed. Walther I. Brandt
(Philadelphia, 1962), pp. 161–94, which publishes the ordinance of the
Leisnig congregation. Martin Luther's reproof of the Wittenberg
congregation for their lack of contribution is given in the standard
biography, Roland H. Bainton, *Here I Stand* (Nashville, 1950),
pp. 351–52. A major monograph on the reformer has been announced:
Ronald J. Sider, *Andreas Bodenstein Von Karlstadt: The Development
of His Thought, 1517–1525* (Leiden, 1974). See also the forthcoming
studies by James S. N. Preus, *Carlstadt's* Ordinaciones *and Luther's
Liberty: A Study of the Wittenberg Movement 1521–1522*, vol. 26 of

Harvard Theological Studies, Harvard University Press, 1974, and
by Calvin Pater, "Karlstadt's Relation to Anabaptism," Ph.D. dissertation,
Harvard University, 1974.

Bibliography

Bibliography

Bibliographical Materials

Several journals provide excellent bibliographical coverage of the Radical Reformation. The *Archiv für Reformationsgeschichte* (1903–) is jointly edited by German and American scholars. Its extensive book reviews and surveys of periodicals has been expanded beginning in 1972 by a separate annual issue on bibliography. *Church History* (1932–) regularly carries articles evaluating the literature, such as George H. Williams, "Studies in the Radical Reformation, 1517–1618," *CH* 27 (1958): 46–69, 124–60, and Cornelius Krahn, "Menno Simons Research, 1910–1960," *CH* 30 (1961): 473–80.

Robert Friedmann crowned many decades of Hutterite research with the aid of Adolf Mais in *Die Schriften der Huterischen Täufergemeinschaften* (Graz, 1965). The latest listing of books and articles is John Hostetler, "A Bibliography of English Language Materials on the Hutterian Brethren," *MQR* 44 (1970): 106–13.

Anabaptist/Mennonite studies are listed in: Hans J. Hillerbrand, *A Bibliography of Anabaptism, 1520–1630* (Gütersloh, 1962); an annual bibliography in *Mennonite Life* (1948–); and reviews and research reports in the *Mennonite Quarterly Review* (1927–) and the *Mennonitsche Geschichtsblätter* (1936–). The *Mennonite Encyclopedia* 1955–59) is the standard reference work, taking over and advancing the data in the *Mennonitisches Lexikon* (1913–67).

Histories of Münster have been assessed by Robert Stupperich in "Neue Quellen: Publikationen zur Täufergeschichte," *Jahrbuch für Westfälische Kirchengeschichte* 44 (1951): 215–17; in "Zur neuesten Erforschung des Münsterischen Täufertums," ibid. 59/60 (1966–67): 225–28; and in his booklet, *Das Münsterische Täufertum: Ergebnisse und Probleme der neueren Forschung* (Münster, 1958).

The most complete recent evaluation of writing on the Socinian/Unitarian movement is provided in these articles by Gottfried Schram: "Antitrinitarier in Polen, 1566–1658," *Bibliothèque d'Humanisme et Renaissance* 21 (1959): 473–511; "Neue Ergebnisse der Antitrinitarier Forschung," *Jahrbücher für Geschichte Osteuopas*, New Series, 8 (1960):

421–36; "Die Polnische Nachkriegsforschung zur Reformation und Gegenreformation," *Kirche im Osten* 13 (1970): 53–66. See also Earl M. Wilbur, *A Bibliography of the Pioneers of the Socinian-Unitarian Movement in Modern Christianity* (Rome, 1950). The publications of the Unitarian Historical Society also contain useful information.

The basic bibliographical guide for the Baptists is Edward C. Starr, *A Baptist Bibliography* (Philadelphia/Rochester, 1947–), which is now complete through the letter P. This incorporates and expands the earlier two-volume bibliography by W. T. Whitley (London, 1916). Both the *Baptist Quarterly* in England and the Southern Baptist periodical *Baptist History and Heritage* publish historical articles and bibliography.

For the Quakers the old compilation by Joseph Smith, *A Descriptive Catalogue of Friends' Books* (London, 1867), 2 vols., has not been replaced. Important historical journals are the *Bulletin of the Friends' Historical Association* (after 1962 known as *Quaker History*) and the *Journal of the Friends' Historical Society* (British).

Source Publications

The outstanding source publication is the series *Quellen zur Geschichte der Täufer* (Leipzig/Gütersloh, 1930–). (The first two volumes used the older term *Wiedertäufer*, now discredited.) The Verein für Reformationsgeschichte publishes the series, with financial aid coming from German and especially American Mennonites. To the thirteen volumes issued thus far will come others: on the Lower Rhine, a third volume on Bavaria, and the *Kunstbuch*. The companion series, *Quellen zur Geschichte der Täufer in der Schweiz* has published one book on Zürich (1952) with three more planned: on East Switzerland, on Bern, the Aargau and Solothurn, and on the disputations between Anabaptists and Reformers. Anabaptist activity in the Basel area is documented in the larger compilation edited by Emil Dürr and Paul Roth, *Aktensammlung zur Geschichte der Basler Reformation in den Jahren 1915 bis Anfang 1534* (Basel, 1921–50), 6 vols. To these may be added the publication of Anabaptist materials in Hesse, edited by Günther Franz and others, *Wiedertäuferakten 1521–1626*, which appeared as the fourth volume of *Urkundliche Quellen zur hessischen Reformationsgeschichte* (Marburg, 1951). The first volume in an English language series called *Classics of the Radical Reformation* has appeared; John H. Yoder translated and edited *The Legacy of Michael Sattler* (Scottdale, Pa., 1973).

Robert Stupperich edited as the first volume in the series *Die Schriften der Münsterischen Täufer und ihrer Gegner* the writings of Bernard Rothmann (Münster, 1970). The older Dutch series *Bibliotheca Reformatoria Neerlandica* (The Hague, 1903–14) contained three volumes (numbers 2, 7, and 10) which were devoted to Anabaptist/Mennonite themes. A new series has been announced to continue the study of the Radical Reformation in the Netherlands, *Documenta Anabaptistica Neerlandica*.

The annals of the Hutterian Brethren have been published several times, first by Josef Beck, *Die Geschichts-Bücher der Wiedertäufer in Österreich-Ungarn* (Vienna, 1883), then by Rudolf Wolkan, *Geschicht-Buch der Hutterischen Brüder* (Vienna, 1923), and finally by A. J. F. Zieglschmid, *Die älteste Chronik der Hutterischen Brüder* (Ithaca, N.Y., 1943) and *Das Klein-Geschichtsbuch der Hutterischen Brüder* (Philadelphia, 1947).

John Smyth's collected works were edited by W. T. Whitley (Cambridge, 1915), 2 vols. There have been many editions of George Fox's writings. Thomas Ellwood was the editor of his journal in 1694 (*Works*, vol. 1) and epistles in 1698 (*Works*, vol. 2); the volume commonly known as the *Doctrinals* (*Works*, vol. 3) appeared as *Gospel Truth Demonstrated in a Collection of Doctrinal Books* (London, 1706). Ellwood's version of the journal was republished many times, and is still useful because of the large number of documents incorporated into it, although he edited more freely than is now considered suitable. The latest edition of the journal is by John L. Nickalls, using some other materials as supplements (Cambridge, 1952). A well-organized collection of original material, with a helpful general introduction, is provided by Hugh Barbour and Arthur O. Roberts, eds., *Early Quaker Writings, 1650–1700* (Grand Rapids, Mich., 1973).

Reading List of Materials in English

General

Davies, Horton. *The English Free Churches.* London: Oxford University Press, 1952.

Durnbaugh, Donald F. *The Believers' Church: The History and Character of Radical Protestantism.* New York: The Macmillan Company, 1968.

Estep, William R. *The Anabaptist Story.* Nashville: Broadman Press, 1963.

Garrett, James Leo, Jr., ed. *The Concept of the Believers' Church.* Scottdale, Pa.: Herald Press, 1969.

Hill, Christopher. *Society and Puritanism in Pre-Revolutionary England.* London: Martin Secker & Warburg, Ltd., 1964.

Jeschke, Marlin. *Discipling the Brother.* Scottdale, Pa.: Herald Press, 1970.

Littell, Franklin H. *The Origins of Sectarian Protestantism.* New York: The Macmillan Company, 1964.

Manschreck, Clyde L., ed. *Believers' Church Conference 1970.* The Chicago Theological Seminary *Register* 60, no. 6 (1970): 1–59.

Norwood, Frederick A. *Strangers and Exiles.* 2 vols. Nashville: Abingdon Press, 1969.

Nuttall, Geoffrey F. *Visible Saints: The Congregational Way 1640–1660.* Oxford: Basil Blackwell, 1957.

Schlatter, Richard B. *Social Ideas of Religious Leaders, 1660–1668*. London: Oxford University Press, 1940.

Troeltsch, Ernst. *The Social Teachings of the Christian Churches*. Trans. Olive Wyon. 2 vols. New York: The Macmillan Company, 1931.

Westin, Gunnar. *The Free Church Through the Ages*. Trans. Virgil A. Olson. Nashville: Broadman Press, 1958.

Whiting, C. E. *Studies in English Puritanism from the Restoration to the Revolution, 1660–1688*. London: SPCK, 1931.

Williams, George H. *The Radical Reformation*. Philadelphia: Westminster Press, 1962.

The Anabaptists

Clasen, Claus-Peter. *Anabaptism: A Social History*. Ithaca, N.Y.: Cornell University Press, 1972.

Dyck, Cornelius J., ed. *An Introduction to Mennonite History*. Scottdale, Pa.: Herald Press, 1967.

Hershberger, Guy, ed. *Recovery of the Anabaptist Vision*. Scottdale, Pa.: Herald Press, 1957.

Horst, Irvin B. *Anabaptism and the English Reformation to 1558*. Nieuwkoop: B. de Graaf, 1968.

Klassen, Peter J. *The Economics of Anabaptism, 1525–1560*. The Hague: Mouton & Co., 1964.

Oyer, John S. *Lutheran Reformers against Anabaptists*. The Hague: M. Nijhoff, 1969.

Payne, Ernest A. *The Anabaptists of the Sixteenth Century and Their Influence in the Modern World*. London: Carey Kingsgate Press, 1949.

Verduin, Leonard. *The Reformers and Their Stepchildren*. Grand Rapids, Mich.: William B. Eerdmans, 1964.

Verheyden, A. L. E. *Anabaptism in Flanders, 1530–1650*. Scottdale, Pa.: Herald Press, 1961.

Wenger, John C. *Even Unto Death*. Richmond, Va.: John Knox Press, 1961.

Zeman, Jarold K. *The Anabaptists and the Czech Brethren in Moravia, 1526–1628*. The Hague: Mouton & Co., 1969.

The Münsterites

Cohn, Norman. *The Pursuit of the Millennium*. Rev. ed. London: Granada Publishing Ltd., 1970.

Horsch, John. "The Rise and Fall of the Anabaptists of Münster." *MQR* 9 (1935): 92–103, 129–43.

Stayer, James. *Anabaptists and the Sword*. Lawrence, Kans.: Coronado Press, 1972.

Stayer, James. "The Münsterite Rationalization of Bernhard Rothmann." *Journal of the History of Ideas* 28 (1967): 179–92.

The Mennonites

Dyck, Cornelius J., ed. *A Legacy of Faith: The Heritage of Menno Simons.* Newton, Kans.: Faith and Life Press, 1962.

Fretz, J. Winfield. "Mutual Aid Among the Mennonites," *MQR* 13 (1939): 28–58, 187–209.

Hillerbrand, Hans J. "Menno Simons—Sixteenth Century Reformer." *CH* 31 (1962): 387–99.

Keeney, William E. *The Development of Dutch Anabaptist Thought and Practice from 1539–1564.* Nieuwkoop: B. de Graaf, 1968.

Krahn, Cornelius. *Dutch Anabaptism: Origin, Spread, Life, and Thought (1450–1600).* The Hague: M. Nijhoff, 1968.

Littell, Franklin H. *A Tribute to Menno Simons.* Scottdale, Pa.: Herald Press, 1961.

The Hutterian Brethren

Bennett, John W. *Hutterian Brethren: The Agricultural Economy and Social Organization of a Communal People.* Stanford: Stanford University Press, 1967.

Conkin, Paul K. *Two Paths to Utopia: The Hutterites and the Llano Colony.* Lincoln: University of Nebraska Press, 1964.

Horsch, John. *The Hutterian Brethren, 1528–1931: A Story of Martyrdom and Loyalty.* Goshen, Ind.: Mennonite Historical Society, 1931.

Hostetler, John A. and Huntington, G. E. *Hutterites in North America.* New York: Holt, Rinehart, and Winston, 1967.

Peters, Victor. *All Things Common: The Hutterian Way of Life.* Minneapolis: University of Minnesota Press, 1965.

The Polish Brethren

Kot, Stanislas. *Socinianism in Poland: The Social and Political Ideas of the Polish Antitrinitarians in the Sixteenth and Seventeenth Centuries.* Trans. E. M. Wilbur. Boston: Starr King Press, 1957.

Wilbur, Earl M. *A History of Unitarianism.* 2 vols. Cambridge, Mass.: Harvard University Press, 1947–52.

The Collegiants

Barclay, Robert. *The Inner Life of the Religious Society of the Commonwealth.* London: Hodder & Stoughton, 1876.

Fuz, Jerzy K. *Welfare Economics in Some English Utopias from Francis Bacon to Adam Smith.* The Hague: M. Nijhoff, 1952.

Harder, Leland and Harder, Marvin. *Plockhoy from Zurik-zee: The Study of a Dutch Reformer in Puritan England and Colonial America.* Newton, Kans.: [Mennonite] Board of Education and Publication, 1952.

Jones, Rufus. *Spiritual Reformers in the Sixteenth and Seventeenth Centuries.* London: Macmillan & Company, 1914.

The English Baptists

Dosker, Henry E. *The Dutch Anabaptists*. Philadelphia: Judson Press, 1921.

Garrett, James Leo, Jr. *Baptist Church Discipline*. Nashville: Broadman Press, 1962.

Payne, Ernest A. *The Fellowship of Believers*. London: Carey Kingsgate Press, 1952.

Torbet, Robert G. *A History of the Baptists*. Rev. ed. Valley Forge, Pa.: Judson Press, 1963.

Underwood, A. C. *A History of the English Baptists*. London: Carey Kingsgate Press, 1947.

White, B. R. *The English Separatist Tradition*. London: Oxford University Press, 1971.

Whitley, W. T. *A History of British Baptists*. London: Charles Griffin & Co., 1923.

The Society of Friends

Barbour, Hugh. *The Quakers in Puritan England*. New Haven, Conn.: Yale University Press, 1964.

Braithwaite, William C. *The Beginnings of Quakerism*. Rev. ed. Cambridge: University Press, 1955.

Braithwaite, William C. *The Second Period of Quakerism*. Rev. ed. Cambridge: University Press, 1961.

Endy, Melvin B., Jr. *William Penn and Early Quakerism*. Princeton: Princeton University Press, 1973.

Etten, Henry van. *George Fox and the Quakers*. Trans. and rev. E. Kelvin Osborn. New York: Harper Torchbooks, 1959.

Lloyd, Arnold. *Quaker Social History, 1699–1738*. London: Longman, Green & Co., 1948.

Nuttall, Geoffrey F. *The Holy Spirit in Puritan Faith and Experience*. Oxford: Basil Blackwell, 1946.

Sykes, John. *The Quakers: A New Look at their Place in Society*. Philadelphia: J. B. Lippincott, 1959.

Trueblood, D. Elton. *The People Called Quakers*. New York: Harper & Row, 1966.

Vann, Richard T. *The Social Development of English Quakerism, 1655–1755*. Cambridge, Mass.: Harvard University Press, 1969.

Indexes

Index of Persons, Places, and Topics

Index of Biblical References